9-26-11.

MW00333569

John,

I thought I was going to finish this book 2 years ago but... Wish Paul were still here to review it.

I hope all is well with you and yours. We are gearing up for a big Alien Con in California next month. Will also visit our daughter and family... fun.

If you find any errors let me know.

In love and white light!

Sean Bartok
(aka NBN)

FLASHBACKS

The Circle and The Tree Publishing, LLC, Copyright © 2015

ALL RIGHTS RESERVED

No part of this book may be reproduced, stored in a retrieval system, or transmitted in any form or by any means (including electronic, mechanical, photocopying, recording, or otherwise) without the prior permission in writing of the publisher, nor be otherwise circulated in any form of binding or cover other than that in which it is published.

PUBLISHER'S NOTE:

This is a work of non-fiction. The names and places in this book have been changed to protect the privacy of the author, his family, and most of those mentioned in the text. The location of many events and institutions have been changed for the same reason. Any trademarks mentioned herein are not authorized by the trademark owners and do not mean this work is in anyway sponsored by or associated with the trademark owners. Any trademark used is specifically in a descriptive capacity. All brand names and product names used in this book are registered trademarks, or trade names of their respective holders. The Circle and The Tree Publishing, LLC is not associated with any products or vendors in this book.

Although the advice and information in this book are believed to be accurate and true at the time of going to press, neither the author nor the copyright holder can accept any legal responsibility or liability for any errors or omissions that may have been made.

COLOPHON INFORMATION:

The Circle and The Tree Publishing, LLC colophon is a pre-existing trademark designed by Sean Bartok. The symbol was inspired by an ancient barrier style pictograph found in the San Rafael Swell, Utah. The figure represents a native spirit connected to the Great Spirit, the circle represents a UFO beam-down track, and the branches represent the sacred cottonwood tree.

ISBN-10: 0997014709

ISBN-13: 978-099701409

www.seanbartok.com

F L A S H B A C K S

An Artist's Memoir of Alien Abductions, Native Spirits, and Enlightenment

By Sean Bartok

The Circle and The Tree Publishing, LLC.

"I am the spirit janitor.
All I do is wipe the windows a bit,
so you can see out for yourself."

GODFREY CHIPS,
LAKOTA MEDICINE MAN

SEAN BARTOK

"A mind that is stretched by a new experience can never go back to its old dimensions."

OLIVER W. HOMES

FOREWORD

BY R. LEO SPRINKLE, PHD: PROFESSOR EMERITUS, RENOWNED PSYCHOLOGIST AND UFOLOGIST

Welcome, Dear Reader, to a wonderful journey, described by a wonderful Writer.

This Author serves as an Artist and Scientist, as well as Professor and Epic Storyteller. He is Protagonist in his inner and outer struggles with many memories and many mysteries.

He provides his Readers with a series of experiences which not only confound him and his family, but also puzzle his friends and colleagues. His decision to write under a pen name came out of the setbacks, and ridicule, that he and his family endured.

In some ways, his experiences are unique; however, in some ways, these events are a model of what is happening to all of humanity. When Disclosure of Extraterrestrial Civilizations occurs, the Author will be viewed as a Pioneer.

Like millions of people around the Planet, the Author has encountered Extraterrestrial Entities (ETs). And, like thousands of people, he has reported these encounters to others. And like hundreds of persons, he has written a book about his reactions to these encounters.

However, as an Artist, with impaired eyesight, and inspired vision, he takes us on a tour of his inner museum. As a Scientist, he displays both the Ugly and the Beautiful: Collections of his motives and actions. As a Professor he informs us-not only of his own educational achievements-he also helps us to develop our own skills and possible choices in dealing with ETs. He is ambivalent about the intentions of the Visitors: Invaders? Intruders? Educators? Initiations? Are they Foe or Friend?

The Author recognizes that changes are occurring. However, the changes seem to be in his own reactions and choices.

The Author ends *FLASHBACKS* on a positive note: "We are not alone in the Universe and...there is life after life." He writes that he and his family, eventually, will benefit from their learning more about their mysterious visitors and their Ancient Ancestors.

This Author is commended for his courage and compassion--and his willingness to share his journey with us.

May we all share Love and Light,
Leo

"The greatest discovery any generation can make
is that a human being can alter his life
by altering his attitude."

WILLIAM JAMES

I

"We can easily forgive a child who is afraid of the dark. The real tragedy of life is when men are afraid of the light."

PLATO

INTRODUCTION

According to the 1991 Roper Organization blind survey and the *Unusual Personal Experiences Report,* one in 50 Americans had been abducted by extraterrestrials (ETs). Paranormal researchers reported that ETs have the ability to induce a state of amnesia in certain memory areas of our brain. I was one of those abducted when I was young but didn't realize it until I was 43 years old. Had my wife, children and I not moved to the country from Denver in 1980, I probably would have never put the paranormal events of my life into a pattern that left no doubt I had been abducted not once, but many times.

This memoir is an account of how the realization came to me that I was a contactee and the effects ETs have had on my life. My first insights were based on the bizarre dreams that I began having shortly after we moved to our new home in rural Colorado. My belief and conviction was piqued even more as the years passed, and as "dreams" and paranormal events continued to plague our family.

In 1983, I met with psychologist and renowned ufologist R. Leo Sprinkle, PhD. After listening to my numerous stories, he confirmed I had been abducted many times. I was not having dreams but flashbacks to those poignant moments when I was with ETs.

Along with the ETs came other mysterious entities, unusual creatures from other dimensions, and Native American spirits. An internationally known Lakota shaman heard about our experiences with spirits and wanted to visit us. He was so taken with the spiritual essence he sensed while visiting that he asked to do his final vision quest on our property. Locals alleged we lived on a sacred Indian healing ground.

I began writing my memoir in 2012 after developing a lung condition from breathing the pastel fixative spray used to protect the artwork I was creating for a gallery in Taos, New Mexico. I thought I was going to die. It was time to record my memoir of paranormal experiences for others who might benefit from what I had to say.

While selecting and reviewing my artwork from the past to the present for inclusion in the gallery in Taos, I became aware of the radical changes in my art, design, and creative work over the years after 1959. I traced those changes and correlated them with my abduction memories, differing life goals and attitudes. I realized there was a relationship between my art and the abduction phenomena. Much of my abduction memories were locked in a state of induced amnesia. My subconscious, however, was evidently intact and spoke to me using the language of vision. It revealed some of what I saw, experienced and was told by my abductors through my doodles, art and designs.

The morning after my abduction from our home in 1984, I discovered a UFO beam-down circular track in the snow containing both alien and my footprints. I took photographs of the beam-down track. These photographs form the basis of the book and, confirm the existence of UFOs. The photographs' content validates to me the relationship between my art and the flashbacks I was having.

Writing is not my forte. It is difficult for me to succinctly express my thoughts and emotions through words, instead of the language of vision-color, form and shape. Once I started writing my memoir, the process became a personal journey of discovery, growth, therapy, and enlightenment. I realized the entities visiting in the night altered and refined my perception of religion, history, science, art, reality, and the origins of mankind.

Like many visual artists, I believe God is in the details of our work. Given this creation philosophy, I have included minutia that will bore many, but may help others paint a clearer picture of the UFO phenomena.

In the book, chapters are years and subchapters are events that took place in those years. Some chapters are long, others short depending on the number of events in a given year. Dingbats (▪ ▪ ▪ ▪) represent a shift in my thought processes, often going from present tense-participant in the moment, to past tense-author with a retrospective view.

In the late eighties and early nineties, I was very vocal and told the press about some of our unusual paranormal experiences. As a result the whole family was sorted out and harangued unmercifully. We endured but were disappointed in the shallow-mindedness of the press, numerous colleagues, some neighbors, and many of the children's classmates. It is with hope the content of this memoir will not put our adult children and their careers at risk, as mine was.

The names of most people, institutions, towns, specific geographic locations, and some dates have been changed. The nature of the story makes it necessary to protect the privacy of my family, others, and myself. I have adopted a pen name for the same reason.

In a more philosophical context, I have always thought it was my civic responsibility to report any abnormalities that seemed potentially dangerous or beneficial to my fellow man. It is in that spirit that I write this memoir.

Sean Bartok

" For those who believe no proof is necessary.
For those who don't believe no proof is possible."

S. CHASE

*"An enlightened person doesn't
ask anyone to believe anything.
They simply point the way and leave it to
the people to realize it for themselves."*

ANONYMOUS

C O N T E N T S

CHAPTER

1

CONTENTS

CHAPTER

2

CHAPTER

3

CHAPTER

4

C O N T E N T S

CHAPTER

CHAPTER

CHAPTER

SELF PORTRAIT, MARCH 1980

"A FLASHBACK IS YOUR
 SUBCONSCIOUS ETCHING
 A NEW CHAPTER IN YOUR
 SOUL'S MEMOIR."

SEAN BARTOK

> *" We need to take dreams more literally and waking life more symbolically."*
>
> R. MOSS

CHAPTER ONE | 1980

THE WOLF | FEBRUARY 17, 1980

Something is wrong! I am momentarily blinded and confused by moving, overlapping, translucent images that overwhelm my vision of the book I am reading. The room I sit in is visually a frenetic whirling mess. Abject fear grips me, first at the base of my spine, then it rips up to my cortex and beyond.

The flashing images that dominate my mind's eye quickly coalesce into a vignette of a small rabbit sitting in a tall grass burrow. Above the contented rabbit is the head of a huge, fearsome wolf about to pounce. The wolf is totally fixated and relishes the thought of devouring his unsuspecting prey.

The hairs on the back of my neck rise with alarm, I look up from my book. As I stand up, I see a light, brownish-green block, perhaps three by five inches, hit the sliding glass door in front and to the right of me. The shape hits so fast and hard that the loud crack causes me to jerk back in response. It then ricochets off the glass and disappears into the night.

The four-foot sliding glass door bows in toward me. The safety glass seems to defy all its normal properties. Instead of shattering into thousands of small pieces, the safety glass appears to mimic hot plastic capable of stretching. I am momentarily in disbelief as the glass bows in towards me.

"What was that?!" my wife, Sarah, yells at me from the upstairs bedroom that adjoins the two-story living room I am in.

"I don't know!?" I respond.

I watch the glass door snap back and return to its normal vertical position. What the fuck! The door's safety glass should have shattered, but miraculously it didn't, what luck! Driven by adrenalin, anxiety, and curiosity as to what hit the window, I regain my courage. I take two giant steps to the glass door that is not more than five feet away.

I quickly unlock the door and open it wide enough to stick my head out into the cold, moonless night. A chilly wave of air rolls into the room. I strain my eyes and ears for the slightest of noises or movement that can tell me what hit the window.

How strange. Not a leaf quivers. The hair in my nostrils stiffen from the frigid air. My visible breath is the only movement in my field of vision. Looking in every direction, I see, sense, and hear nothing.

It's cold outside, 10 to 15 degrees Fahrenheit. The night is moonless, and it is eerily quiet, a soul-sucking quiet. I cannot hear anything running through the snow or the dry oak leaves on the ground outside the construction zone of our new house, or beyond. I look all around until the night air chills me. I am puzzled and relieved that nothing really damaging happened to me or the house.

Living room, loveseat and sliding glass door

I close the door, and as I do, I notice our black and gray short-haired tabby kitty, Molly, sitting not more than two feet from the fixed window next to the slider door. Molly stares into the living room with a calm, pensive, introspective gaze. She is motionless, except for the last several inches of her long, thin tail, which repeatedly curls open and closed. Her tail's rhythmical motion is hypnotic, like the movement of a fuzzy metronome. Molly is normally fearful of her own shadow, yet tonight she must have sat through the whole event. Molly did not run in fear. Very puzzling, how could she still be motionlessly sitting there by the door. Is Molly catatonic?

I walk away from the door and then realize how hyper, anxious, and confused I am. It then occurs to me that perhaps an owl, seeing Molly by the door, and not knowing what glass was, dove down from one of the trees outside to attack her, hit the window, and ricocheted off the glass door into the night.

That scenario is a good, logical explanation, but I know an owl striking the window that hard would have left an oily impact print on the glass, and a dazed or dead owl on the ground. I see no such evidence, and besides, the object was light brown. It was rectangular in shape and had brighter green, horizontal, coarse stitching across its width.

I am determined to continue reading, but want some protection in the event that whatever hit the window might return for another peek or…? I will be ready with a little surprise of my own.

Feeling edgy, I go upstairs and get my .38 snub-nosed revolver from our bedroom. I load it with hollow points and go back down to the living room. I wonder if our neighbor across the road is out and about window-peeping. Perhaps he was up close to the window peering in at me and had his hands cupped around the sides of his face to diminish the glass's glare so he could see me better. When I sensed his presence and looked up he turned to run and hit his forearm or elbow on the window. The guy is an asshole, and we have a little feud going over the enforcement of the subdivision covenants. All the while, I can't get the thought and feeling out of my system as to the sudden and overpowering mind's eye image of the rabbit and wolf.

■　　■　　■　　■　　■　　■　　■　　■

Was my higher self or subconscious giving me flash cards from the sidelines? *Get moving, stupid…get the hell out of there!* Great fear gripped me for no apparent reason, and I wondered how could it start at the base of my spine and go up to my spinal cortex? Why didn't the feeling move in the opposite direction as I had always thought? Was it body over mind or mind over body? Perhaps that night, it was body over mind. And why was I compelled to look directly into the path of the brownish-green object as I stood up? I could have looked in any direction. The mysterious object hit the window in line with where my head had been when I was seated. I was not sure whether the object was directed at my head, or that the whole thing was an accident.

Another puzzling element was how I knew to be fearful of something outside the window when my head was down and my eyes and mind were fixed on the book I was reading. Did I see the object outside the window out of the top of my head? Ridiculous! I had heard of a Hindu belief that a third eye resides in the top of one's head or on the forehead. I had little knowledge of Eastern religious concepts, only that I thought it seemed like a strange idea.

I did believe that in order to become fearful, one had to see, hear, smell, or touch what caused the sense of fear. I believed in the logical fear hypothesis of psychologists James and Lang. These two researchers postulated that we see the bear and we then run or fight. The motivation to run or fight comes from the visual sensory input and then is transferred through the mental process. With the sight of a bear, we mostly think *RUN*, as the fear of being maimed or devoured is a real possibility.

Yet, I was frightened out of my wits before I saw anything with my eyes. Unbelievable! However, researchers Cannon and Bard said that was the way fear occurred; you're running, then you see the bear! Crazy. How could that process of generating fear be possible? Did my body rule my mind? Bullshit, not in my naïve worldview of practical neurology. Or could my spinal column have part of my mind embedded in it, and that's why the fear began near the tip of my spinal column and moved toward my brain?

Perhaps the concept of chakras and the third eye was not as far off the mark as I had always thought. Maybe both sets of researchers were right. But what made me see the wolf and the rabbit in my mind's eye? Those powerful eidetic images were generated internally, like a lantern slide between the eye and mind, or maybe I had a subliminal uprush. Allegedly, an eidetic image and/or a subliminal uprush is accepted to be a subconscious answer to a difficult question you are grappling with. Some people call the subliminal uprush experience an "aha!" moment. Never before did I have an "aha" moment as brilliant as this was.

To my cognitive knowledge, I had not been grappling with a problem that would prompt such a foreboding message veiled in symbolic form. In graduate school, I studied concept formation and the types of images associated with creative and visual problem solving. I learned how to coax images up from my subconscious. Up to this point in my life, I had never generated images with this intensity. I was amazed at the prospect of having such an intense experience with no apparent effort on my part.

I didn't know the basis for the creation of the phenomenon or the symbolic logic of the wolf and the rabbit. I was just sitting there reading the Bible and BOOM! I was instantly overcome with great fear, mental and visual chaos, confusion, and physical turmoil.

As a seasoned graphic designer and educator, the symbolism of the wolf and rabbit was obvious. I had never had a reason to have such a great sense of fear…and for what? I knew who the rabbit was. At the time I wasn't consciously fearful of anything. There was nothing to be fearful about in the part of the Bible I was reading.

On the horizon, however, there were some really big issues to make me circumspect and a little anxious, such as; the pending lawsuit with our contractor, the rattlesnakes that proliferated the grounds around the house and beyond, the defenses I needed to construct to protect the children from snakebites, and the hunt for furniture that would allow us to readily see a rattlesnake under or around it. God forbid, if a snake got in the house through one of the six outside doors.

Not only was I anxious about the outside landscaping I needed to do to allow us to readily see rattlesnakes in the immediate yard, but also the logistics of the daily 100 mile commute to and from work, the working relationship with my new colleague in the design department, and lastly, my career in the visual arts at the university.

As a professor of graphic design at the university, the mantra was publish or perish. Publish in my area of the visual arts meant I was responsible for producing graphic design work that would win gold medals in regional and national competitions. I was also responsible for producing students who could enter the field of graphic design upon graduation. Living out in the middle of nowhere, I was, as they say, screwed. I had no studio space to work in, or a client base to work from. I was committing professional suicide by living so far away.

But I felt the risk was worth it to get the family out of Denver, and away from the growing unhealthy brown cloud of smog that hung over the city and the epidemic of drugs that were infiltrating the elementary schools. I was also fearful of a nuclear holocaust occurring in Denver or at the NORAD facility in Colorado Springs. In 1970, I read Buckminster Fuller's book: *Operating Manual for Spaceship Earth*. Since reading his book, I had been obsessed with the desire to live energy free, "green" and as self-sufficient as possible.

In 1980, my dream could become a reality. Our new home was a two-story, stage-three passive solar structure bermed into the foot of a mesa, with entry doors on both levels. We were located west of Castle Rock, halfway between Denver and Colorado Springs. Best of all, Sarah could for the first time in her life have her horses on our own property.

I did not consciously fear that we would fail in overcoming these obstacles created by moving to the county. So why did these two powerful, iconic images of a wolf and a rabbit that denote ultimate predator; consummate prey, brutal vs. gentle; active vs. passive overwhelm my conscious thoughts? Wow! What a night, but that night I was not to be deterred from my mission of reading the Bible from cover to cover in three evenings. I sat back down in the leather loveseat in front of the sliding glass door and continued reading. My .38 was tucked snugly between the two cushions of the loveseat, out of sight and at the ready if the prowler, or whatever it was, returned.

This night was the first time I had ever sat down and intended to read the Bible

Our homesite nestled in the trees at the foot of the mesa

from cover to cover, but tonight was also different for another reason. Tonight was our first night in our new home and much to my chagrin, I could not get the faintest of TV signals from Colorado Springs or Denver. There was a sense of disbelief. How could we not receive a recognizable TV signal? Then I realized the cliffs around the house that would protect us from the shockwaves of a nuclear holocaust, also kept us from receiving signals.

We were not TV addicts. The only TV we had at our previous house was an old 17 inch portable. We did like to watch the news and particularly the weather forecast and highway driving conditions. Our children, Scott and Breana liked the Saturday morning children shows. I enjoyed watching college football games on Saturdays. In 1980, TV was pretty much an intellectual and cultural wasteland, so the loss of television was a very good thing for the family.

But this night I was unusually anxious, and wanted to anesthetize my mind with some network nonsense before I went to bed. With no TV to watch, I sought out whatever I could find to read.

As it turned out all my books were at the office, or packed away in storage boxes in the mechanical room of the house. The only book I could find to read was Sarah's Bible, the King James version, which we kept on the nightstand by our bed. I had never read the Bible. I had perused through it from time to time, mostly looking at the pictures. What could you expect from a right brained visual artist?

When I was interrupted by my strange experience, I was reading Genesis I and no one was getting smote down or screwed over in any other violent holy manner. I had no reason to be fearful of God or a wolf. I was wading my way through all the early fornicating, begetting, and trying to remember the names of the begotten. The rhythm of reading the text was almost hypnotic. I had to stop often to keep my concentration sharp and clear.

From the time I was five, I had diligently said my nightly prayers. While it could be said I was not religious, it was not because I did not try. In my youth, I would go to various friends' churches looking for a god to replace the one I had created on my own over the years. I always came away disappointed by the usual revelation that if you didn't commit to a particular church's philosophy, getting into heaven would be problematic: "My God is better than your God," or "We are the chosen ones," mentality

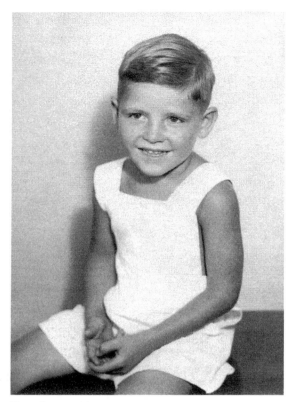

Me at 5 years old

ruled. For some unknown reason, I was preoccupied with getting to heaven at the end of my life.

Years later, I often attended Bible class after school. I was an eager and needy student. The God I had created was universal in his fair treatment of all male and female mankind, and did not discriminate against any human no matter their color, race, age, or religion. The God I believed in and worshiped through evening prayer was completely benevolent and never took reprisals against man. He was supportive of anyone who abided by the Golden Rule, and the secular aspects of the Ten Commandments.

We were here to better our culture, and the lives of our fellow man. God let us live here, but was too busy to bother about our daily personal wants. It was my premise that failure to abide by those simple rules made getting to Heaven problematic.

My God did look familiar. He had a light complexion with no warts or zits. He had long, flowing, medium brown hair with golden highlights. He had blue eyes, Nordic features, and his hands were always clasped in prayer. For some reason he looked just like the painting of Jesus that hung on the wall of Miss Brown's living room where we met for Bible class. My spiritual beliefs were very provincial by everyday religious standards. I didn't know about the churches' need for money and power over others. I was not out to smote anyone, or group, because they did not believe as I did.

I consciously tried to be as good of a person as I could, but I occasionally broke the Golden Rule and the Ten Commandments. I was eager to learn how to be a better person through the teachings of the Bible and Christ, but not the human-invented dogma that laced most Western religions. You don't have to be an old sage to spot the hypocrisy between the theory and practice of most religious groups. As a child, I remained spiritual in my beliefs about life, but I was not religious in that I did not identify with any denomination. I was intellectually somewhere in between Native American animism and Buddhism, and looking for a spiritual home I could devote myself to.

As I sat on the loveseat, I continued reading the Bible into the early hours of the next day. As I read the King James version of the Bible, parts of the Old Testament kept coming to mind. I wondered why did the early Christians sacrifice animals, in particular bulls? Who were these people drifting down out of space? How could they ride on chariots propelled by fire? Why did Moses' hair turn white and he appeared to be glowing after he returned with the stone tablet with the Ten Commandments inscribed on it? And how come Jesus, son of God, looked like a fair-haired, blue-eyed Anglo Saxon and not a dark, almond eyed, Roman-nosed, curly-haired Jew from the Middle East? I wondered how could all the religious people I knew be so unimaginative and believe this fantastic, romantic tale?

As an outsider, the Bible struck me as being an incredible story; one far too imaginative for most of the conservative religious people I knew of to believe in. These people were a real contradiction. Show some Bible belter an abstract painting by Mondrian or Kandinsky and they were befuddled, turned up their noses, and went for a Grant Wood. Yet these same people could readily eat up Biblical stories like pudding. Maybe my inability to believe some of these stories was because I had not been taught what to think as some of my traditional religious friends had been.

It took four more nights and I finished reading the *King James Edition of the Holy Bible*.

CHICKADEE IN THE NIGHT | FEBRUARY 20, 1980

I awake in the night to the two tone whistle of a **Black Capped Mountain** Chickadee. It's loud, distinct, clear, but slightly mechanical sounding. The whistle comes again, and my ears instantly triangulate and lock in on the position of the sound in the dark bedroom.

What the hell! I think. I quickly crawl over Sarah and reach for the light switch, which is near her side of the bed. Leaning over and on her, I flip it on and illuminate the entire room. I look directly at the area of the bedroom the whistle sound came from. The space is halfway between the west patio sliding glass door and the balcony area of the bedroom that overlooks the living room below.

I get up and walk to the area where the whistle sound came from. There is nothing there. I am puzzled; I distinctly heard a chickadee whistle from this point. I scan the whole bedroom and see nothing. I look out into the second story space of the living room and see nothing.

Sarah is still half asleep and quizzically asks, "What are you doing?" I tell her what I heard, turn off the light, and go back to bed.

West bedroom with bird cage and sliding glass door

▪   ▪   ▪   ▪   ▪   ▪   ▪   ▪

Later in the year, I hang a bird cage in the space where I heard the chickadee sound come from, conceptually catching it. I have never had this kind of experience of sound coming from nowhere before in my life. In the past if I heard a sound it was the cat or dog, the furnace, or other natural phenomenon that occurred for some reason around the house. The source of the sound could be logically ascribed, rationalized, and pinpointed.

It took me some time to go back to sleep that night. I kept wondering how I could have heard the wild bird sound in our bedroom. There was no question I heard the sound, my hearing was excellent. In fact, my acute hearing skills almost got me inducted into the Navy during the Vietnam conflict in the 1960s.

In 1949, a neighborhood friend and I were shooting dragonflies out of the air. One flew over my head and my friend missed. I was accidently struck in my left eye with a BB, shot from his BB gun. It hit the pupil of my eye and an eerie copper-colored imprint emerged.

At nine, I did not blame my friend for shooting me in the eye. In a way I felt like I had it coming. I had been shooting everything in sight with my BB gun for years, perhaps this was my payback for all the harm I had inflicted on unfortunate animals. I didn't know about karma, but I would have understood the concept.

"Isn't that a shame," the doctor would always say each time my mother took me to see my eye surgeon after my most recent surgery. His constant use of the phrase, "Isn't that a shame," made me think that I should be ashamed of myself. So I began to develop an inferiority complex. I was clearly not as good as others who were whole. I was definitely damaged goods.

When people looked at me, I would turn away so as not to let them guess what was wrong with me. In high school, I almost flunked a course because I didn't make sustained eye contact with my journalism teacher, Miss Langley. She took my shyness as a negative sign, and a lack of interest in her class.

Early on, my mother told me not to stare or look at anyone for long periods of time. My left eye tended to wander and others found that distracting. When people became aware of my wandering eye, they always developed a shocked look. I could immediately tell that my "stock" had plummeted and I was treated differently; like I had been suddenly written off someone's "special" list.

Mom must have straightened my journalism teacher out because Miss Langley changed my final grade from F to C and I was allowed to graduate from high school in 1958. Mother seemed to be shocked at Miss Langley's behavior, but my shoes were filled with similar experiences from the time I was ten. I didn't want or seek sympathy, just the chance to be treated normal and as an equal.

In an attempt to compensate for my obvious deficiency, I dressed and tried to look as nice as my budget permitted. I knew I had to be better at anything I tried just to pull even with the rest of my peers. I realized that if you are handicapped, you have to be twice as good at what you excel at just to be considered equal.

I found great solace in playing basketball. My above-average skills compensated for my affliction. I eventually became the co-captain of my very mediocre high school basketball team. On the court, my teammates treated me as an equal, and that small achievement proved very important in keeping me on an even keel. I was offered a basketball scholarship to a small, private Liberal Arts and Sciences College in central Missouri.

Of course, I did not like what happened to me, and I would like it less as I grew older and grasped the full implications of being blind in one eye. After most of the early operations, I was hospitalized for two weeks, to convalesce. I was restricted to lying motionless on my back, my upper head bound in bandages covering both eyes to ensure a "successful" outcome to the surgery.

While I didn't blame anyone for my condition, I sometimes silently wept, filled with remorse and self-pity. One of the orderlies evidently saw my tears running out below the bandages over my eyes and whispered something like, "Suffering teaches you about the human heart and forces you to plumb the depths of the human spirit in a way normal life can't. Suffering will make you wise beyond your years." His unwelcomed words were of little comfort to my young ears who already realized my carefree childhood days were over. A great pall swept over me and gloom set in.

In the old days, the hospitals had definite visiting hours. Few people were allowed to visit patients without permission during no visiting hours. Thus, the patient could rest and theoretically make a speedy recovery. Undisturbed rest was considered important to the successful recovery after an operation. During those no visiting times, the checker-patterned asbestos tiled hallways were relatively empty.

For me, who had to lie motionless on my back, listening to the radio was the only entertainment I had during the long boring hours of convalescing. Once the boredom of listening to the radio set in, I began listening to the walking patterns of the few people going up and down the hard-tiled hallway. I began to identify the footsteps of the nurses, orderlies, doctors and visitors, and of course, my mother, who stayed by my bedside as much as her free time allowed. After two weeks of intense listening and internal anguish, came the disappointment of another botched surgery.

After the bandages were taken off and I could see again with my good right eye, I would eagerly see if the sounds of the people who helped me convalesce matched the image I had developed in my mind's eye. I was usually surprised to see how far off or close I was in matching the voice and footstep sounds to physical characteristics of the person. It was during these times convalescing at the various hospitals that I developed a keen ability to hear, locate, and identify minute sounds that most listeners did not pick up on. I acquired the ability to imagine in my mind the images of what people looked like by their voice, footsteps, and touch.

During the buildup to one of the North Vietnamese offensives in 1964-65, I was called up by the local draft board to be tested before possible induction into the military. After all the written tests and the physical, I was pulled aside and told I had exceptional hearing and that I would be assigned to work as a sonar operator on a submarine or a destroyer. Allegedly, I would be stationed in the Bay of Tonkin inside Vietnamese waters.

I was not happy to interrupt my graduate studies, but thankful that I would be in a relatively safe environment during the conflict. Several weeks later I received a letter from the draft board. I was relieved of reporting for training and active duty. I can only assume the draft board rediscovered I was legally blind in my left eye and I would be a risk to others working or serving with me. I thus kept my 4F military status, and continued my graduate studies.

■ ■ ■ ■ ■ ■ ■ ■

Later this night, or early the next morning, after hearing the Chickadee whistles, I awake to Sarah shaking my left shoulder.

"Sean! Wake up!" she excitedly whispers.

"What's the matter?" I whisper back.

"I heard the chickadee whistle too!"

"Where was it?" I asked.

"Outside the sliding glass patio door!" she replies.

"What's going on around here?" I ask, "What did it sound like?"

"A two tone whistle…I only heard it once!"

I ask if it sounded mechanical. She says, "Yes, but it also sounded real."

To me the whistle sound had a slight mechanical metal resonance to it. But, who can be sure in the middle of the night?

I'm with some strange people who are very old, ancient. I am aglow with admiration for their brilliance and abilities. They are extremely tall. It's night. We are walking up a hill; I cannot see directly in front of me due to the nearness of the ancient one ahead of me. I see very little out of my peripheral zone. The trail we walk looks strangely like the path we take to get to the top of the mesa to the immediate west of our house.

It's dark, and I can't really see too much of anything. From time to time I vaguely detect familiar landmasses, mountain mahogany plants, cobble rocks locked in rhyolite shards, cactus, barrel cactus, scrub oak trees, yucca plants, ant hills, and other familiar sights.

But I think I am some place I have never been before. My emerging view of this world is of a vignette with limited range of vision that blurs out to the edges. My euphoria is laced with tense anxiety and wonder. We slowly move up this path that has many switchbacks. I intuitively seem to know who I'm with. I don't know why though or what we are doing on the side of this mesa? Mountain? Hill? No one has a name that I know of. No one speaks. I sense they are my friends, or at least friendly people. For some reason, we stop walking up the path.

I think I am with two people, but I'm not sure. Could there be more than two individuals? I continue to be confused and foggy as to why and what I am doing here with these incredibly tall people whom I cannot see much of. I am right behind one of the tall ones. I can only see his humongous back. My nose seems to be literally at the bottom of what should be his scapula. He must be over seven feet tall. But I don't know, maybe he is much taller.

I cannot move my eyes around, nor can I move my head much. As time passes, I cannot see much out of the region of my fovea. All peripheral vision is now very blurry and then dark. I am very irritated by the circumstances I find myself in.

I'm confused; I don't know where I am or why I am with these tall people, who are wearing such strange clothing. The back of this individual's clothing looks like it is made of several layers of cloth. At first, I think the layering is similar to the back of an Australian drover's coat. Yet it appears to be diagonal from his right shoulder to the left side of his back. The fabric layers are not straight across the back like a coat. Then

I realize it's more robe-like and made from a medium weight beige material similar to prophets' robes from Biblical times. But I'm having such a hard time mentally dealing with the situation that I can't be sure. I feel like I'm coming out from under anesthesia after an eye operation.

I have not seen or remember any faces long enough to describe their structural features. I know they are ancient and I feel like I have been with them before. I am so confused and the whole experience seems to slip in and out of some kind of reality I'm not used to. I am intellectually and physically dwarfed, I feel insignificant in their presence.

We stand facing what looks like the slope side of a tall mesa. The ambiguity of the experience is bothersome and continues to frustrate me. It's irritating that I cannot tell where I am or exactly who is with me. With great effort, I twist my body around and look behind me to see where we might have started from.

To my surprise, I see a line of people who are way down below, apparently on the same trail we trod. These people carry old-fashioned fire torches above their heads to light the path on the hill. The torches furiously burn, and the people look like peasants found in Boris Karloff's *Frankenstein* movie.

As the group and their burning torches come closer, I suddenly see the grim face of the leader under the bright flickering torch light. In this surreal scene, our eyes meet, even though he is a long way away. I immediately become aware that the group I am with has done something horrible to someone they love. These people with their torches and strange, old peasant looking clothing are after us!

I am suddenly gripped with great fear for my life! My heart is now going crazy and feels like it is going to jump out of my chest. Damn! They're out to kill me, and whomever I am with. We are being hunted like animals. I am not an observer of this scene; I am part of the scene!

I erupt up from the bed, I'm sweating bullets and my heart throbs. I'm confused and don't know where I am in this dark room. I look over and see Sarah peacefully sleeping by my side. My mind slowly begins to realize I have just broken out of a bizarre dream. I'm greatly relieved, but still feel confused and anxious by an experience that is too real to be a dream. But what else could my vision have been? My heart still pounds as if writhing to beat its way out of my chest. My fuzzy mind asks, *Did I have a dream or something else?* My mind is not sure.

West bedroom, outside patio and sliding glass door

I prop up on my elbows in bed and stare blankly out the west bedroom patio sliding glass doors in front of me. My heart still races and I'm still sweating. I've never had such an intense dream like this in my life. My train of thought is interrupted by the roof rafters above me creaking. Immediately, I think, *The wind must be blowing hard from the west, causing the rafters to sway and creak.*

Suddenly, I am brought around to full alertness by a soft light that sweeps across the second story wall of the living room and into the bedroom. The faint light is brief but long enough to get my total attention. It takes my focus off the intense, bizarre, and vivid dream I have just had.

There is much building going on in the neighborhood. All the new homeowners are on the lookout for thieves who might steal bunks of lumber waiting to be turned into homes. I am on the alert now and awakening from the fog of my alternate reality.

Then, from out of nowhere, a bright elliptical light appears about eight feet outside the bedroom patio door. The light is approximately 18 inches long by ten inches wide. It slowly moves from the left into my field of vision. I think, *Holy shit!* There is obviously some son of a bitch prowling around our house again! I believe it is a person holding a flashlight at waist high level and then the circular light becomes an ellipse.

Our bed faces the west patio sliding glass door and we can see the scenic cliffs of the mesa above us. This is our fourth or fifth night in our new home and we do not have any window coverings. Whoever is outside can look right in on us if they continue coming toward the door.

The terror of my dream converts into an adrenaline surge. The person outside the house is approaching along the west wall and moves north to our vulnerable patio door. After the strange events of the first night in our home I have relocated my .38 to a new place in between the box springs and the mattress on my side of our bed. I frantically reach down and pull it out and into position to shoot. The feel of the gun gives me courage and conviction. I am no longer the prey or the potential victim. I am now a highly-motivated and accomplished hunter intent on capturing or shooting whoever is spying on us.

The light stops moving north toward the door. On my belly I slide, snake style, over Sarah's sleeping body on my way to the glass door. I wake her and whisper, "Take cover, there's going to be a fire fight, get under the bed now!" She makes no response. I focus on the light and wiggle as stealthily as I can over the soft, sound-absorbing carpet. The bright elliptical light is fixed, constant, but vibrating ever so slightly. It is very cold outside and perhaps the holder is shivering or has the tremors. The light is very clear, bright, and there is no apparent beam making the elliptical spot on the ground.

I approach the patio door and morph into an aggressive bushmaster itching to put an end to this bothersome prowler. I am now in control and eager to apprehend whoever is outside the house. The eight-foot sliding glass patio door has been bayed out 30 inches and the sides are solid walls. The open space at the top is shielded by another piece of glass canted down from the parapet of the house at a 45 degree angle and joins the vertical sliding glass door. The roof of the bayed out region is glass, allowing us to view the dramatic bluffs above the house. I cannot be seen behind the 30 inch wall that forms the bayed out area.

I crouch for a moment eagerly waiting for my unsuspecting prowler. I cock the revolver and slowly reach up and ready myself to disengage the door's lock. Before making my predatory ambush attack, I quickly look behind me. Sarah is awake but still in bed! She must have thought she was dreaming! DAMN! I change my plan to keep her out of the way in case there is shooting. I'll unlock the door, quickly slide the door open with one powerful thrust, jump outside, land like a Samurai warrior on two stable feet, and scream, "FREEZE, ASSHOLE OR I'LL SHOOT!!!"

I'm ready, almost eager to shoot. I'm psyched and mentally prepared to defend myself and family. If he moves and does not obey my command, I will not hesitate to shoot. I'll unload this .38 on whomever I see. I do not want to kill anyone, but this prowling around our house late at night is going to stop. I silently switch the lock latch on the door into the open position. As I do, the mysterious light suddenly sweeps around counter clockwise to the west, then the south, and is immediately out of sight! Shit!

Front, south side of the house

He must have heard me and is now moving south along the west side of the house. If I move quickly I should be able to intersect this prowler as he comes around the west side and cuts across the south side, or front of the house, and eventually to the road beyond. He will escape if I can't catch him as he goes by. The front, south side, of the house has two second story balconies with sliding glass doors. I have the strategic advantage if I can just beat him there.

I run to the first balcony that gives me the best platform to shoot from. The new thick, plush carpet absorbs the sound of my running feet, and I doubt I have been detected by whoever is also moving to the front of the house. As I race to the balcony door, I morph into a cat like predator who has one intention, and that is to shoot whoever is coming my way.

I go from hunted to hunter. My snub nose .38, with its two-inch barrel, is relatively accurate up to twenty feet. I think if I miss the first shot, I'll just empty the revolver as fast as I can and hope for a hit, then retreat to reload. From my new position, the prowler will be in my range if a conflict develops. I noiselessly creep barefooted out on the balcony that overlooks the intersection of the west and south sides of the house.

My position is much better than before. The solid balcony sides are collectively sheathed in six layers of thin concrete and stucco finish, all on top of an inch and a half of plywood. I would have some protection now in the event the prowler chooses not to freeze. I hear or sense nothing as I move out to the balcony's edge.

I slowly peer over the handrail and look down expecting to see my prey, but no one is there. I strain my eyes to scan the visible area for any evidence of a human form. Nothing. I listen intently, no sounds. Then I hear the faint sound of tires rolling over loose road gravel. I follow my ears and look south toward the subdivision entry and see a sheriff's patrol car coming in our direction toward the house. I think, *The first faint light washing across the west wall of the house must have been their car headlights as they entered into the subdivision.* Everything is clear now. The light I saw, and was chasing, must have been the patrol car's spotlight shining in our direction. The car must have stopped at the entry to the subdivision and scanned the area with a powerful search light. A flood of relief rushes through me.

I could have been killed if I had gotten into a shootout with someone quicker, a better shot, or shooting with a .357 magnum. I would have been blown right off the balcony! Hamburger! Or I could have killed a curious neighbor. The realization of what a foolish thing I had done quickly dawns on me as my adrenaline rush subsides and rational thought emerges. My hyper-aggressive act is completely out of character for me. I have transformed into someone I do not recognize. The great sense of relief I feel almost makes me giddy. Why have I become so territorial, so intense, and so eager to kill?

At that moment, Sarah yells, "Do you see the lights?"

I do. I see the sheriff's headlights slowly making their way along the subdivision's winding road toward us.

I yell back, "Yes, I see the lights."

Sarah calls out again, in a more excited voice, "Do you see the lights!!??"

Watching the patrol car weave its way closer to our home; I say again, "Yes, I see the lights!"

She yells again, "Do you see the lights!!??"

For no apparent reason I'm getting really aggravated now. I was anxious before, now I'm almost angry, pissed. I think, *How many times is she going to ask the same question?*

But she demands an answer to her question, yelling once more, "DO YOU SEE THE LIGHTS!!!???"

I don't answer, she must be deaf. The door from the balcony is open to the inside, and she should very easily hear my enthusiastic response to her excited questions.

I watch the patrol car make its way to our end of the subdivision. I then reason, *I'll bet they saw the kids' night light shine on the north-east side of the house through the glass patio doors and decided to come check the situation out.*

I feel very secure now, and happy that our neighborhood gets periodic police protection. I stand on the balcony until I start to calm down and get cold. It is 10 to 15 degrees out and I'm barefooted, in my underwear, and standing on the very cold brick floor of the balcony. I go inside, believing the patrol car will come up our driveway to see what the light from the children's room is attached to. I move quickly to the upstairs entry door and open it.

I am now on the north side of the house and the ground level that the driveway is on. I wait at the open door for four or five minutes. I'm getting really cold now and finally give up waiting for the deputy to come up our drive. I shut the door and go into the children's room.

Their bedroom is closest to the upstairs entry door. Scott and Breana are both sound asleep. Their room is on the northeast side of the house and has the same type of patio sliding glass doors that our bedroom has. I wonder how they could have slept through the entire "do you see the lights" business. I'm still anxious, confused, and have a slight

Children's northeast bedroom patio door

headache, but I'm wide awake. I go downstairs to the kitchen and have a peanut butter and jelly sandwich with a glass of milk.

As I eat, I am still perplexed as to the dream I experienced earlier in the night. Psychologists say we dream all night. In my entire life I can only remember having had two reoccurring dreams that I could vividly recall. Both were easy to interpret and occurred when I was under a lot of stress or extremely worried.

One of my two dreams always occurs when I am afraid of something bad happening to me. I am in a canoe with lots of other people who I do not know. We have no oars and are drifting down a mountain river at great speed. All of the sudden we approach a Niagara Falls-sized waterfall. As the canoe begins its death slide down the waterfall I wake up. I have had that dream many times, but it is not as intense as the one I had earlier in the night, about the tall ancients.

The canoe dream was short, an impossible situation for me to even consider being in, very Salvador Dali-esque. Tonight's dream was long, very real, electrifying, haunting, and perplexing, almost tangible. There does not seem to be a moral or hidden meaning that I can decipher or understand. The contents were just a snippet of time that illuminated an event that came out of nowhere and ended in an incongruous conundrum.

What a bizarre dream that will always be tattooed to my soul. A dream I may never have again. My head aches, I take two aspirins and go to bed. Sarah is fast asleep and will be getting up early to make her long fifty-mile commute to work. I do not wake her to talk about the sheriff's patrol car checking on the subdivision. The whole incident was benign and not worth waking her to discuss. I'm innervated and settle into an uneasy sleep.

By the time I wake the next morning, Sarah is long gone. She has gotten up, dressed herself and the children, made breakfast for all, loaded them in the car, dropped them off at daycare on the way, and she is now in class teaching her first of five classes in photography. Whew! What a woman. I always ask to help in the morning, but she says, "There's no use getting up, I can handle it."

We both share the load equally in far different ways. This academic semester, I get up later, go to bed later, and teach three days a week. I need every bit of creative and planning time I can sequester to get all the work at home accomplished. It's February, and spring will be here before I know it, so I've got to have a plan for snake-proofing the outside and inside environments, to insure the children's safety.

Once I get over my sense of guilt for not helping her this morning, I call the dogs for their morning meal, before I get ready for work. We got them a year before we moved out to our new home in Plum Creek Valley. They are Labadors and littermates. The two are charged with helping to protect the children from rattlesnakes. Allegedly, the vibrations they make while playing with the children, along with their sounds and smells, will keep snakes out of the immediate play area. Of course, they are hunters and curious about anything alive in their territory.

I try calling Huggy and Charma and to my surprise, I have no voice, just squeaky raspy sounds. My throat does not hurt though, and otherwise I feel fine. Why I can't talk, I do not know; perhaps I got colder than I thought standing outside with no clothes on.

At nine a.m., I call the Art Office and squeak out my reason for not coming into work. I leave brief instructions for the secretary to give to my students. I feel good, and I go to the Castle Rock lumber yard and buy materials to construct storage cabinets in the downstairs mechanical room. As I unload my first batch of 2x4s and begin carrying them over my shoulder to the house, I am immediately riveted by the overpowering feeling that I'm being watched with great intensity. I snap to attention and look up and to the west.

For some reason I look directly at a small figure looking down on me from the rim of the mesa some 1,000 visual feet away. My gaze is inexplicitly locked onto his. This strange person is trespassing and is just standing there looking at me. I am confused by the feeling and body language he presents from his lofty position. I am not sure if he is looking at me with an air of great superiority or is concerned about the family's presence here. I decide to aggressively stare him down to visually let him know I do not want him on our property.

After what seems like a long time, the weight of the 2x4 studs cut into my shoulder. I psychologically blink, and intuitively know he does not. I feel bested, in this undeclared staring match. After I turn my gaze away, I look back and notice he unfolds his arms and relaxes them naturally by his side. I only now observe his arms look very long. While I have been staring, I have not been seeing.

As I walk toward the door with the lumber, I think about climbing to the top of the mesa to run the trespasser off. It takes 25 minutes just to get to the top of the mesa. I decide it's not worth the effort. I will probably never see the person again.

I'm wasting my time and continue into the house, downstairs, and into the mechanical room with my load. As I set the lumber down on the concrete floor, I realize what a strange physique the guy on the bluff had. The figure had an abnormally large head, long torso, short legs, and arms that came down to his knees, not mid-thigh as they should. I bust my ass getting up the stairs and out the door to take another look at this individual. He is gone. I think, *Jesus, what a strange-looking guy.* He stood, staring down at me in such an arrogant, but quizzical manner.

I have taught anatomy and life drawing classes for ten years, as well as illustrated the human figure for clients, and I know what the classical cannon of human proportions are. This guy was really screwed up by Greek ideals of human proportion. How come I didn't notice his strange proportions when I thought I was staring at him? Why did I have to get downstairs before it dawned on me what I was really looking at? How strange. Again, I think about rushing up the path to the top of the mesa to meet him. It will take too long, giving him time to get into his car and leave. I need to keep my focus on what I am doing. I go back in the house and work on the framework of the storage cabinets the rest of the day, and then cook dinner in preparation for Sarah and the children's arrival. My voice mysteriously comes back by the time Sarah and the children get home around 5:30 to 6:00 p.m.

Sarah barely enters the front door when she asks, "What did you think of those lights last night?"

I think, *Well here we go again.* Instead I say, "It's great the sheriff's patrol cars are going through the neighborhood at night."

I can tell by her incredulous facial expression that she is confused by my matter of fact simple answer. She explains what she had seen while lying in bed looking out the west patio door toward the top of the mesa and it's totally different than what I saw. I was looking south, Sarah was looking west, and we were both seeing lights. No wonder there was such confusion in our "do you see the lights" conversation.

▩　▩　▩　▩　▩　▩　▩　▩

Shortly after the light in the yard swung around and disappeared and I ran to the south side of the house, Sarah saw a different set of lights. According to her statement, given six years later to Ethan Rich, Assistant State Director for Colorado MUFON (Mutual UFO Network);

"The first light appeared to oscillate from above the house. It was a single beam of white light approximately four feet in width, and would appear out the north and west windows every ten seconds or so. Why it appeared to be oscillating from above the house was that the beam was passing very low on the bluff, actually passing only about 50 feet outside the windows. From my perspective in bed, if the beam had come from the front of the house, the beam would have washed across the north bedroom wall as it passed. The south bedroom wall has a partial overlook of the living room below. Any light coming from the front of the house would shine on the bedroom wall. There was no light showing on the bedroom wall, it just showed outside the north and west windows. The light made only about five or six revolutions and then it quit as abruptly as it had begun.

"No more than a few seconds passed before the second round of lights started up. I saw them through the west [*bedroom*] sliding glass doors. They were on top of the bluff and appeared to be in a fog or were themselves whirling clouds. This seemed odd since the white circling light showed a clear view outside the house, no fog. They were bright pink and blue lights in oscillating clouds whose movement reminded me of time lapse cloud photography. The kind we have all seen, which when viewed, gives a look of extremely fast moving, in this case, oscillating clouds. The burst of lights lasted only seconds and then the night became black again. There were no sounds that I recall."

※　※　※　※　※　※　※　※

Wow! How exciting that we, or Sarah, had seen what could only be a UFO! How fantastic! We had heard about UFOs but never thought about seeing a craft from another world ourselves. We wanted to believe in them as saviors of our humanity. They were a romantic wish fulfillment, our salvation in an insane cold war with Russia. The press was always eager to point out that only nut jobs, weirdo freaks, wackos, and people with overactive imaginative minds saw UFOs.

As we ate dinner that night, after her revelation, we talked about the light by the house, my misinterpretation of it, the lights on the rim of the mesa, and what it all meant. We didn't have a clue as to what this sighting meant to us then, or in the future, but we were just excited to have seen a UFO! We were not frightened and did not verbally dwell on the event.

Privately, the memory took over my mind like a Kudzu vine; its tendrils growing into every nook and cranny of my thoughts. I felt very special, euphoric and thought they visited us because our house lived up to Corbusier ideals, "A true house should be a machine for living." From that night, the experience was always very close to the surface of Sarah's and my consciousness. We felt very special to have seen lights from such an object and to have witnessed an unusual event as the craft blasted off or somehow disappeared. But, since I was outside that night, why didn't I hear the sounds of the blast off? Then I realized, Sarah didn't say it blasted off. Maybe it didn't blast off, but just lit up pink and blue and disappeared in an animated fog on the spot. Could it have stayed there as an invisible thing or gone someplace else without being seen leaving?

Our only recent reference to UFOs back then was Spielberg's very romantic movie on the topic, *Close Encounters of the Third Kind*. We now knew from our own experience, we were not alone in the universe, a most exciting, comforting thought and feeling.

It's my regular day off to do my own creative design work and curriculum planning. I get up and hike to the top of the mesa to the place where Sarah said she saw the pink and blue lights. I scour the entire rim of the cliffs and find nothing that I think is out of order: no burn marks, no weeds or grasses bent away from a center point, no rocks, cobble, or pebbles moved from their usual position. Mosses and lichens are all intact. There are no footprints in the sand or gravel.

What I do find is chilling, there are three small scuff marks on a large piece of cap rock near the edge of the mesa. The rock's dark, weathered patina is barely scuffed and the light-colored parent material below is hardly visible. I cannot say that the marks are true physical evidence. Another person may say that they were made by natural causes. The marks are right where Sarah said she saw the lights. The almost imperceptible marks are roughly one and a half inch by three-quarter inch in size. When visually connected, they form a triangle that is approximately six feet between each leg.

When standing in the center of the triangle, I see a straight path down into our bedroom. The first thoughts of the potential purpose of the visitors cross my mind. Was last night just an anomaly? My thoughts turn to the UFO sighting and the strange events prior to and after the actual blast off or…? Perhaps the UFO just disappeared into a different dimension.

■   ■   ■   ■   ■   ■   ■   ■

How eager I was to rationalize and confuse the lights of the sheriff's patrol car with those the UFO emitted. There was no way a search light could have displayed a focused beam around the west side of the house. The car was a mile away, and the light would have had to penetrate through the foliage of a 30-foot juniper and then through the branches of several oak trees, plus through the southwest corner of the house. How could I have thought the ten-watt nightlight in the kid's bedroom could be seen from the same distance? The officers would have had to see through the house to the light's location on the back side of the children's bedroom. I concluded that the only light from the patrol car were the headlights that washed softly across the west wall of the living room when it entered the subdivision.

I also jumped to another conclusion and made an everyday rational gestalt out of the unusual bright vibrating elliptical light. I conveniently rationalized the noise of the rafters quaking and squeaking on the roof above me when there wasn't a breeze to be had that night. The rafters were responding to the weight of a craft or person shining the light down on the ground near the west patio door. How humorous it must have been to the ETs in the mothership on top of the mesa to watch me creeping around like a cat after a light reflecting off of a watch crystal onto a wall. It was also funny to think that I unwittingly hunted a UFO right over my head with a snub-nosed .38! If ufolks laugh they must have been in hysterics.

No wonder the light disappeared just as I prepared to jump out and say, "Freeze asshole or I will shoot!" They must have told those on the roof I was about to come outside, thus ending the strange cat and mouse game. Well, I wasn't too embarrassed at my response, and I could see how the game was pretty funny.

My mind then flashed to the person I saw on the mesa top. In retrospect, he appeared to be wearing a tight jump suit. The suit was essentially the same light brown color as the object which struck the window the first night we moved into the house. When it dawned on me that the color was the same, a cold front from Hell swept across me.

It didn't take long to connect the dots to create the ominous picture emerging in my mind. These people were watching us, but why? I was smart enough to know they weren't hanging around just to have fun playing games with me. Could the dream of the ancient ones, that woke me up have been a metaphor for the real events of the evening? Could the people coming up the trail after us with torches have been a metaphor for the sheriff's patrol car winding its way into the subdivision? Was it a premonition? Perhaps the sheriff's light and presence scared the ufolks away, and the whole veil of the surrealistic dream was lifted when the patrol car approached the entrance to the subdivision. Was there some kind of mysterious relationship between my dream and reality? Maybe I had actually been with this pair of ancient people before and I was having a flashback, not a dream. There were so many similarities between my dream and the real events of the night. I would think about that night for years, and perhaps will for the rest of my life.

Why were people wearing old-fashioned clothing in my dream? And why were they using torches instead of flashlights? An impossible thought tickled my conscious mind. Could I have traveled with these tall ancient-looking people back in time to the mid-eighteenth century? Had we somehow provoked peasants into hunting us? How bizarre an idea! How could an uncertain romantic skeptic like me even consider time travel, let alone experience it? Could Sarah and I have stumbled onto the existence of people from another world when we bought this property?

Two days later, I learned a very important lesson. I went to work the day after my regular day off, and proceeded to tell the school's secretary and a few faculty members loitering in the faculty office about the UFO visit. Just talking about the evening's events made me excited. I got goose bumps and became very animated. For a moment, I experienced euphoria again. It felt good. The chairman of the department came up and listened to the last half of the story.

When I used the word UFO, it hung in the air like an invisible vapor that only a few could imagine or comprehend. Some rolled their eyes in disbelief that a word like that could roll off my conservative lips in this academic community. I could tell other faculty were intrigued by my story but were afraid to comment. When I finished, the chairman caustically said, "Well, that makes a good story," implying I made it up just to stay home in our new house. Our secretary seemed embarrassed for his thoughtless remark. She turned and went back to her office.

With the chairman's caustic and ignorant remark, I became a little bit smug knowing what I knew. I instantly became a galvanized believer in the reality of UFOs. From that moment on, I also knew to keep my story to myself and to only share it with close friends and more open-minded people. Later, I developed the philosophy of: *if they ask, tell; if not, keep your mouth shut.* And that is what I did for many years.

GURGLES IN THE NIGHT | MARCH 2, 1980

Several days after we saw the lights, I awake in the middle of the night to the sound of water being poured into a pipe that seems to be about eight feet long and inclined at a slight angle. In muffled gurgles, it flows down toward the other end of the pipe. I don't hear water come out the end of the pipe and fall to the floor below, just the gurgling sound. I can tell it's coming from the living room, and is about 15 feet off the floor.

Poor Sarah. I crawl over her and turn on the lights. She is pummeled in the frantic process and wakes up. I go to the balcony area that overlooks the living room, but I see nothing, no evidence of a pipe or fluids on the floor below. I guess I should have known there would not be anything, but I'm the eternal optimist and expect to see something.

I turn off the lights and go back to bed. I can't sleep and the sound haunts me. I have heard a similar sound before, but I can't place it. After much reflection, it occurs to me the sound is like that of a plumber checking the draining ability of sewer lines being installed in a basement right after the concrete wall forms are removed.

▩　▩　▩　▩　▩　▩　▩　▩

How did I know this? The summer of my fifteenth year, in 1955, my parents said I needed a job. I was very respectful and always obeyed my parents. I had my driver's training permit and was mobile, bored, had a girlfriend, and eager to make some money. Dad said, "Why don't you go down to Watersedge, and look for a summer job?"

We lived in a subdivision ten miles away. Watersedge was the closest urban area where a teenager might expect to find work. One of my friends at the time worked at a Dairy Queen there, so maybe I too could find work in the area. I drove to Watersedge and ended up at the Trails End Motel. The motel sat in the sleaziest part of town. I was attracted to the place by its gigantic metal and neon sign; a replica of James Fraser's painting of an exhausted Indian on his horse, titled, *Trails End*.

From the time I was ten, I had heard rumors I was part Indian. I didn't know

Me on the right with my braves, at 8 years old

what part, but I liked the idea. I had great admiration for the hunting and survivor skills of Native Americans. I also liked their dress and lifestyle. No one else in the family shared my view, and the allegation was always spoken in hushed words.

Naturally, I was attracted to this big sign of the exhausted Indian sitting on a worn out pony. I went into the office and asked the old, dried-up sour puss working the front desk if she might have some work for me. With a little effort she said, "Maybe," and called for Herman, her husband. Herman was a short, jovial, and portly German about

50 years old. He looked ancient, and I was reminded of a 1950s red-faced, red-necked, blue-collar, Coca Cola bulbous-nosed Santa Claus wearing a pair of stripped carpenter's overalls. Herman didn't have a lot of hair, just a fringe above his ears and around his lower cranium. He looked like he belonged in the scriptorium of a fifteenth century Italian monastery. I immediately liked Herman.

He scrutinized me and asked how old I was.

"Fifteen," I said.

"You're too young; you don't even have a Social Security card."

I retorted, "I am a very hard worker and would like a chance to prove myself."

After much grousing around, he finally said, "OK, let's see what you can do with the backyard, the grass needs mowing."

His wife gave him a strange look even considering her eyes looked like they had been dipped in alum. They were tinged with red, tight, squinting, and shifty. She said nothing, it was just the look that made me suspicious.

Herman took me out back of the motel and got the old power lawn mower out, gassed it up, and dusted it off. The mower had not been used for a long time. I was confident I could mow his grass, since I had been cutting our grass at home for many years.

Herman led me and the old lawn mower to the fenced-in back yard. There was hardly any grass to be mowed, just small patches here and there with tall grass along the edges of the chain link fence. Various weeds, rye, and crab grass were spread intermittently over the entire yard. The rest of the space was barren Missouri clay dirt covered by hundreds of piles of dog crap. The backyard was where they kept their giant and beloved boxer, Oscar.

Herman said, "When you finish, come to the office; Gwen will pay you."

I saw very little to mow, except these piles of dog shit with tall clumps of hearty rye grass growing around the edges of older piles. The only way I could mow the clumps was to go through the piles of crap. I had no idea what they fed that big boxer, but it didn't look like he had missed any meals.

Once I started mechanically mowing back and forth across the yard, mowing lots of dog shit and a little grass, the stench became almost unbearable. Each time I ran over a pile of crap there would be a big dull WHOP sound, and crap particles would fly out the discharge side of the lawn mower and splatter back all over my legs and beyond. I needed the money and a job. I would do anything to finance my romantic activities. After an hour or so I finished. My lower pant legs and shoes were covered with dog shit.

There was a water spigot with an attached hose mounted to the side of the motel. I washed my shoes, pants and the mower, and went back to the motel office to get my pay. Herman was very jovial when I came into the office; he must have liked the way I leveled all that dog shit. The yard looked like someone gave it a medium yellow-brown crew cut as the areas between the piles were covered by a veneer of freshly mowed yellow-brown crap. Recycled Purina Dog Chow, no doubt.

Herman paid me and gave me a fifty cent tip. I was elated. Then Herman said I was the only one who would mow that grass and asked if I would like to work for him on a more permanent basis. Of course I said yes. Evidently Herman believed mowing the yard was a rite of passage for new help.

Herman was a plumber by trade, and he needed an assistant to help him plumb new homes. I had no idea what he wanted me to do, but I said I could do the work. The rest of the summer I either mowed neighbors' yards or worked for Herman plumbing new homes. I loaded and unloaded his old oxidized green Chevy panel truck with plumbing supplies. I also threaded pipe, dug trenches for sewer pipes, put oakum in joints, ran back and forth to his truck getting tools, and did all the heavy lifting of pipe and supplies.

One of my biggest jobs was keeping Herman company and laughing at his folksy jokes. I could tell he reveled in enlightening me to the ways of the world through his funny stories. He liked me and I liked him. I was the son he did not have and he was the father I longed for.

It also turned out Herman led a double life and used me as a decoy to appease his wife and allow him to see his younger, sexy girlfriend. He would have me meet him at the motel office where Gwen would see me and think Herman was going to work. He would usually say he had to do "service work" so he could take his big ass yellow Cadillac and a few tools to tighten this or that leaky faucet or whatever. I never saw Herman do any service work on inanimate objects, but I was sure something was getting serviced.

He would always go to the same rundown Craftsman-style cottage home out in the country. Herman would swagger up the steps to the front door, and go inside without knocking. What balls! I would end up on my back in the very low crawl space of the house scooching around through cat shit, cob webs, spiders, roly-poly bugs, ants, old construction bits and pieces, feathers, and old smelly dried up rat and mouse crap and carcasses.

I could hear much through the naked, un-insulated, one-inch floorboards of the house above my head. The undersized two by six inch floor joists would begin jumping up and down as portly Herman and his lady danced and carried on with great zest, joy and delight. I couldn't see, but I could imagine what was going on right up above my head. Then all would go quiet, and that was it for an hour or so. I was left there in the dark, blindly scooching around on my back with my nose on the floor joists, hoping I wouldn't run into a copper head or other poisonous snake while dragging a hot work light on the end of a 50 foot extension cord that habitually went on and off at the most inopportune time.

My job was to follow the plumbing in the crawl space and look for leaks. By the end of summer, I had gouged a grove in the dry, filthy dirt under all the plumbing in Herman's girlfriend's house. It took me a few trips to realize I was Herman's cover in his romantic tryst with a woman whom I never saw and who would always remain a mystery to me. I was not judgmental, I could see how he could be lonely; his wife was a real grouchy bitch with boobs that could pass as mud flaps.

What does all this nostalgic bullshit have to do with the noise on the February night in 1980? One of my other regular jobs with Herman was to help install the sewer plumbing in new homes. We were the first people to work in the basement after the concrete wall forms were removed and the framing of the upstairs had begun in earnest.

Normally there was very little light in our work area, and we were grubbing around in an ungraded basement strewn with old rotten lunch leftovers, human fecal matter, and construction debris. Herman must have had his own mental laser level in his head. He always instinctively knew when we were on grade to make sure the plumbing worked properly. Fortunately, being on grade was his problem, not mine. I just did what I was told to do and daydreamed about my girlfriend.

Herman let me dig the preliminary sewer trench toward the septic tank inlet pipe while he gave instruction and contemplated the final grading of the trench. As I recall, we had to have one-eighth inch of fall for every eight feet of pipe run.

As we connected one length of pipe to another, we tested the flow ability of the drain pipe by temporarily adding a vertical elbow to the near horizontal drain pipe, then he would pour water down the pipe to see if it would flow at the right speed to the other end of the pipe where it would run out on the bottom of the trench.

It was at that time that Herman simplified the plumbing process for me. "Sean, all a plumber has to know is; shit runs downhill and paydays are on Friday." Since then, I have noticed that real experts can always reduce a complex profession, process, or concept into a few poignant phrases like: E=mc². If people start speaking in complicated jargon they are amateurs or are trying to confuse you into believing their profession is very hard, complex, and sacred.

■   ■   ■   ■   ■   ■   ■   ■

The sound the water made trickling down the pipe then, when I was 15, was the same sound I heard earlier that February night. The noise was so loud I didn't dream it, and why should I dream of such a miniscule event in my life that happened so long ago? I heard water running down a pipe, figured out the reason for the sound from my experience as a plumber's assistant, but wondered why did it just pop out of midair like the two toned whistle of the chickadee had done many nights earlier. For the moment, there was no answer to my question. I needed an articulate expert or more noises to be able to establish a pattern that would lead to an answer.

I am like most designers; we seek to discover patterns that can link elements of a problem into a definable whole or gestalt. Once the patterns manifest themselves and links are made between the intricacies, the solution to the problem automatically emerges. Bucky Fuller once said to me while I attended a design conference, "To define the problem is to solve the problem."

I did not realize at the time how long and how many noises it would take before I had a recognizable pattern or inkling as to the meaning and importance of the sounds. In 14 years I would think I knew how noises popped out of nowhere. I fell asleep and did not know if the sound repeated itself later in the night. Sarah did not wake me to say she heard the water trickle down the pipe that night.

HUMMING | MARCH 15, 1980

It is the middle of the night. I wake to the sound of a low oscillating hum. It is like an electrical motor that rhythmically and slowly changes its frequency up and down. I cannot pinpoint where the sound comes from. I'm tired of being suckered by a noise only to have it stop when I make the effort to get out of bed.

I listen to the humming for ten minutes, and it does not move or change volume. It is constant, but I still cannot pinpoint the source. The sound seems to fill the whole house. The thought occurs to me that there is an electrical short somewhere.

We are in a legal scuffle with our builder over his lack of performance in finishing the house. We first took occupancy of the house on Valentine's Day, 1980, instead of Christmas, 1979, as we were supposed to do. On the first day we turned on the water in the lavatories upstairs, water came out the ceiling downstairs! So I think that our contractor's electrician had somehow screwed up the electrical wiring, and a short was causing the humming.

I get out of bed without crawling across Sarah. I do not bother turning on the light this time. With the lights off I figure I can focus all my auditory senses on the sound. I silently move around the house and end up in the family room near the balconies on the front of the house. Predictably, when I get to where the humming is loudest, it quits. I stand around for another five minutes waiting for the sound to begin again, but it doesn't. I'm wide awake, a little anxious, restless by now, and decide to look outside to check on the weather.

I turn on the outside flood lights and go out on the balcony where I first searched for the nonexistent prowler several weeks earlier. To my surprise, a beautiful, quiet spring storm is in progress. The snowflakes are very large and falling slowly to the earth.

Days earlier, I put dichromate flood lights on the porch handrails that cast colored lights on the snow as it falls. Dichromate lights emit almost pure light in hues of red, green, and blue. When they are all turned on and overlap each other, the results are secondary colors in the areas where two primary lights intersect one another. By way of example, red and blue lights overlapping will give you the sibling of the two parents, magenta. If the lights mix just right, you get secondary and intermediate colors in the entire visible electromagnetic spectrum. In a big snow storm, the effects of the colored lights on the falling snow are spectacular. Of course you can't get the color as brilliant as when mixing pure sunlight, but dichromate lights give you a good imitation of nature's electromagnetic phenomenon. I use the lights in my Introduction to Design class when we study the theory of light and color.

Right now, it is absolutely silent outside. I can only hear the slight hissing sounds of snowflakes hitting the super-hot flood lights.

As I marvel at the color show I move the lights around to change the color patterns in my visual field. I happen to look down on the ground in front of the living room. There is a circular area in front of the two stories of glass, defined by the changing depth of the fallen snow. Inside the circular shape, the snow is maybe five inches deep. Outside the circle, the snow is eight to ten inches deep.

I am amazed and instantly realize that a circular object has damn near stuck one part of its curving edge clear into the living room! The roof has a five foot overhang in front of the living room and the circular object had projected itself that far under the overhead roof line. How long the object was there I do not know. I am aware of the notion of flying saucers, and obviously to me, that is what had been parked partially under the overhang by our living room window.

Evidently, when I wandered into the family room listening for the humming sound, I was detected by the inhabitants, and the saucer shape must have silently moved away, leaving a nice circular track in the snow below it. The craft or circular object made the print by blocking the snow from falling under it while parked. A distinct image from the first night flashes back to my mind's eye, maybe I am the rabbit and should be worried about the wolf. Perhaps my subconscious showed me the image of a wolf to warn my anesthetized frontal lobes.

As I stand there staring at the circular impression in the snow, I wonder about the people who man these strange crafts and if they come to do the Lord's work. Do they have a god? Do we share the same god? Or are they our god?

Do they have a heart? Are they warm blooded? What phylum do they come from, and what do they think of us as a species? Are they coming into the house?

I do not move, transfixed by the strange phantom circular shape in the snow down below me. This ominous shape would symbolically represent so much more than I am capable of comprehending at this moment.

My mind is trapped in its own silence while my will seems paralyzed. I emotionally back pedal into the bedroom, take two aspirins, lie down, and tell myself the circle is a natural phenomenon caused by ambient heat from the house and strange wind currents.

By morning, the circular shape is blurred by additional snow and drifting. By the time Sarah gets home from school that evening, the print is nonexistent and has been replaced by a two-foot snow drift that banks itself up against the sliding glass patio door. I begin to realize how I had rationalized the origins of the circular print. I am back to square one and don't have a clue about who was visiting us.

Sometime that week, it occurs to me what a nice shape a circular patio would make in front of the living room. I have been thinking about what I am going to do with the patio in this area, and a circular shape will fit very nicely. After all, the house is based on basic modernist elements: cylinders, tetrahedrons, cubes, and rectangles. In early spring, I create a circular-shaped patio out of brick pavers.

Circular patio

* * * * * * * *

What a fortuitous event the UFO imprint inspired. That was not the first, nor the last time, my art/design work had and would be directly affected by images, phenomena, materials, and experiences that I was not visually or conceptually cognizant of at the time. It would be 1983 before the light began to dawn in my mind as to the origins of some ideas leading to concepts generating meaningful artwork. I could only wonder how many humans created extraordinary designs, written inspirational music, produced innovative architecture, developed revolutionary ideas, etc., as a result of a little help from our "visitors."

One can readily see other direct influences that designers have responded to in creating for our contemporary culture such as the Walt Disney movie, *Frozen*. The characters look like alien hybrids with their large eyes canted at an angle, small nose, small mouth, and enlarged head with fine hair. Other alien influences may include the wrap-around sunglasses that look like ET eyes, amniocentesis, and then of course, our stealth bomber. These are a few obvious examples of how man has been influenced by ufolks. As they say, "monkey see, monkey do." In a year, I will experience a more subtitle method of planting ideas in human minds by our mysterious night visitors.

THEY'RE BACK! | APRIL 3, 1980

I think I am sleeping in our bedroom. I wake to see three lights the size of pinpoints coming toward me from what I believe is outside the west patio door. The lights shine through what I assume are the off-white drapes that now cover the glass patio doors.

At first, the lights are small; a bright one in the middle flanked on both sides by less intense ones. The three lights are in a row, mathematically arranged on the same horizontal axis. They appear to be about a foot apart, but everything happens so fast that I really can't be sure of size and distance, nor exactly where I am.

The lights come at me through the glass doors 12 feet in front of the bed, so fast that I only have time to lift my upper torso enough to reach below for the .38 tucked between the mattress and the box spring. I am stopped halfway in the process and cannot move. I then literally feel like I am liquefied and melt into the mattress, or whatever I am lying on. I have only time to say to a sleeping Sarah, whom I cannot see, "They're back!" The feeling of melting into the mattress is very soothing, warm and reassuring, a pleasant sensation. I am evidently anesthetized by the lights and lose consciousness. I do not remember anything after that.

The morning after brings with it a worrisome schism. Did I dream what happened or was it a real experience? One part of me thinks, *What a bizarre idea. How can such an event happen to me? What does it mean? Who are they? What do they want? What do they look like?* The other part of me tries to deny everything. As the day goes on, I say to myself, *Nah, nothing happened last night.*

Life goes on. I have no bruises or broken bones to verify something was done to me without my knowledge or permission. The experience is just too much for my cognitive mind to logically rationalize. Nothing appears to have changed, but I know deep in my soul something happened to me.

■ ■ ■ ■ ■ ■ ■ ■

From that point on, I never stopped thinking about our mysterious visitors, morning, noon and night. My days had no beginning or end. I was sure that we had become the focus of the beings who visited us in the night. The euphoria and excitement that came with Sarah's first sighting of the UFO turned to fear, panic, and anxiety. For the first time I was frightened. There was no one to protect us, only ourselves. If we told the police we had a UFO problem, they would laugh themselves silly and call us kooks.

This was 1980, people didn't openly talk about UFOs without paying a horrible emotional price for doing so. Religious zealots and half-wits seemed to rule the media and the media itself didn't want to talk about topics that would upset the populous. People wouldn't buy or watch shows which featured unpleasant topics. "Keep 'em stupid at all costs," must have been the mantra of the press. These self-indulgent reporters who were so full of themselves were quick to judge, ridicule, and humiliate the contacted who had no proof of the horrendous experience they had endured. Contactees would be labeled pathological attention seekers, and over imaginative nut cases, or worse. Careers could be ruined as a result of the mention of knowledge or belief in UFOs, aliens, or God forbid, abductions

On my way to work the next morning, my mind was consumed by thoughts of the dream or flashback from the night before and what to do about the problem of being abducted and not knowing what was being done to me. My preoccupation with the problem lasted all day, and on my way home, I had an epiphany.

Prior to moving into our home I often took our young Labradors duck hunting in the Plum Creek basin west of Castle Rock. There were many beaver ponds on the creek and the migratory ducks stopped to rest and eat on their way south.

Jump shooting was difficult, and I believe we only got two ducks over the entire season. I was not concerned with how many birds we got. I just wanted to give the dogs a chance to get some exercise doing the thing they do best, hunt ducks. Their natural hunting ability was remarkable and their enthusiasm for the hunt gave them and me a lot of pleasure and exercise.

On one hunt I shot a mallard. It fell in a beaver pond upstream on Plum Creek. When I got to the pond where I knew the duck fell, Huggy, our male Lab was already swimming randomly in the beaver pond looking for the downed duck. When he could not find it on the surface, he began swimming around in a big circle, gradually tightening the circle. Finally, he came to a point in the shrinking circle, dove underwater and came up with the duck. He brought it to me, laid it at my feet and looked up at me. What a dog!

Weeks later, we were jump shooting some ponds further south and I heard a flight of teal coming our way. I crouched down and froze, Huggy did the same. The ducks flew overhead, Huggy kept his head down and did not look up. If flying ducks saw the whites of your eyes or felt your gaze, they would often flair, veer off, and escape. How he knew not to look up I'll never know. As they passed over and presented a more fixed target as they moved away, I rose up and got one shot off. I missed the bird. Huggy stood up and gave me the "stink eye" as if to say, *How could you miss an easy shot like that?* God, he was a natural born hunter and never ceased to amaze me with his natural skills.

Charma, our female Labador, was another story. She liked to hunt anything on legs, and often ended up chasing rabbits, squirrels, or smaller creatures that caught her interest. Her inclination to hunt legged animals would be a valued asset in the future. She screwed up many pheasant hunts by chasing a jack rabbit right through the best hunting spots, flushing pheasants way ahead of us.

The solution to my more important problem was obvious, thus, my "aha" moment. I needed to go "duck hunting." The house was the duck blind, the UFOs were the ducks, and I was the hunter. What a simple solution to thwarting the unwanted visits.

At that moment I felt hopeful. I had not realized how depressed I was that these people, or beings, could do as they would with us. I was helpless to defend our home, but now I felt empowered. I was out to get one of our unwanted visitors and rid ourselves of their presence.

I had my epiphany on Interstate 25, about halfway between Denver and Castle Rock. I stopped in Castle Rock and got a five pack of twelve gauge double-ought buckshot shells. The shells were for my equalizer; grandfather's Winchester Model 12 pump action shot gun. At the time, it was the nastiest firearm of its kind on the planet. In my youth, I had read in more than one hunting magazine that this gun, with the kind of ammo it was loaded with, could stop a mature male African elephant when in full charge.

I had also begun to think that entities who came for you in the middle of the night, and didn't want you to know who they were, or what they were doing to you, were perhaps evil and to be avoided or destroyed. If they were innocent of any sinister acts, I thought, *Why didn't they just come up and knock on the door and say, "Hi! Can we come in and talk?"* Their openness would have made things so much easier, and I could get my sleep at night.

But now I had a simple plan I could execute, provided I woke up in time to get a shot off. I was confident I would wake up, after all hadn't I always awakened before when they came to the house? The visitors got lucky the last time. I would have to become a very vigilant hunter if I were going to get or meet my quarry.

Our visitors had only one pattern so far, they came quietly in the night. But I didn't know what time intervals they preferred to visit us. I needed to know their visiting periods and habits to succeed. To find out their visiting times I would have to stay awake every night until I either got a visitor, or they established a nighttime pattern I could use against them.

Years of the long nights began for me with that realization. Not knowing their visiting patterns, I would have to stay awake each night until they came. From my college years, I was used to studying until eleven o'clock each night, and then I would go to bed or take a break and continue working or reading. I continued that work habit until I was almost 60.

Staying awake was not difficult for me. The first part of the night I would review my day's work, family and social issues, home and personal needs, then try to conceive solutions to any problems I discovered. After that, I would think about how I was going to design the interior and landscape the exterior of the house to make it easy to see snakes. I visualized the materials and processes involved and then decided how to go about constructing this or that imagined solution. The permutations and processes of a given solution went on and on until I could narrow down the costs verses aesthetics and my capabilities of implementing the idea. I would move onto dealing with my professional conundrum of producing graphic design in a clientless vacuum. Lastly, I'd fantasize about the night project of capturing or shooting an alien.

I had no earthly idea what I was hunting. I supposed they must look like the weird creatures on the cover of the *National Enquirer*. The *Enquirer* even put Jimmy Carter's head on the body of an alien, so they could take any form. I did most of the grocery shopping, so I saw that type of publication each time I checked out of our local Safeway. My other models were the strange but similar creatures I had seen in *Close Encounters of the Third Kind*.

And then there were the creatures that appeared in all the science fiction movies of the 1950s that featured aliens. Most of those were such jokes they were laughable at best, except for the tall vegetable alien creature in *The Thing*, which scared the bejeezes out of me and my childhood buddies. There were also some popular songs of the fifties that sparked an image in my mind of what I might encounter, like "A One-Eyed, One-Horned, Flying Purple People Eater," and "Ain't No Haint Going to Run Me Off." I never knew what a haint was, but I could identify with the fanciful lyrics of the tune.

The only thing I knew was that my plan of attack was simple, stay awake as long as I could and at the first scintilla of a sound, jump into action. I wouldn't wait to say, "FREEZE OR I WILL SHOOT!" I would just make sure it wasn't Sarah or one of the children and then point and shoot in one fluid motion. I planned on shooting it in the stomach, saving the head for research and sale. I assumed I could catch our intruders after they opened the upstairs entry door and came in the house. I saw myself hiding or lying in wait at the intersecting corridor of the upstairs bathroom and entry hallway. All I had to do was step out into the hallway, turn to the left, and empty the gun on whomever or whatever was there.

After that, I would rush outside and attempt to capture the small transporter craft. If there were a door I would shoot inside the craft with the twelve gauge and try to disable the complex electronics I envision inside. I knew I would need to reload the shot gun, turn on all the outside lights, and call my neighbor, Joe, for help. I would wrap the body in sheets and try to get to Joe's house and put it in his horizontal freezer for safe keeping. Then I would go back to the house and guard the craft until the sun came up. I felt confident that Joe, a retired military man, could go to town and get some camo-netting to cover the craft with in the daytime to visually hide it until I could move it to a garage or barn in Monument. I was ready for the hunt and the kill.

DREAM ON | APRIL 5, 1980

We are in a legal battle with our contractor over the house. He refuses to finish the house or do any final landscape grading. I refuse to give him his final payment until he completes all the contract work, including the flying staircase on the east side of the house. Of course, our builder put a lien on the house.

We have spent every cent we can afford on the house and have little to spend for a lawyer to defend us. I don't worry; I think we will be vindicated. However, I know we can only hold out for maybe a year before the courts will order us to pay up. Our attorney tells us that by law, our contractor only has to finish 80% of the contracted work to demand his final payment.

Long story short, we need some money, and if I manage to bag one of these aliens, I feel sure we can sell the corpse to the *National Enquirer*. They can stuff the little bugger and haul him all over the nation doing promo work for the magazine. I can kill two birds with one stone; get these aliens out of our hair and earn some money to counter sue our contractor. Countersuing will make me as happy as getting rid of our unwelcome mystery visitors, but I don't know what I can countersue the guy for.

At first, I only dream about what I will do with the alien carcass and the complications of getting the body to the locker plant in Monument. Monument is a small town south east of us where I can keep the body frozen and intact until I cut a deal with the *Globe* or *Enquirer*.

As the nights roll by, my fantasies of such a clandestine sale grow into complex ordeals and intrigues about the mothership and their attempts to rescue their dead comrade. The price for the little guy raises exponentially until I am filthy rich. I fall asleep with that daydream running in my head, but it isn't long before my daydream takes a quantum leap in complexity and financial possibilities.

BOOM! | APRIL 6, 1980

It is late at night or very early morning. I awake for some reason and half sit up in bed. At once, I see lights through the off-white drapes covering the bedroom patio doors. LIGHTS! I look through the drapes, the lights are small and dim but I can see the colors are pink and blue. They rotate around a cylinder or sphere and are horizontally arranged. The radius of the circle they travel around must not be over four to five feet in diameter. Someone else, like Ezekiel, might describe the lights as "wheels within wheels." The rotating lights are about four feet off the ground and move north at a slow rate of speed. They go past the west patio door and turn the corner of the house and head east. I then see the lights go by the long, narrow north window of our bedroom.

The lights are not more than eight feet from me as they go by the window. I can't believe it; I barely begin my vigil, and here they are! Instinctively, I grab the .38 and bust my ass getting to my post. I cock the revolver, hold it stiff armed, firmly with both hands, and point it at the floor. At the right time, all I have to do is step around the corner, bring my weapon up into position, then empty the gun on whatever is coming down the hallway.

I have no fear; I am eager, and excited to terminate whatever has been mentally, and perhaps physically, violating us. I do not consider this as murder. I feel as though killing something that could very well be evil or dangerous to my family is okay with my God. In short, killing one of these night visitors means no more to me than killing a rattlesnake. I feel morally justified in what I am about to do.

I wait, straining my ears for the slightest hint of a door lock mechanism moving, or the knob turning, or the slightest hint of the door hinge squeaking. Fifteen to twenty minutes go by, my focus does not wane, and I hear, feel, and smell nothing. After about thirty minutes, which seems like an eternity, I slowly stick my head around the corner and look down the very dark hallway to the upstairs entry door. I scan the whole area with my eyes and ears, without moving my head. After several minutes, my eyes adjust to the dim light in the hall.

I am stunned to see that the front door is open by perhaps an inch. What the hell! I know I locked the door before going to bed. Every night I diligently make my rounds and check all the doors in the house before turning off the lights for the night. Why is it open only an inch or so? Those rat bastards, I must have startled them, and then somehow they sensed I was waiting for them, and retreated. I continue to stare at the door in disbelief that I have somehow blown a perfect opportunity to get a shot off, or to know what these beings look like. After another tense fifteen minutes or so, I cautiously walk to the door and open it to look out.

BOOM! For a millisecond, I feel an explosion of white light go through me like millions of particles. I am blinded by the most brilliant light I have ever seen. That is the last thing I remember that night.

Waking the next morning, I am aware something happened to me, but have no memory beyond the lights flooding my eyes. I don't feel, look, or think any different than normal. I begin to realize they somehow know what I do in the house and can anticipate my every move. How else could they have anticipated my aggression last night? Maybe the house is bugged. I scour every inch of the house, from the drapes to behind paintings, in search of any foreign objects or sensors. I find nothing.

* * * * * * * *

That was the second time they sensed I was about to do something aggressive towards them. Maybe they had some infrared sensors that looked right through the walls, doors, or roof of the house and could see us whenever they wished. I would continue to follow my only course of action, that's all I could do. Selling the house and moving was not an option, with the pending lawsuit and no money to begin to build or buy again. Besides, I appeared to be the only one having these dreams and seeing things that didn't make sense. I didn't seem to be worse off since we realized they were visiting or observing us. I was plagued by the thought of what these people looked like; what they were doing to me, and how they knew I was there in the hallway waiting for them.

I began to fear their next visit. I became anxious day and night from then on and was no longer confident I would win this battle. The brilliant light and events of that night were the first thing I thought of in the morning and the last thing I thought of at night. To fight depression and fear, and to stay awake at night, I ramped up my plans which now included the capture of their little transporter craft. I started off dreaming the craft would be worth a million dollars, but as the nights went by, the relative value of the transporter escalated into the tens of millions. Then I discovered a fighter jet of the day cost 100 million! Jesus, the alien transporter would be worth much more. The thought of liquidating our debts, of becoming independently wealthy, and sharing our good fortune with family and others, kept me going. I began to realize that the reality of getting an alien or craft was very slim, but I continued my nightly vigil.

ON THE WALL | APRIL 10, 1980

In the middle of the night, I wake to the dogs barking out in front of the house. I listen for some time and then reluctantly go downstairs and let them in. They are so grateful and their eyes are filled with both fear and joy. I try to keep them outside, our new house is still precious, and I fear they will crap on the new carpet. They have a warm doghouse on the northeast side of the house, and being Labs, can stand the cold weather. The two normally stay outside at night.

I put them in the laundry room adjacent to the downstairs bathroom. The room is small, six feet wide by ten feet long. The dogs are happy to be inside and quickly settle down on the soft bedding I provide for them. I go back to bed and I don't hear a sound out of them or anything else all night.

As usual, I get up after Sarah and children are already gone. I don't know if Sarah knew the dogs were in the laundry room so I go down and open the door to check and see if they are there. Huggy and Charma bolt out and nearly knock me down. Along with the dogs comes the unmistakable stench of dog crap.

I immediately realize why. About five feet up on the east wall is shit that looks like the result of one of the dogs being held up against the wall and pressed there so hard, he/she defecated on it. Another possibility is that one of them was thrown against the wall with great force and crapped all over it.

The drizzly feces ran down the wall almost to the floor. What the…! I have never seen anything like dog crap splattered all over a wall before. How horrible for one of the dogs. I go to the kitchen door, the two are dancing around wanting out…now!

Neither one of the dogs seems worse for wear with no broken bones or apparent physical wounds. I let them out and clean the wall and the floor. I wonder how someone could throw a 50 to 75 pound dog up against a wall when there is only six feet of throwing distance. The situation is so impossible I don't know what to think. The dogs' barking must have been in response to something harassing them last night. But how did whatever it was get in, and why did it come into the house to punish or quell the dogs? I did not hear them bark once they came inside. I heard nothing opening the slider door downstairs last night.

I am baffled, and my determination to shoot one of the harassers is renewed by the wrath taken out on two gentle animals that are of no threat to them. Is this a not so subtle warning to me? The aliens also give new meaning to the passive-aggressive act of "kicking the dog." I vow to be "at the rat hole" next time these gutless bastards pay a visit. My anger and need for revenge is the only thing that keeps me together today, and I long for a rematch.

The night after the dogs were abused, I wake to see the same pink and blue rotating lights go around the west patio doors heading north and then turn the corner and go along the north side of the house heading east. If anyone could have a pre-rapture experience it is me, and this moment is the cause. I immediately reach under the bed and get the shotgun, loaded with number two buckshot shells. This is going to be retribution, assholes.

I silently roll out of bed on my side and tippy toe to my station at the intersection of the bathroom hall and entry hall to wait for our abusers. I lean up against the hall wall with the shotgun in the ready position and pointed up. I click the safety off. This time I am going to wait until Hell freezes over before I go out to "play." This time *Thor* is with me and will be hammering 1400 foot pounds of deadly power per second of hot lead down the hall to greet whoever hid behind the white light five nights earlier.

My plan is the same, except I am not going to open the front door until after I shoot the bastard in the hallway. I will have two shots left to go after the craft and take out anyone else who is in the way.

One step forward and I'm in the hallway to the front door, spin 90 degrees to the left and BANG! My "million dollar baby's" guts will be all over the floor, and I will then charge out the door into the night and avenge our dogs' tormentors with some more kickass, hot buckshot. After the retribution ends to whatever is outside, I'll take the craft however I can. I keep thinking a shot to the instrument panel should ground the transporter craft. Then I will reload the shotgun and wait for the mothership to do whatever. Hell! I might as well think big; I'm out manned, out gunned, and surrounded by minds far superior to mine. However, a mothership should be ten times as valuable as a commuter craft. With a lot of luck I'll get them all. I'm excited and intoxicated with my desire to kill and end this lopsided contest.

I wait; my finger is on the trigger. The single minutes turn into thirty, then thirty turns into an hour of holding the heavy nine pound shotgun. Staying ramped up and focused that long is difficult for a hyperactive person like me. I begin to reflect on the history of the powerful gun I am holding.

The gun originally belonged to my grandfather, my surrogate father and hero. Grandpa Johnson was a Miami County, Kansas premier coon hunter and all around great guy. He and his three-legged dog, Ike, always won the Miami County Fair field trials for coon hunters in the late forties and early fifties. Grandpa was the president, or some kind of muckety muck, of the Miami County Coon Hunters Association. He had coons in wire cages scattered all over the back yard at his and Grandma's farm.

In other cages were opossums, always snarling and flashing their nasty, pearly white, thorny-sharp teeth at the slightest provocation. Those scary, beady-eyed, baby-fine hairy bastards could chew your fingers off if you got them too near. The coons were more or less indifferent and nervously paced up and down in their cages, swaying their heads back and forth waiting for a jail break that would never come.

These caged coons had a date with field trials in the upcoming county competitions. The coons were also in cages so his pack of dogs could get the scent first hand and know what to look for in the field trials. Ike, however, usually won the county competitions. With only three legs, he was always last in the pack after the scent, but he was thorough, took his time, and always was first to tree the coon, or scented pelt, that the other coon dogs overshot in their competitive enthusiasm for the hunt.

Grandpa was without a male to pass his passion for hunting and fishing on to. My aunt was unable to have a child. My mother, of course was not incapable, and so when I came along, I became the focus of his passionate affection for a hunting heir. At age five, he bestowed upon me his trusty .22-caliber carbine. He took me out onto the county road, away from the house, to show me how to shoot the insulators, off the telephone poles.

As we stood on the gravel road looking up at the insulators, I prematurely pulled the trigger and almost shot his foot! He was taken aback for a moment, but undaunted. Later that day, Grandpa took me into town and bought me a Red Ryder lever action BB gun. I was ecstatic, and began my tutelage as Grandpa's *protégée* in earnest. I hunted days, and dreamt of hunting at night. I read *Field and Stream, Argosy, Outdoor Life,* and any other hunting and fishing magazines that described how to effectively hunt. Whenever I was around, Grandpa talked hunting and told me stories to help me refine my mental and physical skills as a hunter. On special occasions, in the winter, I got to go coon hunting with him and his cronies at night.

We were usually part of a large group of hunters that coalesced to form a hunting strategy, and then fragmented into small groups that tended to spread out after the dogs were let loose on a coon's scent. We drove around in his old Dodge pickup that smelled of ancient dirt, grease, gas, motor oil, tobacco smoke, beer, and B.O. We frequently stopped to listen to the dogs chase the unlucky coon over hill and dale, and usually down a creek, thick with tall grasses, sycamores, cottonwoods, elms, papaw trees, and low shrubs.

While there was great interest in whose dog lead the charge, and predictions as to whose dog would "tree first," there was a lot of cigarette smoking and "pulling" on a bottle in a brown paper bag. As the evenings morphed into late nights, there was a lot less interest in coon hunting and lot more interest in such topics as marital and in-law problems, new John Deere farm implements, and who would win the KU/KState football game. All topics were very interesting to my young ears. But nothing beat getting out of the hot smoky truck and heading toward the baying dogs that had finally treed a coon. Grandpa always held my hand, and invariably, we stumbled over a plowed corn field headed toward a wetland to rendezvous with a large sycamore tree, a worn out coon, and baying dogs on a cold moon lit night. I held his labor-worn, leathery hand and he held his fabled Winchester Model 12 Pump Action shotgun in his other hand.

※　　※　　※　　※　　※　　※　　※　　※

Standing here in the hallway, I now hold that same gun, and hope to bag a quarry far different than any, I thought at the time, that Grandpa had ever encountered or sought. This gun is more than a gun; it is a memory stick for me, and as I wait and strain all my senses for a sign of my foe, I again lapse back into other memories of hunting with Grandpa for quail, pheasants, ducks, squirrels, rabbits, and coyotes.

※　　※　　※　　※　　※　　※　　※　　※

If it were alive and moved, had a bountiful pelt, or was edible, Grandpa hunted it, and his quarry didn't have to be in season. When I was with him and we weren't hunting or fishing, he was showing me off to his cronies and their friends. I loved to go to town with him. We always ended up in the bars that lined the north side of the Paola, Kansas town square. We started on the west end of the block and hit every bar as we moved east.

He had friends in every bar and they always bought me sodas that I never got at home, and gave me money for the coin-operated electronic shooting game, "Shoot the Bear." While Grandpa "shot the shit" and drank draft beer, I shot the crap out a mechanical bear that responded to infrared beams of light that emitted out the barrel of the gun. Each shot that hit a special spot made the mechanical bear move backward, forward, turn, stand up, and growl. Once the bear stood up and growled you could keep shooting it in the stomach to keep it in a vertical position. With each successive shot you scored crucial points to win free games. If you were good, and I was, you could score enough hits to win an endless number of games.

Once I started, I could keep shooting and winning free games until Grandpa had enough beer and bullshit at that bar. We would move on east to the next bar and repeat the process. By the time we hit the last bar, he was high and I was sick from drinking too many cream, grape, orange, and cola sodas. It was time to go home to a tea toting grandma who would invariably be puckered up, pissed, and speechless. God, poor Grandpa, he always paid the price for taking me to town with him for a little communion with his drinking and hunting buddies.

Grandpa kept his old Dodge truck and many of his farm implements under a big sycamore tree about a hundred feet east of the farm house. The shade from the tree gave some relief from the scorching summer Kansas sun. On many hot and humid August afternoons, I would play under the tree in the dust with my toy cars and trucks. Out of the corner of my eye I would often see him casually saunter to the driver's side of his truck and slightly open the door while looking over his shoulder in the direction of the house. With great stealth and dexterity he would slip his hand under the front seat of the truck and pull out a can of hot Falstaff beer. With his back to the house he would shield the beer at his breast, open it, and then in one calculated motion, lift that hot beer up to his lips and without pushing his head back he would suck that hot beer down in one big sucking motion. Grandma would not allow any form of alcohol in the house. I began to realize why Grandpa was such an avid coon hunter.

＊　＊　＊　＊　＊　＊　＊　＊

I have been standing in the hallway for what seems like hours, waiting for our intruders. Reminiscing about Grandpa, hunting, and this powerful gun I hold, keeps me awake, my courage up, and my belief that I can go head to head with whatever is on the other side of the upstairs entry door waiting for me. The hours slowly pass and the dark night begins to give way to a distant morning glow. I am fighting the creeping horrors of falling asleep while on the watch to protect my and my family's lives.

I finally give up waiting, and decide to walk to the entry door. This time I turn on the porch light and peer out the door's peephole to the outside world. I see nothing. Going outside, there is nothing to be seen. I am relieved, but disappointed to have missed another opportunity to rid ourselves of whoever is bothering us. I also begin to realize how hard it is going to be to keep up this intense, nightly vigil. I go to bed shortly before Sarah gets up to start her and the children's day. For weeks, I am haunted and perplexed by the aliens' ability to know where I am and what I am doing. Now, I am on the alert for any small element that could be a sensor to keep track of us around the house.

■　■　■　■　■　■　■　■

I was bothered by the idea that maybe the second time I saw the lights I had a flashback again. A flashback so strong that I went through the motions thinking the commuter craft was going by the house once more. But in reality, I was awake and having a secondary flashback. Then maybe I actually saw the craft the second night but it was just going by and cruising around the base of the mesa looking for more homes to visit. I wasn't sure what to think about the lights. I would just keep myself in the open position and stay alert. One thing I knew for sure, I had suckered for sound and lights in the past, and always found nothing. So now, instead of the house being the duck blind, I decided to retreat to a smaller area to defend or hunt from, our bed. Our bed became the duck blind and I would let whom or whatever come to me, unless I was positive that I would find something or someone elsewhere in the house.

CLICKS IN THE NIGHT | APRIL 15, 1980

My nightly vigil continues, and I begin to know all the noises the house makes. I also recognize many other sounds, like the one Molly, the cat, creates climbing up the wooden batts on the corner of the patio garden door frame, climbing back down, and then the soft thud of her dropping to the ground.

Among the myriad of definable natural sounds, I begin to pick up on an almost inaudible clicking of something walking around on the wooden parquet floors in the kitchen and adjoining dining room downstairs in the south east side of the house. Our bedroom opens into the second story of the living room and that room in turn, opens into the dining and kitchen area. The noise is not footsteps, but claws, cautiously clicking on the hardwood floors. The number of claws touching the floor per step sounds like four distinct clicks. Judging by the sound, there are three claws near one another and a fourth one farther away. The fourth claw is, as I auditorily visualize it, at least 18 inches away from the three clicks. I keep my vigil but do not go to see what makes the sound. After a while, I hear these sounds every night.

One night, I finally go down to see what is creating the noise. I leave the lights out and just quietly slip down to the kitchen area. I move south down the large corridor. I

hug the wall leading up to the kitchen on my left and reach with my left hand around the corridor wall to the light switch in the kitchen. In my right hand is the .38 ready to go in case I am threatened. As I blindly reach around the wall to turn the light switch on, I'm frightened. I don't know what I will see, and

Corridor with kitchen entry on left

God forbid if something grabs my hand while I am reaching for the light switch. I would pass out or go totally ballistic from anxiety realized.

Boom! I turn the light on and don't know what to expect, but I see nothing. I'm relieved. I take a big, well-deserved breath. The claw sounds suggest to me that whatever I am hearing belongs to a very large creature, and I'm not sure the .38 is capable of dealing with such a beast.

The shotgun is too bulky to quietly schlep around the house. Carrying the .38, I can have my hand on the kitchen light switch and shoot with my free hand if necessary. The shotgun doesn't allow me that kind of flexibility.

I stand motionless in the kitchen for five minutes or more. While I don't see a thing, I feel like something is watching me with great curiosity, intensity, and is unsure what to do in my presence. I hear, see, smell, or feel nothing, but I get edgy and know there is something alive in the room watching me. I psychologically blink. I should not leave the room, but I do and go back to bed. Walking away, I feel the riveting energy of something visually following me back upstairs.

Night after night, I hear the claw clicks on the kitchen floor, and I sometimes go to see what it is. I always find nothing but sense that something invisible is there. More than one time I press the issue, moving slowly and thoroughly around the kitchen and dining area with authority. I extend my naked arms and feel for any changes in air density or temperature. Each time I go down to the kitchen, I am just as anxious as I was the first time, but I keep thinking something will show itself some night. I'll be there to see what it is and do whatever must be done.

After weeks, I think the clicking sound belongs to some kind of humungous bird of prey's hard talons. The three clicks are the talons on the front toes of the foot, and the click that seems 18 inches away is the talon on the back toe. I cannot imagine a bird that large. The nightly clicking goes on for years; I eventually ignore them, and conclude that I probably will never know the source of the noise. Whatever makes the talon sound is invisible to my eyes and beyond my imagination at the time.

THE BLUE BUNNY | APRIL 18, 1980

I awake to the excited voice of our seven year old son Scott. "Daddy, Mommy, Daddy, Mommy," he excitedly half whispers in my face. I am lying on my side and my face is near the edge of the bed at the same height off the floor as his mouth, that is talking to me. My eyes are still closed. His breath is sweet and warm and his face is right in mine. I open my eyes to a surreal image.

Scott is wearing his last year's Halloween costume, a full one-piece, blue fleece pajamas with a hood. Sarah sewed ears on the hoodie. He appears to be a big, fuzzy,

Scott

blue bunny. He is very cute in the rabbit jammies; he is also very excited. In the dim light I see the wide-eyed expression on his face and I can tell he is waiting for me to respond.

"What is it, Scott?"

"Some little people just ran out of my bedroom!" he says.

Shit! I can't believe it, the thing I feared most was that the visitors would also find the children interesting.

I was more than alarmed, but calmly say, "Oh, Scott, you were probably just dreaming."

I get out of bed and scan every atom in the environment looking for any sign of something out of the ordinary, like a ufolk or something I can vent my outrage on.

Even though I am upset, I keep my composure and lead Scott back to bed, comforting him as I go with the idea that he has just had a dream. Scott accepts my story and I tuck him back in bed. Breana is still asleep in the bottom berth of her bunk bed. I tell Scott I will go around to make sure nothing is in the house. He asks me to shut the closet door; he believes something is in there. Jesus, how Scott's off hand observational comment will haunt me to my grave.

I check the closet, shut the closet door, then go through every room in the house. I find nothing. I go back to his room and tell him I have looked everywhere and that there are no little people. My report comforts him and he goes back to sleep.

I am shaken to the core with sorrow and guilt by what he has seen. I know he did not have a dream. I could cry, and I do inside, but there is no way out for us until the legal problem with our builder is concluded. Even then, for us to sell a house that is not totally finished and based on a design which is a little extreme for the average person will be difficult. Selling the house will take months, and moving may not stop the alien intrusions in our lives.

I go back to bed realizing that all my efforts to defend the family have been in vain. I do not go to sleep, but lie awake the rest of the night trying to figure out what to do.

The next day all was back to normal. I didn't ask Scott what the little people looked like as I didn't want to ignite his remembrances; he might become traumatized. If his experience were as benign as I thought mine had been, we could hold out until something concrete presented itself. I could shoot one of the aliens, sell it, and we could get the hell out of there. Had I known then what I would find out six months later, we could have moved into a new home compliments of our lender, Golderado Savings. However, if "ifs and buts were candy and nuts" what a fine Christmas we would have had in 1979.

I felt maxed out when it came to being vigilant and I didn't know what else to do, other than get on some form of drugs to keep awake. Every night I stayed awake as long as I could, and daydreamed about the possibility of shooting one of the visitors and capturing the commuter craft. However, I had not had a "dream" since Scott told me he saw the little people leave his room. Foolishly, I thought, *Maybe they are done with us.*

STRANGE TRACKS | APRIL 22, 1980

We receive 186 inches of snow during this winter of 1979-80. The lower part of our driveway is now strewn with canned goods that fall out of the paper bags which come apart in the driving snow storms. Storms always manage to blow in as we come home from work and try to get to the house. Our driveway is 800 feet long and runs west to east. The major snowstorms this winter sweep in from the west. They blow from the tip of the north edge of the mesa and then curl back around the east end, coming at us full tilt from the north. The fierce winds often fill the lower part of our drive with three to five feet of snow.

Early on, we try to power our way up the drive by hitting the snow drifts hard with the cars. Invariably, the cars ride up on the deep drifts and then sink into the snow, locked in tight. We usually get stuck 50 to 100 feet up the drive which only complicates the issue of ingress and egress when the storm blows over. We learn quickly to park at the end of the drive and walk to the house. Sarah holds Scott's hand, I hold Breana's, and we plow our way up the drive at night through the deep snow.

Usually a blizzard of blowing snow from the north hits us on our right side. Most times we are also carrying groceries in paper bags. We keep the children on our lee side, shielding them from the driving wind that cuts through us like razor blades. We carry the paper bags on the windward side. Because the bags are warm from their stay in the car, the driving snow quickly melts on them, and before we know it, the wet paper bags begin to fall apart.

Canned goods tear through the bags, and soon an avalanche of food pours out onto the deep snow. The cans are only seen again when I shovel the drive, or when the snow melts in the spring. The children are tough, and I can't remember them ever crying as we make our way through the subfreezing, cold winds and snow drifts to the house some 700 feet from our abandoned car.

It is after one of the heavy spring snowstorms that I see something strange in the snow. I am dressing for class, and on this particular day I wear a tie. As I walk around the family room tying my tie by feel and experience, I happen to look south out of the upstairs doors that access the two front balcony porches. I look at the neighbor's house to the south and the long gentle hill that rolls down to the ravine.

The distance between the ravine on the lower north end of the hill and our neighbor's back yard, is about 350 feet. The snow on this hill measures approximately a foot and a half to two feet deep. About 100 feet west of our neighbor's back yard, I see a trail of large, circular tracks that come down the gentle hill toward the ravine. Once the large tracks reach the ravine, they stop. I don't know what to make of them. Did they originate from the ravine or vice versa? Either way, the prints are there. It's getting late, so I finish dressing and go to work. Tomorrow is my day off and I will go see what made the strange tracks.

About ten o'clock the next morning, I venture out into the snow and hike south across the ravine and look at the tracks. Each track is roughly nine feet in diameter, a near-perfect circle. The center of each circular print is about nine inches deep, even though the prints are in snow that varies in depth from one to two feet. The nature of the snow does not change. There are no swales or shadow zones that can make the snow structurally different, softer or harder, affecting the depth of each print.

The middle of each circle is the deepest while the edges are very shallow. Overall, the print has a shallow, catenary, concave cross section; like a spherical balloon has been pressed down into the snow with the same amount of pressure each time. The average distance between the circular shapes is about 27 feet, although some are a bit less.

I can't conceive of how the tracks were made or by whom. There is no logical explanation for their existence. There are no human footprints but mine in the area, so I feel the prints are not the work of a prankster trying to stir our imagination. We have not spoken to anyone about the strange events occurring around our house, since I told our secretary and the Art Department Chairman about our first night's lights and visitors. It is also impossible for a person to mitigate tracks in one to two feet of snow. You don't leave tracks; you leave a plowed path.

I go back to the house, and over the next week, the circular indentations are covered by successive snows and drifts. I never see prints like them again. After some strange and terrifying things happen to the dogs later in the spring, I will eventually conclude I know what could have made them.

RATTLESNAKES ON MY MIND | APRIL, 1980

S pring break comes, and on my days off I shop for living room furniture we can see under in case a snake gets into the house. Also, I am looking for a couch that will extend to the floor and not allow a snake to crawl under it.

I buy a used baby grand piano. Sarah is now teaching the children how to play it. The piano takes the place of television as a source of nightly entertainment and education. Sarah is a great mother and has an infinite amount of patience when it comes to helping the kids with the piano, homework, and their emotional and physical developmental needs.

Sarah does the hard, important work. I get off easy and do the grunt work I think necessary to help keep the children safe from snakes. Over my spring break, I landscape the broken ground around the lower half of the house and prepare it for patios and a sod grass front yard. Laying thousands of brick pavers, I create a circular patio in front of the living room inspired by the round UFO print in the snow. On the west side of the house I construct a ten foot, circular retaining wall and create a beautiful brick patio there.

In front of the kitchen and dining room sliding glass doors I make a patio out of flagstone. Our contractor does not give me enough space under the door jams to lay brick pavers so I opt for thinner flagstone material to resurface the concrete pad there. I create another patio on the east side of the house out of large brick pavers. All the patios are linked together so we have patios all over the place for the children to play on. The pavers are laid in a basket weave formation; their geometric, linear pattern of dark tones make it easy to see a curvilinear, light-colored rattlesnake on their surfaces. Rattlesnakes do not like smooth surfaces like the bricks have, especially when the bricks get hot in the summer.

▦ ▦ ▦ ▦ ▦ ▦ ▦ ▦

In the 17 years we lived there, I only saw one snake approach a brick patio. It was a magnificent, six foot, shiny bull snake. This beauty came to the edge, flicked his long tongue, moved his head around to survey the area, and left.

In winter, the pavers gave us additional ambient heat by radiating energy upward in front of the house. Warm, radiant energy moving past the collector windows was better than cold air sapping the house of heat. The only possible problem area was the large flagstone portion of the front patio. The edges of the lighter colored flagstone slabs were more irregular and a snake could be harder to see. Luckily, we never had a sighting of a snake on its surface. The large, flashed pavers on the east side of the house were similar in form, color, pattern, and function to the other pavers; and never once was a rattlesnake seen on that patio either.

Towards the last of April, I veneered the concrete wing wall that was to support the upper portion of a flying staircase to the house. It was the genesis of our lawsuit with the contractor. I faced this eight by ten foot area with horizontal tongue and groove cedar that matched the west and east ends of the house.

When I was not working on the outside building or landscaping, hauling bricks and flagstone from 50-75 miles away, or shopping for furniture, I hunted rattlesnakes around the large cap rocks that had broken off and rolled down the steep slope of the mesa. Where the rocks came to rest, the land was more or less flat. To hunt on the steep slopes was more dangerous. You could be struck from above your waist by non-rattling snakes warming themselves on the horizontal shelf rock. Not all rattlers rattled, and when surprised, they could strike before totally identifying the nature of the intruder.

Spring approached and the days got warmer. I continued to move forward making the outside safe for the children before the dreaded snake season began. The race was on to have good rattlesnake proof play environments for the children by summer vacation.

HUGGY BEAR AND CHARMA BEAR | SPRING 1980

When we first buy the property in 1978, we celebrate Scott's fifth birthday there. The party is disrupted by the discovery of four rattlesnakes in just that one afternoon. What a depressing realization that we have a real problem in my nirvana. The next Monday, I call several government agencies to see what can be done to get rid of the snakes. The best advice we get is to get some dogs. We call the Humane Society and tell them what we need dogs for, to protect the children. We also want a dog that can take on a rattlesnake and survive, if bitten. The suggestion is to get Labradors. They are good hunters, affectionate friends for the children, and large enough to absorb a snake bite and still live. The important element is to have dogs that can create ground vibrations which irritate the rattlesnakes and keep them away from the children's play areas. The Labs' penchant for chasing balls or sticks is thought to create vibrational havoc for the rattlesnakes' delicate ground sensors.

After several weeks of watching the want ads in the *Denver Post*, we notice an ad for a free adult Labrador. We have to interview for the dog. His name is Huggy Bear. He is a super large dog with a great chest for breaking icy waters while retrieving downed geese. His pedigree is impressive. After a couple interviews and the approval of the owner, we are given Huggy. He weighs over 100 pounds and has gone to obedience school. As it turns out, he needs more obedience training because of his very bad temper. How the owners could give him to us knowing we have two small children is beyond me.

God, he is a magnificent animal. I take him with me whenever I can just for company and to bond with him. Huggy sits in the front passenger seat of the Bronco, his butt on the seat and his front feet on the floor. His head is as high as mine, and he easily looks out the window and seems to intelligently survey the surroundings as I drive around, mostly going to our property. While he likes me, I can tell he still misses his previous owner. I feel somehow obliged to make him happy and go out of my way to pamper him.

One night he growls at Scott for barely touching his front paws. I scold him. Huggy bares his big canine teeth at me. I immediately yank him by his choker chain and lift him up off the floor while yelling, "No!" He keeps growling, writhing around and snarling. Finally, his tongue turns blue, his eyes bulge, and he almost passes out before he quits growling. That is it, Huggy Bear has to go.

The next day, I take him with me to the property. I park outside a Quick Shop in Castle Rock. A very nice-looking woman walks up to me and I swear she asks if I would like to breed to her…bitch. I tell her I am flattered, but married. Ha! She blushes, and I laugh. She has a good sense of humor and does not have children. Perfect. After some funny small talk it turns out she saw Huggy (not me) sitting in the seat of the Bronco and wants to have him breed to her female Labrador. I say, "I will give him to you and your hubby for two picks of the litter out of the breeding." She agrees. I follow her home and leave Huggy with her. Her husband is ecstatic. He is a big goose hunter, and for him Huggy is a dream come true.

Months later, we have nine little Labradors running around in our back yard. Huggy Bear's new owners move to Portland, take him, and leave us with the puppies to sell. The black Lab puppies look like a gaggle of black, fathead minnows moving in one cohesive mass around on the green grass of our current home's backyard. If one of them sniffs a bug, they all rush to sniff it too. They are such innocent creatures, and fun to be around.

Sarah decides the best way to find the picks of the litter is to throw a ball out in the yard. When she does, the largest male takes off after the ball and retrieves it. She puts red nail polish on the tip of his tail. She throws the ball again and a beautiful, smaller female Lab retrieves it. Sarah marks her tail with red nail polish as well. We sell the rest of the puppies, and send the money to Portland.

We name them Huggy Bear II and Charma Bear. Huggy II is smaller than his father. At maturity Huggy II weighs about 75 pounds. He is gentle, loving, very smart, gregarious, an incredible hunter, and obsessed with retrieving anything.

He is also a great brother to his much smaller sister, Charma. More than one amorous male gets his comeuppance for even giving Charma a friendly sniff. Charma weighs about 50-55 pounds. She is an incredible hunter of animals, but not birds. Birds are Huggy's specialty. Charma doesn't care to fetch either; she is shy, introverted, cunning, and has a passive-aggressive personality. Fortunately, she is also an intense watcher and enforcer; Huggy is a gregarious participant.

The two are inseparable and they both love to be with the children and the family. You have to throw his ball to get retriever-intense Huggy out of your face. The kids perpetually throw sticks, balls, dirt clods, or anything for him when playing outside. The furious activity and scent of Huggy thrashing through the brush or the yard help keep snakes away from their play areas. Charma stays near the kids and is close in for protection.

Breana and Charma Bear

She is not afraid of snakes and kills bull snakes that venture too close. Together, the two dogs are perfect protection for the children when they play outside.

By the end of the first summer in our new home when I yell, "Snakes!" both dogs run around the yard sniffing for any scent of a snake. Conversely I say, "Bird!" and both run around looking up in the blue sky and trees! What a great pair of dogs. They are truly a godsend. However, we never rule out the possibility of an accidental or freak situation that results in one of the kids being bitten by a rattlesnake.

I always have a great sense of dread as rattlesnake season approaches. When it does, a

Scott and Huggy Bear II

state of high anxiety and total vigilance prevails after the first snake of the season is seen. The veil of fear lifts by the last of October when most rattlers are in their winter hibernation mode. Coincidentally our other reptilian "neighbors" seem to begin and end their "visitations" during the snake's winter hibernation and spring awakening time. One can say we unwittingly morph from hunter to the hunted.

You never really know what Huggy and Charma are barking at in the night. There are so many animals traversing the area between the three ecological zones we inhabit. There are the riparian zones of the Plum Creek Basin, our wetlands around the subdivision pond, and the spring creek in the ravine. The prairie zone of the high plains steppe sweeps away from our front door to the creeks and ponds below. The mountain zone includes our home and the mesa to the west and north. In these three ecological zones, bears, cougars, raccoons, coyotes, foxes, deer, elk, and antelope reside. Naturalists allege that most of the state's creatures, large and small, call our area of Colorado, home. We love all the wildlife, but when the dogs bark at night, we have no idea what they are contesting. We often yell at them to quit barking.

Huggy becomes so paranoid about barking, he rarely makes a sound. When scolded for barking, he gets this guilty look on his face like he has committed a mortal sin. Huggy is so intelligent and desperate to please, that I believe he understands all we tell him and does what we ask of him. Sometimes, I swear he can read my mind.

His conscious unwillingness to bark presents some real problems. If we let him out at night, we have to stay awake until we hear him pawing on the upstairs entry door. I often go to the door five or six times before he finally shows up to come in. Charma's personality is completely different. She can't care less about pleasing us. Her world is all about pleasing and satisfying Charma. If she wants inside, she barks. If she sees anything she barks until we make the right response. Fortunately for us, she is Huggy's spokesperson, and our most vigilant guardian.

RATTLESNAKE HUNTS | APRIL TO OCTOBER, 1980

My rattlesnake hunts always begin close to the house. Each time I circle the house I increase the radius to cover as much ground as I have time for. Hunting close to home is my priority. I hunt so often, I begin to think I can smell rattlesnakes. It turns out the mountain mahogany plants gives off a pungent odor about the time snake season begins. The thought of one of the kids being bit in the throat, as an unfortunate female homesteader was in James

Michener's, *Centennial*, haunts me.

By the end of summer vacation, 1980, I have killed 40 large brood snakes. These female snakes were probably the progenitors of the vast number of rattlesnakes that live and hibernate in the rocks behind and around our house. My fear of rattlesnakes is far greater than the threat of our night visitors.

Prairie rattlers are said to only reach four feet in length, but the brood stock I killed consistently measured five and a half feet in length. After a while, we begin to eat the snakes out of a respect for them, and to appease my building guilt in killing so many innocent snakes. Like all reptiles, they "taste a lot like chicken" when breaded and deep fried.

Several years later, I quit counting after killing 80 of them, but the snakes just keep coming. I do not give up my diligence in hunting them until Breana and Scott are in college.

▩   ▩   ▩   ▩   ▩   ▩   ▩   ▩

We built the house to take full advantage of the southern exposure during the cold months of the year. The winter sun not only heated the house but also the large rocks surrounding it, and helped keep the house warm long after the sun went down. The rocky west and north canyon rim wrapped around us and kept the cold west and north winds away by funneling them right over the top of the house and around the shoulders of the mesa. The lack of prevailing winds also kept the little box canyon warmer in the winter than surrounding land masses. The rattlesnakes liked the same environmental qualities we did. For eons, the snakes hibernated on the warm south slopes of the sun-drenched shoulders of our canyon.

The prairie rattlesnakes came out of hibernation in late March to early April and moved down to the prairies to hunt rodents and birds during the summer months. Near October 17th each year, they made their migratory trek back up the rocky slopes of the mesa to hibernate in holes, burrows and dens, or under large rocks and rock shelves west and north of the house. Their biannual migration seasons were the most dangerous times of the year for the children.

▩   ▩   ▩   ▩   ▩   ▩   ▩   ▩

During our first fall living on the property, I kill a group of eight rattlesnakes under a rock in a shallow den with one shot. They are all intertwined and squirming around one another like a can of balled up fishing worms.

I discover the hard way that rattlers often hunt in pairs. On one of my hunts, a large rattler buzzes at me from its perch on top of a large, flat piece of mesa cap rock. I go after the snake but it drops off the rock and slides under its perch and out of sight.

Over the months, I had distributed eight foot, light-weight, wooden fence posts around the outer back yard. I use these as pry bars to lift heavy rocks. I stick one end of a post under the rock where the snake disappears. Immediately, I hear it buzz at me from the back of the rock. I lift up on the post and the rock comes up off the ground toward me, like a clam shell opening.

To my surprise, I have pinned a snake's tail under the wooden pole. This very large snake is livid, hurt, and comes lunging out at me. Its first strike misses my hand by inches. Rattlesnakes are not supposed to be able to jump more than one third the length of their body. This snake does not know that rule and extends itself to its full length each time it strikes at me. The snake is like an animated, fast-moving yo-yo with a wide open mouth which had large white fangs trying to bite me. It repeats its lunging strikes several more times before it wears out and I kill it with my pointed shovel.

I am totally fooled by there being a second snake under the rock. I think the snake I saw and was after, buzzed at me from the back of the rock, but in reality, there were two snakes under the rock. I did not expect the snake I was after to be right in front of me ready to strike.

It seems that the large females generally rattle at me, some as far away as fifty feet. The smaller, darker-colored males are more unpredictable because they don't always rattle. Over the years, I have many close calls with male snakes while walking in the tall native prairie grasses.

While the house is being built, I put all the small pieces of scrap wood in a pile out to the west of the house. I want to use the wood for kindling as soon as we put in a fireplace. The scraps are scattered randomly in a pile. One day I set about sorting, organizing, and stacking the scraps into nice, even stacks.

Months earlier, I had covered the pile with a waterproof tarp. The tarp is now partially covered with new scraps and intermingled with old ones. When I get to a point where I can remove the tarp, I use both hands to grab it and shake it out like a sheet or dirty rug.

I snap the tarp, and at its highest point, a two foot male rattlesnake shoots further up in the air almost straight over my head. Totally surprised, I watch the snake go up into the air and then come down. For a brief second, we are literally eyeball to eyeball with one another. Then the rattler flops on the ground by the toes of my shoes. I jump back, he collects himself and begins to rattle and dance where my feet had been.

I catch the snake and put him in a five gallon carboy glass jug we previously used to brew beer and wine. I want to study him and see how far away I have to be before he starts buzzing at me. I continue cleaning up the pile of scraps but am soon interrupted by another snake rattling at me. After a little digging in the wood scraps, I find a second snake. The two snakes were probably hunting mice in the wood scrapes. This one scares me, until I see it is only a three foot bull snake imitating the sound of a rattlesnake with its mouth. What a smarty pants! The bull snake fooled me. I catch it as well.

I decide to see if another wife's tale is true; a bull snake will eat a rattler. I drop him in the jug with the rattlesnake and put some small mesh screen wire over the top of the neck of the jar and wire it in place. The two snakes stay as far away from each other as possible.

I am disappointed they didn't immediately go after each other. After a while, I become disinterested and continue organizing the pile of wood scraps. I clean up the pile and leave the area. Several days later I go out expecting to see a very fat bull snake, but all I find is the rattlesnake. The bull snake, a constrictor, was capable of extending itself up and pushed the screen wire off the end of the bottle and escaped. Later, I take the bottle with the rattlesnake in it and let him go some ten miles away on some uninhabited ranchland.

Snakes seem to be everywhere at times. On one trip up to the top of the mesa to picnic, I kill three rattlesnakes before we are 100 yards from the house. The last one I kill, I discover by a large, flat rock. After killing it, I cut the snake's head off with my shovel, which is also my walking stick, and put the head on top of the rock. At the other end of the rock I put the rest of the snake's body. I think if a hawk sees the body, it might take the snake away and benefit from its demise.

I am going to bury the snake's head when we come back down from the mesa. The head still has venom and can be dangerous if carelessly handled by a child, or eaten by a dog, or other animal. The two parts of the snake are five to six feet apart.

After the picnic, we walk by the rock and are mystified to see the stump end of the body has moved to within two inches of the snake's head. The body is weaving back and forth over the severed head. Very strange, no wonder some Native Americans hold snakes in reverence. The snakes seem to be as Native Americans will say, "Waken" or sacred.

By late spring it is double down time. I bust my rear dealing with creating a safe environment for the children: *co-developing* a new graphic design curriculum at school; *writing* resumes for senior design students; *administrating* the submission of student graphic design work for inclusion in the Art Department's senior show and the Art Directors' annual student design competition*; preparing* my work for the Art Directors annual competition; *arranging* portfolio reviews for students with Denver professional graphic designers; *visiting* with student internship sponsors before assigning a final grade; *writing and designing* promotional material for the Design Conference in Chicago class; *posting* advertising around town; *recruiting* students for the CDA; *securing* scholarships for needy and deserving design students to attend the CDA; *arranging* for student housing in Chicago; *arranging and administering* final reviews for student portfolios; *teaching* two design courses; *developing* a working relationship with my new colleague; *co-raising* two children; *grading* the front yard; and *installing* an eight-zone sprinkler system in the yard upstairs and the garden level down below, all while *staying* awake as much as possible at night to deter any ET (extraterrestrial) intruders.

■　■　■　■　■　■　■　■

Perhaps I was too tired to know if anything was going on around and in the house, but it seemed nothing unusual happened for a long time after Scott reported seeing little people running from his and Breana's bedroom. Maybe the warmer temperatures were not to our visitors' liking. To my knowledge, all visitations and bizarre dreams temporarily stopped, and something else began making its presence felt.

The year before we moved to Plum Creek Valley, Sarah and I spent two weeks touring Switzerland. I visited a premier graphic design school in Basil and talked shop with the professors there. The scenery and architecture was amazing, and I absorbed every bit of it and wished the USA could adopt the same design criteria and sensibilities the citizenry of Switzerland ascribed to. I was in love with all I saw and the only thing I could afford to bring back was the use of red geraniums on the balconies and patio areas of our home. Naturally, I loaded up the balconies' wide handrails with red geraniums in light orange clay pots. The light gray color of the stucco balconies and the front façade came alive with the splash of rich greens and bright reds. The bright red blossoms brought life and visual energy to the rigid minimalist exterior masses of the house.

※　※　※　※　※　※　※　※

The dogs are no longer sleeping in their dog house now that the temperature at night is fairly warm. I awake in the night to the sound of them barking at something. They are at the front of the house and I can tell they are focused on something in front of them or south of the house. After they bark for five minutes or so, I reluctantly get up and let them inside. They wag their tails and tell me they are very happy to be in. Both are the sweetest of dogs, but I don't want another accident with crap on the walls. I put them out on the family room balcony. I leave the glass door in the open position and shut the slider screen door. This is the same deck I have described before, when we saw the lights and I thought I was going to intercept an intruder. It's also above the area where I saw the large circular UFO print in the snow by the living room. I make the dogs comfortable with soft bedding and they do not bark after that. All seems well and I go back to bed and fall fast asleep.

I do not know how long it is after that, but I wake to the sound of the balcony screen frantically, erratically, see-sawing back and forth. I hear whimpering and whining dogs, scratching noises, and geraniums in clay pots shattering on the flagstone patio below. I bolt out of bed and run toward the commotion. As I do, I hear the screen door still jiggling back and forth against the door jamb at a frantic rate, and then I hear a big heavy dull THUD!

I arrive at the screen door in time to see Charma with her chest balanced on the porch's ten inch hand rail. She is frantically peddling her back legs in mid-air trying to get a toe hold on the interior wall of the balcony so she can push herself over the edge of the handrail and away from whatever is terrifying her. I rip open the screen door and grab Charma by the tail as she gives one final push, and is headed over the hand rail and sixteen feet down to the hard flagstone patio below. She will suffer sure death or brokenness beyond repair. She has knocked the pots of geraniums off the handrail as she tries to get away from whatever is coming out of the house.

As I pull a yelping Charma back over the hand rail by her tail, I see out of the corner of my eye, Huggy going psycho on the inside corner of the balcony. He is as far away from the screen door as he can get and is freaking out. Huggy's face is filled with great fear, and he is shriveled up in the corner. I wrestle Charma to the floor of the balcony and push her inside the house into the family room.

Son of a bitch, I don't know what went through the screen door. Whatever it was, scared the hell out of our two dogs. The hackles on my neck were infused with fear witnessing the dogs' terrified facial and body language. What was the thing? It was invisible to me, but horrified the dogs as it wiggled see-saw style, through the fine mesh of the screen.

I let Huggy in. He has his tail between his legs. Both dogs are in shock and wander around in a daze with their tails and heads down. They don't look at me. I spend some time cajoling and loving them, using soft, kind words of appreciation and affection. I want to show my fondness, support, and concern for them. After a while, they lie down on the carpet and begin to come back to reality. I close the glass door to the balcony and make sure they know that I have. To my way of thinking they are now safe from whatever had frightened them.

■   ■   ■   ■   ■   ■   ■   ■

From that time on, the dogs slept in the house if they wanted. I was at a loss as to what the hell see-sawed itself through the screen door. Why didn't I see anything go through the screen or out on the porch? What made the big THUD sound after it got through the screen? By then, we had endured five months of insanity. I knew these dogs didn't frighten easily and now they were terrified. Huggy had always been fearless and had recently decimated the big Doberman that lived in the house across the road from us.

There was no way to hunt what I could not see. I went to bed and pondered what had gone out of the house right through the sliding screen door. Whatever it was, it was transparent but dense enough to have to wiggle its way through the screen on the door. Was it inside all along, or did it come in with the dogs? Did the thing come in through the screen door while they were on the porch? Why could the dogs see whatever it was and I could not see anything? I was not frightened by this mysterious event; it was just another conundrum that will haunt and tease my imagination for years to come. I would then have enough experience to make a guess as to what the entity was.

As the end of the spring semester comes to a close and finals begin I had used all my personal creative time on building decks, patios, and making the grounds safe for the children to play on. The last area downstairs to complete is the laying of beautiful, luscious, cool green sod. By hand, I grade and smooth the ground in the front of the garden level and put in a sprinkler system to irrigate the new sod to be delivered later today. It is important to have a manicured yard to help keep rattlesnakes at bay. Rattlesnakes don't feel comfortable traveling in short grass, or open areas, where they are vulnerable to attack by hawks, eagles, falcons, the dogs, and other predators.

This day is very sunny and I am out on the bare earth in the downstairs soon-to-be front yard giving it a final raking before the sod is to be delivered. A little after ten o'clock, Sarah comes out of the kitchen slider door and calls me to the phone.

"The secretary is on the phone and she wonders if you are coming to your final."

"Jesus!" All of the sudden I realize I have a ten o'clock final with my senior design class!

"Tell her to hold them and I will be there in 45 minutes," I say.

I cannot believe I have blown off the final and totally forgotten about my students. I have been with them for four years and truly care about each of them. They are like my children. I have never missed a final in my entire teaching career.

I quickly dress and leave for school some forty minutes away. I am in a total panic as I race north down our county road that intersects Motsenbocker Road, which will take me east to Castle Rock and then to I-25 north to Denver and downtown to the university.

I don't know how fast I am going, but I have a strong tailwind and I am going much too fast for the gravel road I am speeding on. As I approach Motsenbocker, I slow and then put on my brakes. The Bronco I drive has a light rear end and soon I am sliding over the loose gravel out of control. As the Bronco slides into the eastbound lane of Motsenbocker, I see, through the thick gray, brown road dust blowing along with me, a car. It is coming at a high rate of speed several hundred feet away in the eastbound lane. I am now fractions of a second away from having a mortal T-bone crash! All at once, my real vision is totally blocked by another image.

In my mind's eye, I see three gnomes at the foot of our bed. It is nighttime. There is one large gnome in the center of the group, flanked by two smaller ones. They are staring at me as if I'm some kind of strange animal or thing that they have never seen before. I sense I am a complete curiosity to them. I am totally confused by seeing them too, and not the road ahead of me.

The blinding image only lasts a fraction of a second. The Bronco finally stops perpendicular to the eastbound lane and I hear the blaring horn of the oncoming car whose driver frantically attempts to avoid hitting me. Through the dust and debris I created with my slide, I come back to my full senses.

I slap the Bronco's gears into reverse, put my foot in the carburetor, and burn rubber backing off the highway and out of death's way. Just as I drive the Bronco off the apron of the intersection, the other car screams by through my dust and burnt-rubber smoke. The driver flashes me a much-deserved middle finger while yelling inaudible obscenities at me. Shit! What a close call. I cannot believe what just happened to me, but no time to think! I take off again driving like a wild man to get to my final.

By the time I get to Castle Rock and onto I-25 headed north, my pulse rate has dropped and my heart is no longer about to jump out of my chest. My mind is occupied by what the hell I am going to tell my students. But I am also still in disbelief as to what my subconscious has dredged up for me to see.

▦ ▦ ▦ ▦ ▦ ▦ ▦ ▦

I just had a subliminal uprush "aha" experience of biblical proportions, the kind Earnest Hemingway allegedly had when composing some of his work. I unwittingly used his method of jogging my subconscious for the answer to a riddle that had been perplexing me since the bright lights subdued me at the upstairs entry door earlier in the year.

A simplified version of Hemingway's alleged methodology of jogging creative insights from his subconscious is as follows: you totally immerse your conscious thought with the problem you are contemplating. Think about the problem day and night. If necessary, deprive yourself of sleep in any manner possible. He reportedly drank tremendous amounts of coffee to stay awake and continue the incubation process of engaging the problem. After three to four days of sleep deprivation and thinking about the problem, question, creative insight, or whatever, divest yourself of the process. At that point, do something totally unrelated to your normal work or social habits like, go bowling or sliding your car out in front of oncoming traffic. If you are lucky, you will get the subliminal uprush or epiphany experience.

My incubation process was the same. I had been thinking about who and what was behind the lights that had totally anesthetized me. I thought about that issue all the time, and I had for months. When I slid out into the road which was something I have never done before or after, my subconscious released the images that temporarily replaced my real time vision.

I was, however, not for a moment, convinced we were being visited by gnomes. Those entities were from the land of fairytales and could not be what was bothering us. I dismissed the notion of gnomes running around the house and couldn't believe my subconscious could show me such a ridiculous answer to my persistent conundrum. A rational, left brained person would say I hallucinated due to sleep deprivation.

I made it to my final an hour late and luckily, my students didn't lynch me for being so irresponsible and inconsiderate. The memory of the image of the gnomes staring at me from the foot of our bed proved not so forgiving. While I couldn't digest the idea that gnomes really existed, I could still see their quizzical expressions as they benevolently starred at Sarah and me from the foot of our bed.

LIGHTNING | JUNE 15, 1980

After a ten-day stay in Chicago attending the Design Conference, I return home and begin working on the upstairs decks, the backyard, and the courtyard enclosure outside the children's bedroom. I enclose the decks and make a grassy courtyard area that is also a relatively safe zone for them to play in. The floors of the decks on the upstairs side of the house are made of redwood and brick pavers. All decks and porches are elevated a foot to keep snakes away from the vulnerable patio doors. Two of the decks are more like porches as they have walls with stucco on the interior. The exterior sides of the walls are sheathed in tongue and groove cedar, as are the east and west faces of the house. By the end of summer the children have decks all the way around the house to play on. The decks are not 100 percent safe from snakes, but with the help from God, the dogs, our habitual "watch out for snakes" mantra, and a little luck, the children can live a relatively normal home life.

Spring and summer evenings are often spent sitting on the upstairs decks watching the lightning strikes around the area. Over the Plum Creek Valley and the towns of Castle Rock and Monument, lightning storms are a common event.

Over the years, we had a water well pump struck by lightning, a horse nearly killed by it, and I had lightning hit near enough to the studio that bolts of electricity shot out of the outlets. Walking from the studio to the house is often a scary proposition on overcast spring and summer afternoons. A shaft of lightning can strike you from as far away as seven miles. The lightning can come from innocent-looking light gray clouds. One electrical strike that first spring is particularly irritating to me.

Initially, when we can't get TV reception in the house, I go on a personal quest to get a TV signal from Colorado Springs or Denver. Some razor-sharp mind tells me to string chicken wire up and down one of the big Ponderosa pines on top of the mesa. He says I am to aim an outside antenna at the mesh of chicken wire and *voila!* I should get a signal off the chicken wire. With great effort, and personal peril, I do as instructed.

I am very zealous and nail 2x4s, four feet long, up and down the trunk of a large Ponderosa pine on top of the mesa that I see from the house. I nail layer after layer of chicken wire up and down the 2x4 ladder I make. The total collector length of the antenna ladder measures 12 feet, and I string over 100 feet of chicken wire up and down the ladder.

The antenna I create is very impressive; NORAD would give me an A for my effort. With great confidence and enthusiasm, I aim the business end of our new antenna, mounted on the roof of our house, at the chicken wire antenna attached to the Ponderosa tree. Bingo! We should have a signal. When I turn the TV on, I see nothing but snow and static. Shit! I go back to the drawing board and develop a new plan to capture a signal. I truck bags and bags of pre-mixed concrete and jugs of water up to the top of the mesa.

I pick the highest rock I can find on our property and mount a TV tower base to the rock with concrete. I attach a tall TV antenna to the tower. I hook 1200 feet of coax cable to the antenna and run it over and down the mesa to the house and our TV. This is a fool proof plan, and I execute it with care and professionalism. Still no TV.

Now, I am told I need an inline coax cable booster to get the signal down to the house. Before I can get the booster hooked up, the whole rig is totally fried by a lightning storm the next day. I think, *No TV for you, Bartoks, back to the books and piano program.* Months later, my big chicken wire signal catcher, disappeared. Perhaps those who operate the big microwave tower on the hill seven miles to the east of us had something to do with its demise. I never find out and don't care. At least the pine tree is spared from getting hit by lightning due to all the wire running up and down its trunk.

▩　▩　▩　▩　▩　▩　▩　▩

Sometime in the first several years we lived in Plum Creek Valley, I read in the local paper that our area had the second most lightning strikes per year in the United States. At the time, the leader in lightning strikes was a place called Gulf Breeze in Florida.

I often wondered if the mesa's cap rock material and encapsulated rhyolite debris had more iron in it than most of the land masses in the surrounding countryside, attracting the lightning. I also wondered if the high number of lightning strikes enticed the UFOs. Perhaps the mesa's cap rock was magnetized as a result of the lightning strikes and the UFOs could somehow recharge their craft from the magnetized rock's granular structure. I thought this because almost every year in the spring and fall, flights of geese would get stuck in the vicinity over our house, honking and flying in the same circular pattern for hours.

I would not have heard the geese had I not been awake listening for unexplainable sounds. The constant honking in the night piqued my interest and imagination. Finally, I linked the lightning to the possible magnetism of the volcanic tuft material that formed the crust of the mesa surface. Perhaps the little lodestone the geese use to navigate during their biannual migration got short circuited as they flew over our home. The geese became confused and flew in endless circles for what seemed like hours, until they somehow broke free of the area's gravitational anomalies that impeded their journey.

THERMAL SIPHONING | SUMMER, 1980

I complete building the walls of the upstairs courtyard area and encapsulate a safe zone for the children. Then I begin building a zero-clearance Heatilator-type fireplace on the west wall of the living room. Our all electric home is using one third the energy of homes similar in size. I am determined to reduce our kilowatt usage even more. The Heatilator fireplace draws cool air from the outside and into a heat exchanger in the back of the firebox and then moves this cold air into the combustion chamber of the fireplace. With this system, interior warm air doesn't escape out of the house and get sucked up the chimney whether the fireplace is in use or not. Most

Fireplace and snake proof couch in living room

fireplaces that don't draw cool air from the outside are sapping the interior warm air for combustion, thus the fireplace takes more warm air out of the house than it is putting in (thermal siphoning).

I also build a one-foot overhang above the mantel area of the fireplace and face the bottom of the overhang with one-eighth inch plate steel. The heat from the fireplace that would normally go up the face of the fireplace is captured in a two-story, five foot by one foot heat chamber. I put a squirrel cage blower inside one wing of the fireplace structure and suck the warm air down and out of the heat chamber and into the side of the room where all the window glass is. This mitigates cool air from radiating through the glass. Later, I devise a simple product to stop thermal siphoning of cool air in the summer and warm air in the winter, a big step toward saving a lot of BTUs and money.

The fireplace looks great on the west wall and produces enough heat to further reduce our energy costs. The structure of the fireplace also braces the west wall and increases its structural integrity. By December, I complete the work that needs to be done inside and outside and I have saved thousands by doing it myself. But there is still that pesky issue of not paying the contractor his last payment. I have used a lot of the money, he alleges we owe him, to make the house complete and safe for the children.

L ate one night, we get a call from the rancher who is boarding both of Sarah's horses. He lives only five miles away near the Plum Creek Grange. Sarah's horses, Rebel and Rogue, had mysteriously gotten out of their pasture and ran or were chased down a county road. Rogue tried to cross a cattle guard breaking three legs in the process. The rancher asks what Sarah wants him to do. She says to put him down. The rancher does.

The tragic event motivates us to build a horse coral about half way down the driveway towards the main road. We don't want to make it too close to the house or otherwise, during fly season, we will have a problem. Sarah has a corral built for her remaining childhood horse, Rebel. For the first time ever in her life, Sarah lives on the same land her horse does. Sarah spends the summer riding Rebel, taking care of the children, taking them on horseback rides, working around the house, and getting ready for her photography and art classes in the fall.

After we build the corral, we get the big idea to connect the south side of the enclosure with a combination studio/barn complex. I need a special place to work and Sarah needs a place for her horse. I design the studio, Sarah designs the barn, and we join the two ideas into a workable plan.

The studio is a stage one, passive solar piece that, of course, faces south. The south side of the studio is sheathed in four by eight foot double paned safety glass. This bank of solar collectors is 24 feet long and cant at a 45 degree angle from the ceiling to 18 inches above the floor.

The inside has a concrete slab floor covered in flashed paver bricks to absorb the sun's radiant heat. The ceiling is Southwest-style, round log beams with two by six inch tongue and groove ceiling material. Above the ceiling is six inches of Styrofoam insulation. Above the insulation is a normal built up roof composed of layers of felt material with tar and gravel on top. The exterior and interior walls are six inches thick with heavy insulation and six coats of concrete and stucco facing on the interior and exterior walls.

There is no overhanging roof line to protect the glass collectors from absorbing the sun's radiation during its trek across the summer skies, so it gets hotter than Hell as the sun's path tracks overhead. In July and August, I sometimes work outside or have fans running to make the room habitable. To help keep the summer heat down I plant fruit trees close to the collectors to shade the glass in the summer.

During the winter days, the studio's warmth radiates through my body; it feels great. The warmth and the sunny room are marvelous to work in. The interior materials and insulation keep my studio space warm until the early hours of the next day. I raise vegetables and flowering plants during the winter.

Studio/Barn facing south

Sarah soon buys a second horse, Flagg. Rebel and Flagg are nice studio companions. When I tire of what I am working on and need a break, I visit them and know they will be very supportive of whatever I have to say. Flagg becomes a regular beer drinking buddy. When he sees me coming with a bottle of beer, he knows he is going to get the last of it. His eyes light up and he comes running toward me with both lips curled back in great anticipation of supping on the fizzy, grainy brew. Sarah would not approve if she knew.

Studio interior

The union of the two spaces works out, and miraculously I get TV and radio signals, all seems well with the universe. I am ready to start my personal design work again. I can't work or feel comfortable until I have created an aesthetically pleasing "nest." Now all I have to do is to reinvent myself from working in graphic design for the printed page to what-I do not know.

Prior to moving to Plum Creek I work on participatory art projects with civic groups like the Denver Art Museum, the Denver Symphony, and The Junior League. During this period, I invent many art related devices that aid in the creation of participatory art projects I am working on. The last device I invent is a highly mobile device for cutting Styrofoam. It allows me to cut the material into all sorts of interesting forms which I then paint white. I put magnetic tape on the bottom of the forms. These shapes with magnetized strips stick to a lightweight sheet metal base. The base mounts to a wall and the shapes can be moved around by the viewer to create a never-ending combination of three dimensional forms and compositions. When I finish my first piece it is four o'clock in the morning. I am so excited that I wake Scott up and photograph him by the work to give it scale. The lighting is really crappy and Scott looks a little frazzled.

I make several more pieces. When dichromate lights are aimed at the wall pieces and turned on, the bas-relief smooth forms create a color field that changes into an infinite number of color configurations. The end result is acoustical light modulator wall pieces which are very modern in form and style. I hang them in heavy traffic areas and by the piano. Perhaps I can create them to sell in interior design boutiques. A good idea, but

Scott in front of styrofoam piece

I know that I need to work in a form and medium that can be termed graphic design, if I am to continue teaching in that curriculum. I always try to practice what I preach.

I don't know exactly how I come up with this idea, but I figure out a new way to work on fabric with colors that are vibrant, light-fast, and easy to use. Perhaps I can create banners on fabric for specialty stores in the area. Banners are in the academic domain of graphic design. I probably wouldn't make much money, but I could compete in regional and national graphic design competitions with banners.

So I throw myself into experimenting with dyes on various fabric materials and I quickly develop processes and techniques that are potentially capable of producing great results on fabric. Now I need a client to work for so I can generate designs to make a little money to pay for the expensive dyes.

There are a lot of obstacles ahead for me and my new process, but I find that perseverance always wins out. Working on fabric is difficult and laborious and I seldom leave the studio until midnight. The most difficult part of the process is heat-setting the pigments to the fabric. To do this, I take a four by eight foot sheet of one-half inch plywood, buy some ironing board covering at a fabric store and make myself a giant ironing board.

After I create a design on white fabric, I pin it to the ironing board. I take a hot iron and start ironing at the top and one side of the fabric. I place the iron on the fabric for one minute applying an even pressure to it. After one minute, I move the iron, making sure it slightly overlaps the previously ironed area. I repeat this process until the entire design surface has been ironed. The colored dyes are now set to the fabric and become fadeless in the wash or sun. Often it takes twenty to thirty hours to heat-set a large banner. When I heat-set, I normally work late into the night on the living room floor of the house. During these times, I often see and experience an unusual phenomenon.

I am on my hands and knees heat-setting the dyes on fabric. It is usually late at night or early the next morning. I normally have my back to the windows and my head down while I iron. I am in the space between the piano room and the living room. I often get the strong feeling that I am being watched from outside the house. At first, I just lift my head and turn in the direction that l feel the strange sensation comes from. For a fraction of a second I see a thin, bright, vertical light that measures four or five feet high and half an inch wide. The light is brilliant. I never see a figure or animate object.

As the years go on, when I get this feeling of being watched, I turn as fast as I can to catch a glimpse at whatever is studying me. The impression I get over the years is that I am seeing into a nonexistent room outside the house that is lit by this brilliant white light. Then the door to this room appears to quickly close and there is no more light. The feeling of being studied is over, and I go back to work.

If the feeling that I am being scrutinized is really strong and persistent, I draw all the drapes to keep my imagination and anxiety under control. Maintaining my focus on the ironing task takes great self-discipline and concentration. One screw up and I can scorch or burn the fabric, ruining countless hours of hard creative work. The light in the night and the feeling of being watched, goes on for years until in 1983, I invent a way to heat-set my work in a more efficient way.

With my new heat-setting machine what had originally taken me up to thirty hours to complete, now takes 15 minutes. I am off to the races and a whole new world of creative possibilities opens up before me. I no longer heat-set my design work out in the living room, but in the windowless mechanical room. The uneasy feeling of being watched and the sudden flash of the brilliant light ended for the moment. I am, however, still watched as I work, I just don't realize it at the time.

※　※　※　※　※　※　※　※

In the late 1980s, a famous Lakota shaman heard from one of our friends, who was writing an article on this shaman for *Life* magazine, of the unusual events in and around our home. This elderly shaman came to visit us and offered his spiritual guidance. He felt such a strong bond with the spirits he sensed here that he told me he wanted to do his last Vision Quest on the property. While visiting, advising, and instructing us, he also performed the *Inipi Cleansing of Bad Spirits* ceremony in the mechanical room. He performed the ritual in total darkness. Sarah and I witnessed the spirits responding to the shaman and the rhythmic movement of his sacred eagle wing. Many spirits showed themselves as chevron-shaped lights to us during the ceremony. Sarah and I were not fearful of the good spirits' presence. I never felt uncomfortable again as I worked in a room potentially full of spirits.

On that same day, the shaman sat at our kitchen table with his back to the sliding glass door. Sarah sat across from him and saw over a dozen chickadees land in the aspen tree outside, directly behind him. They stayed there the entire three hours he sat at the table, probably wanting to be near this great Sioux shaman. Had the kitchen slider door been open, I had no doubt they would have come inside to be even closer to this very spiritual man. Up to that point we had only seen one chickadee around the house since we moved there. The rest must have come from the forest south of the house, or did they just materialize? We later found out the chickadee was a favorite spirit bird of the Sioux and Plains Indians. This revelation brought back the memory of the night Sarah and I heard the chickadee whistle in our bedroom shortly after we moved into our new home.

Summer is over; we are back at school again. We accomplished a lot over the summer. I spent my time in the studio generating experimental fabric pieces. Sarah had a nice barn with hay storage and protection from the elements to keep her horses in. Scott was developing his racing skills going up and down the drive in his go cart.

Breana's grandpa built her a rabbit cage. She now has her first rabbit to take care of and to nurture her work ethic and sense of responsibility. Breana emulates her mother's great devotion to caring for her horses and all living things. She also loves her mother's horses and is a young cowgirl on her way to becoming a gifted equestrian.

Late summer is uneventful, or we are not aware of anything unusual happening. September, however, proves to be a different story.

I wake to Scott whispering to me, "Daddy, Mommy, Daddy, Mommy." Once again, he is talking directly into my face in the middle of the night.

"Yes Scott." I say. I'm hoping he is not going to tell me there are more little people running out of his and Brenna's room.

"Daddy, Mommy!" he excitedly says again.

"What is it Scott?"

"Someone was playing the piano!" he exclaims.

"I didn't hear anything."

"I heard it," he insists.

I ask him, "What was the person playing?"

"What Mommy likes to play." Scott says.

Often in the evening, Sarah likes to play many pieces, but her favorite is *Fur Elise*. Well, someone playing the piano is better than small people running out of his room.

"I'll go down and check it out and see if anyone is there," I say.

I take him back to bed, shut his closet door, and go look around. I don't find, feel, smell, or see anything out of the ordinary. I go up and confirm to Scott that all is okay and that I am glad he came to tell me what he heard.

He is one of the most observant people I have ever been around. When he walks into the studio and my paint brushes have been moved three feet away from where they were the last time he saw them, he will ask, "Why did you move the brushes?"

He is the only one in the family who has found Indian artifacts on the property, mostly when he is with us on a hike. We don't see the artifacts, but he does. I do not want to squash his inquisitive mind, so I encourage him to tell me whenever he sees or hears anything that attracts his attention. I am at a loss as to what he has heard. Did he have a dream? I don't think so.

He is not given to lying or making up stories. He doesn't have the benefit of TV to plant absurd creatures and stories in his young mind. I believe he has heard something, just like the night I heard the chickadee whistle in our bedroom.

JOINED AT THE HIP | SEPTEMBER 12, 1980

It is September; fall semester begins. I am at home on my day off. The day is marvelous, bright, and sunny. The house is now efficiently heating itself from the direct radiation of the sun, supplying warmth that is all consuming, comfortable, clean, and free of charge. I surmise that the window solar collectors are two to three weeks ahead of themselves. We are getting too much heat too early. This means that our contractor did not position our house seven degrees east of magnetic south like I had instructed him to do. We must be ten to twelve degrees east and are catching the sun's direct rays a week or so before we should. This means that in the spring, when it is still cold, we will not get the two more weeks of direct solar radiation we need to effectively heat the house. Other than that, I am content with the house heating itself in the winter and cooling itself in the summer.

I sit on the downstairs bathroom stool reading art department memorandums before I go to school. The door to the bathroom is open and I can see out to the hallway, the piano, the living room, and into the patio and the trees beyond. Charma is stretched out on the living room floor basking in the sun's rays and heat. She is very comfortable lying in the sun near the piano and is in doggie nirvana.

As I read, I notice some movement out of my peripheral vision. I look up and see Charma slowly getting up and coming in my direction. She looks strange. I stop reading and watch her as she approaches. Charma has a weird look on her face and is moving in a very tentative manner, as though she is walking on eggs.

As she approaches, our eyes meet and she seems relieved for a second. I notice her head is slightly down and she then rolls her eyes up and back in her head as though there is something directly behind her. When I see her roll her eyes back so she can look over her shoulder, her eye movement really perks my full attention. She gingerly walks right in front of me and then sits down on my left side. She rolls her eyes up and gives me a fearful look. I get the idea and I look around and scan the whole bathroom. I see nothing, I hear nothing, I smell nothing, nothing touches me, and I feel nothing except tension. Charma's body language is so obvious that only a fool could not tell she is frightened and is seeing something that is apparently after her. The room is absolutely quiet and filled with the fear Charma has brought with her.

I get a little edgy and my butt is going numb, so I get up. Charma follows me out of the bathroom, up the stairs, and outside. We could have been, as they say, joined at the hip. As soon as we are outside, she seems to be all right and jauntily dog trots off toward the studio. I go to classes and give the experience little notice, but I am getting the feeling something really unusual is going on, or maybe Charma is paranoid.

THE SPARKLER | OCTOBER 5, 1980

I wake to soft flickering pink and pale blue lights slowly washing across the mirror and walls of the upstairs Jack and Jill lavatory corridor. This east/west corridor joins our bedroom on its east end and links to the north/south hallway that goes to the upstairs entry door. Off the north wall of this bathroom corridor is a door leading to the bathing area. In this room are a Jacuzzi and a toilet. The door to this area is open. Above the Jacuzzi is a series of skylights.

The lights I am seeing from my bed must be coming from on the roof near the skylights. The rotating pink and blue lights are coming down through the skylights, into the bathroom and spilling out into the east/west corridor. I know and recognize the lights and what I think they mean. I nervously watch the lights and do not move.

Then I see a beautiful lime-green light enter the east end of the lavatory corridor. The spherical light is soft and glowing as it moves towards me. Green is not my favorite color, but I am hypnotized by the sheer beauty of this lime-green colored light. For some reason I do not leap up out of bed and pursue the light. However, when I do decide to

Skylights in upstairs bathroom

get up from lying on my back, I am mysteriously stopped. The soft light continues toward me and I pass out or lapse into unconsciousness.

I rouse from my "sleep" and the soft lime-green light is in back of me. I can sense that I am now not alone and there is someone behind me, but I cannot see anyone. It is then that I realize I was not in our bedroom when I first saw the lights. I never lie on my back to sleep and I am not on my side of the bed, but rather on the side where Sarah always sleeps. Now I am troubled and anxious about where I am, who I am with, and where is Sarah? The room seems to be dark, not light as were the other rooms I dreamt of, or were in.

Then I realize there is a thin, silver, shiny tube about six to eight inches long on the right side of my temple and optical chiasm. Great anxiety rushes through me and I am reminded of the times I have gone under the knife for eye surgery, while on my back in operating rooms. I cannot move. My eyes are rolled as far to the right side of my head as possible. I can feel my eyes bulging. I see a small hole in the end of the silver tube next to my temple area.

Suddenly, the silver tube spews a steady stream of bright, deep red sparks from its open end. I try to jerk my head away from the tube and the red sparks, but I am held in place by some unknown force. This sparking wand, with its four to five inch emission, is being passed back and forth from my temple and optical chiasm area to the back of my head. As the sparks come back into view, the tube looks like a sophisticated sparkler that emits a controlled, hemispheric spray of deep red sparks. I am fearful, anxious, and frantically try to digest what is happening to me. I feel and smell nothing, but I know this slow, systematic back and forth movement of the sparkler is doing something to me.

I think, *Maybe they are trying to fix my eye!* I am hopeful, almost euphoric. If anyone can fix me and make me whole, it would be these strange, mysterious people. Shit! They are on the wrong side of my head! I can't use my vocal cords to talk, so I think with all my mental force, *WRONG SIDE! WRONG SIDE! WRONG SIDE!!! YOU'RE ON THE WRONG SIDE!!!!* I cannot move any part of my body, except my bulging eyes. Grabbing this magic wand and switching it to the left side of my head is not an option; I cannot move. I mentally keep lamenting, *Just give ME the fucking wand!* But they do not seem to listen or pay attention to my mental pleas.

The unseen abductors continue to go about their business and keep the wand on the right side of my head. I am totally exasperated and frustrated with their continued back and forth movement of the sparkler on what I perceive to be the wrong side of my head. I slip back into unconsciousness, or into my real shitty, frustrating, interactive dream.

※   ※   ※   ※   ※   ※   ※   ※

The next day, I was haunted by that strange dream, or flashback, I experienced the night before. I was baffled as to where I was when I woke to the pink and blue lights and the beautiful lime-green light that came down the hall. While everything in my physical environment appeared to be in order, I was still confused.

I was lying on my back on Sarah's side of the bed. That was wrong on two counts. Where was Sarah during this period of time? And I never slept on my back. I always slept in a semi-prenatal position, facing whichever direction was to the outside of the bed. In our bed I slept on the north side of the bed on my right side.

The biggest issue was how someone could run this magic wand back and forth laterally from my temple to the back of my head from behind me. Our bed was up against the east wall of the bedroom and a person would have to reach through the wall to accomplish this.

On the other hand, I was flattered and encouraged that whatever these entities were, they might have been trying to remove one of my great sorrows and make me whole again. Maybe I had a wish fulfillment dream and was merely deluding myself by thinking I was being helped by benevolent external forces using medical magic our cultural could not conceive of to fix my eye.

While I had no proof of that ufolks' visit, a large birthmark on the back of my head disappeared. Over my lifetime, the birth mark had gone from a two dimensional blotch one inch in diameter on the back of my cranium to a growth that was three dimensional and would get sore from time to time when combing and brushing my hair. Whenever I got a haircut I always warned the barber not to get aggressive with a brush or comb in that area of my head. Even doctors warned me about the birth mark being cut by a barber. They feared I could bleed extensively or get blood poisoning from contaminated clippers or scissors cuts.

The circular birthmark had overgrown its boundaries and could be lifted around its edges. The mark often hurt and became problematic; the thought of getting it removed had entered my mind. After that night, the birthmark was gone. How it disappeared was a medical mystery. I felt I had physical proof that these people tried to help me. This humanitarian act was an endorsement to me that while their different appearance and habits frightened us, they were in fact benevolent. At least I could see the positive benefits of their medical expertise and apparent helpful motives.

I could not help but think about the summer before when we were just beginning construction of our home. I was out visiting the site on the day the trench from the electrical transformer to the house was being dug by an operator riding a small trenching machine. Electrical wires to the house would be run down this trench. The young operator and I talked briefly as the conveyor blades of his trenching machine made steady progress digging from the transformer to our house.

As we talked, the trenching machine all of a sudden nearly ground to a halt and lurched up out of the ground. It then settled down and moved forward with little resistance. The trencher lurched again and slowed down as it bored through harder material once more. The trencher then resumed its slow plodding movement through the dry, hard ground. The operator was visibly excited and said, "We must have gone through the walls of a kiva!" I said something silly and in a skeptical tone like, "Oh really?" My body language and attitude must have told the operator that I didn't believe him. I had a general knowledge of what a kiva was but construction on the house was running way behind. I was there to goose things up and get the construction show back on the road. My apparent lack of rapt interest in the importance of a kiva, and his keen interest in the history of the land, probably made him think I was a very ignorant, insensitive twit.

He caustically quipped, "You realize you are building your house on a sacred Indian healing ground." I'm sure to him I was clearly not a student of Native American history and he must have wanted to shock me, and put me in my place. He quickly calmed down and told me about how he and his wife hunted arrow heads and Indian artifacts around our property for years.

He alleged that in recent times, ranchers brought their sick livestock to this site and tied them in special spots. After several days, the animals would be healed of their afflictions. While I found the operator to be very compassionate and seemingly an expert about his hobby, I didn't take him seriously. My young, ignorant mind told me he was an amateur anthropologist, not a main stream scientific expert from a university. How could he know about a kiva below the surface of the ground?

The trenching operator went on to tell me about all the artifacts he and his wife had found on the mesa above our house, and on the grounds at the base of the mesa. In fact, while he was digging the trench, his wife was up on top of the mesa looking for new artifacts that may have washed up out of the ground after the last heavy rain.

He alleged that the bluffs above our house, and our neighbors' in the canyon south of us, were ancient buffalo jumps. A buffalo jump was a place where Native Americans stampeded small herds of bison across the mesa and then over the mesa cliff sides to their subsequent death below. The Native Americans would then butcher and harvest the dead and dying bison at the base of the mesa.

I was not indifferent to the operator's experience and interest in the impact of Native Americans on and around our property. But I was more focused on motivating some lazy butts toward getting our construction goals back on track. At the time I did not appreciate the potential impact of his words. I now give his words credence.

Perhaps ufolks had been coming to this site for centuries and working their magic on the Native Americans. Maybe the shamans' use of rattles, medicine bundles, charms, and the laying on of hands to heal the sick was a naïve attempt to emulate the ufolks healing with things as simple as a mysterious silver sparkler. Or maybe they befriended the Native Americans and taught them how to manipulate energy fields and forces that are unknown to us "civilized" people, to actually heal tribal members. I kept asking myself, *What could be so special about us or this site to keep the ufolks coming back?*

T
he dark cloud that has been hanging on my emotional horizon for ten months is now directly over my head, threatening to rain on my little parade. It is time to pay the contractor his last installment, even though he does not finish building the house as specified in the agreed upon blueprints, written contract, and verbal instructions. All my moral protests over the last months have fallen on deaf legal ears, hell bent on making me pay for something I didn't get.

My lawyer is the son and brother of two lawyers who had worked for us in the past. The son, Carl, is fresh out of law school and has no passion for the project. I suspect his father asked him to chaperone me into ethical oblivion, and keep me from doing something legally stupid that will cost us more than this final payment. Over the months, he often calls to tell me what is happening. I tell him all that is wrong with the house and what I am doing to mitigate the problems. I can tell he can't care less. He really frustrates me. My attorney wants to meet with Ralph, our contractor, and his lawyer in his lawyer's office at four o'clock December 23, 1980. They are going to horse me into paying Ralph his final payment. I almost get sick at the thought, and my stomach is all riled up.

Whenever I've been commissioned for a project, I don't get paid until I complete it. I am not going to pay until our contractor finishes the house. That means completing the exterior east facade which includes a flying staircase from the upstairs ground floor to the garden level below. Our contractor is to grade the yard and put in concrete steps to the garden windows and the upstairs front door. I have already done everything except the flying staircase. I prepare a bill to give him for my expenses.

I have given up several changes that are wrong headed, but I will not budge on this flying staircase issue. This simple little house is, could be, a classic modern home constructed along the lines of the Bauhaus, Corbusier, and modernist tenants. The house has already been compromised by concessions I made to expedite the project and get us moved in by Christmas 1979.

I allowed the parapet height to be increased, and now the house seems heavier and does not visually float as intended. The visual tension of the front façade is also lost when the balconies were not cantilevered, and instead were supported by three static pillars. The balconies do not appear to mysteriously hang in midair as I intended. The visual tension between the home's design elements and the airy qualities of the original idea is lost. Now these "suits" are going to make me give up the dynamic diagonal I know would activate the rectilinear space frame concept the house was designed around.

Each time I talk to my attorney it is agony; I know he is escorting me to the executioner. When he talks to my contractor's attorney he probably says, "Just give me some time. Sean will come around and Ralph will get his money very soon." Screw Ralph; Hell will freeze over before that happens. Besides, I have already used most of the money on the outside of the house, the studio, and the piano. But one thing I notice over the years is that I always do my best thinking when my ass is backed up against the wall.

I get the idea to completely analyze all the receipts and find out how much was spent on what, and if there are any discrepancies in the withdrawals by Ralph from Golderado Savings, our lender for the construction loan. As I refresh my memory, it occurs to me that Golderado Savings can't issue Ralph any money from the construction account until I sign off on the itemized list of expenses based on a handful of receipts Ralph brings me each pay period. After I approve the itemized list of expenses, Ralph is issued a check for that amount from the bank.

▓ ▓ ▓ ▓ ▓ ▓ ▓ ▓

During the summers of my high school and college years, I worked as a carpenter building small houses near my parents' home in Missouri. I had started as a laborer working with Herman and others. By the time I was in college, I worked as a finish carpenter. Dad and I built a 3,000 square foot summer home on the banks of the Arkansas River when Sarah and I first moved to Colorado.

I knew much of the process of home construction and the use of materials and subcontractors as I looked at copies of receipts that Ralph submitted to the bank. I began counting every piece of lumber and nail needed to construct the framing and the subfloor, etc.. Laboriously, I went through the house plans, documenting and cross checking all the materials, labor, processes, and services used to build our new home. I knew down to the last nail how many it took.

▓ ▓ ▓ ▓ ▓ ▓ ▓ ▓

On the day of reckoning, December 23, I leave the house about 3:30 p.m. and drive north toward Denver on I-25. As I get to the escarpment above the Lincoln Avenue exit, the sun is almost nonexistent. It is blotted out by the thick, brown cloud, caused by auto pollution and an air inversion that keep it over Denver. I could swear I see filaments of brown, stringy, smoky particles linking the brown cloud in a horizontal mass that is nauseating to look at. I feel a little redeemed; the children could be living in this crap that is walled up against this big hill just south of Lincoln Avenue. The smog menacingly tries to get over the hill to Castle Rock. Perhaps I have saved some of the children's lung tissue from being damaged, but at what cost?

I drive down that long hill past Lincoln Avenue and am absorbed into the sea of smog, and at that point, conceptually, I break out the ancestral long boats. I cannot wait to come ashore and encounter my persecutors.

Not all lawyers' offices are created equal. Ralph's attorney's office is a dingy, dinky hole in the wall. His office is located somewhere about the fifth floor of a dirty, faceless brick building in northwest central Denver. The office is so grimy, it seems like all the light in the room is sucked up by the dark walls. The walls are hungry for a breath of fresh air and light.

In this small, dingy office is a Nazi gray metal desk and four non-descript matching metal chairs covered in puke green Naugahyde. Hermann Goebbels must have been the interior designer. I now know why Ralph's attorney called me: "PICKY, PICKY, PICKY" over the phone the night the line in the sand was drawn and we both dug our heels in and went to legal war. I should countersue him for polluting the environment with his crappy office and subsequent shitty attitude toward those who demand better. This guy is so used to living in a world of grungy crap, that anyone who expected more was PICKY.

His office has one small vertical window that looks out into a bleak, brownish-black night. I can barely see Christmas lights across the way, dimmed by the density of the brown cloud's daily visit, and the filmy grit deposited on the windows. The office is a disgusting, depressing, and visually degenerate environment to work and conduct business in. One week in this environment and I would flagellate myself daily, or better yet, break out five gallons of white paint, a brush, and roller.

Everyone is there but, of course, not my attorney, who soon calls and says he will be late. Ralph's lawyer says, "Let's go to dinner." What a bazaar scene, we three go down to a greasy spoon, a 1950s Edward Hopper type grill and eat dinner. We are the only ones in this lonely restaurant. For me, the air is tense but the two of them are very casual. We have been fighting over this issue for almost a year, and I have nothing but simmering hate for these two people. Many nights I go to sleep dreaming of accidently meeting Ralph in some primeval forest. One of us doesn't make it home.

Now he sits right across from me casually having a greasy, open-faced roast beef sandwich. The thought of attacking him with my butter knife and fork runs through my mind. There is sporadic small talk about mundane life issues, but not the case. Finally, we return to his office and my attorney is there. Ralph's lawyer tells me what the law is and why I should cut a check for the last part of the agreed upon payment. My attorney sits there looking blankly at me, his mind elsewhere. I go through the litany of grievances I have and what I have been forced to do to mitigate the inequities of the contractual obligations Ralph owes us. I tell them nothing new.

They smile with their eyes at each other as though it is a done deal; I am going to pay. I then go into what I find in my research. The house has 1500 lineal feet of tongue-and-grove cedar siding; Ralph bills me for 3000 lineal feet. He uses one 24 foot glue-laminated beam that measures 6x18 inches in the house. I have been charged for a beam 45 foot long that measures 12x24 inches which is not in the house. The rafters of a huge Safeway grocery store could be propped up with a beam of that size. Ralph also uses seven skylights in the house, but bills me for 14. The list of overages and fraudulent acquisitions go on and on.

My lawyer, at last wakes up, and realizes we have these guys by the short hairs. He now gives me reassuring smiles. Ralph's lawyer scooches down in his high back Naugahyde chair and studies his pencil. Ralph is looking down and won't make eye contact as I read the list of unnecessary, unauthorized, and illegal expenditures. When I finish, I put the laundry list in front of his attorney, and say nothing except "Fraud." How dramatic!

There is lots of shuffling around by the three and all requests for the last payment are dropped. His attorney alleges that the score card is even.

■ ■ ■ ■ ■ ■ ■ ■

My attorney said little of substance and missed the really big issue. Of course, I didn't think about a possible lawsuit against the lender and Ralph for fraud at the time.

We could have had a free house. Had I or my attorney realized the contractual infraction, we could have taken the issue to the courts. But I was 40; young and stupid, enervated by the whole process, and just wanted to go home and forget the ten month ordeal. I did not get my beloved flying staircase, but Ralph did not get his final payment.

The lawsuit had been the big road block to moving from our new home and perhaps away from the strange events that happened early on. After that meeting, the road block was gone, however, neither Sarah nor I, ever talked or thought about putting our home up for sale and moving. I don't believe now that the decision to consciously leave was ours to make. Perhaps we were suffering from the Stockholm Syndrome and had bonded with our night visitors and now saw everyone else as the problem. There was no reason to move.

"Everything is determined, the beginning as well as the end,
by forces over which we have no control.
It's determined for the insect, as well as for the star.
Human beings, vegetables, or cosmic dust, we all dance to a mysterious tune,
intoned in the distance by an invisible piper."

ALBERT EINSTEIN

*"We seem near
to the great fact;
the mysteries of
mysteries. The first
appearance of new
beings on this earth.*

CHARLES DARWIN

CHAPTER TWO | 1981

OFF THE WALL | JANUARY 8, 1981

Christmas has come and gone, and the winter semester is quickly approaching. I have scheduled myself to teach the first course in the History of Design at the university in the upcoming semester. It is evening, we eat dinner and I sit at the kitchen table reading from my textbook. I sit with my back to the kitchen's sliding glass door and the patio outside.

Kitchen table and sliding glass door

Sarah asks me to feed the dogs. If we feed them at night, we usually tuck some of our dinner scraps into their regular dog food. I take the two bowls out to Charma and Huggy Bear. I put Huggy's bowl near the south side of the house, not far from where I am sitting. I then take Charma's bowl of food around the corner to the east side of the house, then come inside and resume my reading.

I barely get back to my reading when I'm distracted by Charma barking at something outside on the east side of the house. Her barking indicates she is

Garden level, east side of house

moving away from her bowl of food and toward the low, gentle knoll to the east. Charma's barking suddenly stops and turns into a sharp, loud pain-filled yelp. Immediately there is a heavy THUD against the east wall of the house.

I see the painting on the wall of the kitchen bounce out away from the wall and almost fall to the floor. The wall has flexed as a result of whatever hit it. I immediately jump up and rush outside. I see Charma in the dim light lying on the pavers near the wall of the house by her bowl of food. She appears stunned and evidently had been thrown by something up against the house. If she had been thrown a foot north of where she was, she would have gone through the triangular kitchen window and have been cut up pretty badly. The THUD I heard was her fifty-pound body hitting the house.

I look up and to the east. There, in front of a tangled mass of fledgling Gamble Oak branches, silent and ominous, stands an enormous translucent conundrum looking at me. I can only wonder, *What the fuck is that?* The strange, eerie shape is about fifteen feet from me, apparently accessing my worth. The frozen, unfamiliar entity then starts moving diagonally in front of me, heading for the plum tree thicket to my right, at the south end of the downstairs' front yard. The distance to the plum thicket is about fifty feet. The only illumination in the area is the ambient light coming from the kitchen and the second story of the house.

This very light brown, translucent shape is about eight feet tall, a foot wide and wafer thin. The entity looks like the profile silhouette of a very slim and shaggy T-Rex. In the faint light, I can make out a horizontal head area, a vertical thorax with two small arm-like appendages sticking out in front, an abdomen, and a long horizontal tail. The form is like a long geometric stylized 'S'. There are no back or bottom legs to this simple, ragged-edged mystery.

I believe the light brown thing is two dimensional, and if seen from its edge, it would be difficult or impossible to see. It would be like looking at the edge of a piece of paper. The shape is about six inches to a foot off the ground and doesn't make a sound as it glides over the crunchy, dry Gamble Oak leaves. The perplexing form moves as though it is on a zipline headed toward the plum thicket and large juniper tree in the front yard. It disappears behind the branches of the juniper tree. The branches do not move as this ephemeral figure passes through them.

After living here eleven months, I am pretty much shock-proof. I view the event and strange phenomenon with rapt interest and curiosity. Remarkably, I am not frightened; the hair on my neck is not standing up, my heart is beating at its regular pace, and I am unmoved by the sighting. Seconds later I think that what I saw must have been a ghost or spirit. I have no known background experience or information on ghosts or spirits; I have never had an occasion to research the topic. Knowing that I will probably not see the shape reemerge from behind the juniper tree, I lean down and tend to Charma. I feel to see if she has any broken bones or tender spots. Miraculously, Charma is unhurt but shaken by the experience. I take the dogs and their food inside the house where they eat and stay all night.

* * * * * * * *

I immediately knew it had to be Charma who was thrown up against the laundry room wall six months earlier. I thought it was this creature who threw her against the wall hard enough to literally knock the crap out of her. How anything could do that in a six-foot span of space boggled my mind. I should be frightened but that would be foolish; there was nothing I could do to deal with such a conundrum.

I was encouraged by the fact that the entity ran from me. Had the thing come toward me, I was not sure what I would have done. It would have been a James Lang-Cannon Bard moment for sure.

Sarah had been saying all along that there were spirits in the house making the strange noises we kept hearing. I was convinced the ufolks were the culprits. Learning how to deal with this new phenomenon was just what I needed to get me down the road of reinventing myself. I acknowledged the spirit's existence but could not deal with an entity that might be invisible. I knew that whatever it was had probably been in the house for some time, and so far hadn't hurt or altered anyone, other than Charma, who was diligent enough to bark at it. The spirit obviously did not like either her barking or it being detected.

A big lesson was learned that night. I was to go after whatever I saw or heard regardless of how ambiguous or horrifying the source was or appeared to be. I needed to be mentally resilient and believe that I was the predator, not the prey. I also had to give off a strong aura and energy field that would put fear in the spirit. I could not pale in the face of the unknown. So far I had instinctively, or out of ignorance, been the aggressor when I heard strange noises.

It was clear I had to maintain that posture to keep control of the situation to protect Sarah and the children. I preferred to call what I saw that night, a *spirit*. The name to me was less threatening and ominous than the word, *ghost*. To call it a ghost might unnecessarily frighten Sarah, the children, and me. Frightful ghosts were often seen in children's cartoons, movies, and novels like Charles Dicken's *The Night before Christmas*. I didn't want to dredge up a terrifying literary ghost in the minds of the children.

I was mystified how the strange-looking entity threw Charma up against the wall. It did not appear to have appendages strong enough to throw her five to ten feet through the air and up against the house. The spirit's shape was so ambiguous, I had no idea what it might be or represent.

Life went on as usual that winter, and I became much more observant of what went on around me. I looked for any visual nuances in our home that might give an invisible spirit away. I couldn't hunt what I couldn't see. Later, when I got into full fabric design and banner production, I hung eight foot by 42 inch sheets of chiffon with my recent designs on them from the ceiling of some rooms so I could detect the slightest movement of air or invisible forces in the house.

THE OLD TIMERS | JANUARY, 1981

With the new Heatilator-type fireplace installed in the house, Saturdays become forage for wood day. The woods across the ravine south of the house are lush with Gamble Oak, the hottest burning wood to be found in the area. The pine and spruce trees are more abundant but do not give off as many BTU's per pound. We need wood that can burn all night to keep the house warm from eleven p.m. to six the next morning.

The whole family is involved and the Bartoks are out on the loose looking for wood. My job is to cut and trim the downed and standing dead oak trees. Sarah, Breana, and Scott drag the logs to the edge of the ravine and I throw the day's tree harvest into it. We then pull the logs up the other side and to the house. Probably, we are doing what the Native Americans that lived here in the past had done for centuries. I cut the long logs into manageable-sized pieces that create warm evenings around the fireplace.

Eventually, we exhaust the supply of dead trees across the ravine, and the band of Bartoks move on up the old toll road path to the top of the mesa. The bounty is smaller, the trek back with wood is farther, but the view of the front range snow-covered mountains from Long's Peak to Pike's Peak is grand. During the foraging and exploring, we find two abandoned farm homes on the mesa due west of our house.

One home looks as if the family was just setting down to eat before they mysteriously disappear or flee the scene, never to return, leaving the entire setting of flatware, plates, and coffee cups on the table. A relatively new Schwinn children's bike hangs silently on the inside door of the barn. An abandoned combine with flat tires and broken out headlights sets parked and decaying along the two-track road that leads to the house from the west. The old, ragged kitchen curtains flutter through the broken window panes over the sink. The nearest home to the abandoned farm house is ours, only three-quarters of a mile away.

We discover a burned out house along the highway to Castle Rock on the west side of the mesa. Local historians allege that the father of the family who lived there went berserk and killed his wife and three children. He then set fire to the house and killed himself.

The only other homestead dwelling in the vicinity is the burned out remains of a two story rock home. Todd, my barber in Castle Rock is an old timer who has lived in the area all his life. He tells me that the father of this homestead had also gone berserk, killing his family and then himself after torching the inside of the house.

Over the years we hear many strange stories from locals. A farmer we buy hay from tells us a tale about his neighbor. He was driving on a county road at night, east of Monument, Colorado, fifteen miles southeast of us, when he saw a bright light in his rearview mirror. He was soon overtaken by this bright light that did not pass him but went up above the cab of his truck and stayed there as he continued to drive down the road. The light, and whatever the craft was, made the hairs on his neck and head stand straight up on end. The cab of his truck was filled with a strange electrical humming sound. After several miles, the light broke off to the south and disappeared as mysteriously as it had appeared. Shortly thereafter, his neighbor's hair turned white. The guy was never mentally the same and he died prematurely of a heart attack..

When I tell Todd where we live, he excitedly relates another client's story to me. His client said he saw a bright light one night go straight up off the mesa west of Castle Rock. The light was brilliant, and once it was sufficiently airborne it made an abrupt 90 degree turn and headed west. Within seconds the light disappeared over the horizon.

My barber then reveals one of his own unusual stories. From time to time, he sees a huge Great Horned Owl sitting on the snag of a large pine tree not far from his home. This story doesn't sound out of the ordinary until he mentions the bird is at least five feet tall, considerably taller than most Great Horned Owls in the area. Oddly enough, he is worried about the safety of his dog, and not himself! His story is a precursor to a similar account our closest neighbor would tell us in 1989. Her story is far more ominous.

Almost any old time rancher or resident we talk to has stories of strange and inexplicable events that defy traditional logic, common sense, and easy explanation. A couple more stories strike close to home. A garage mechanic tells me, that in the 1960s, campers saw a classic UFO silently glide down a canyon from the south and exit the north end of a valley toward Daniel's Park. I look into this and find a newspaper article confirming the story of campers seeing a UFO in the Daniel's Park area around that time.

Todd, the magnet of all wild stories, also claims a rancher who lives on the west side of our mesa had a chilling account of waking one morning to find his 1,500 pound bull dead and laying upside down in the top of a large cottonwood tree close to his barn. The bull had been mutilated and was missing his anus, tongue, eyes, and blood. Judging by the way the limbs of the cottonwood tree were broken, the rancher thought the bull had been dropped from the air into the top branches of the tree. The Sheriff came out to make a report and attributed the death of the bull to the work of a cult group in the area.

Possibly, if the death was explained in this manner, the rancher could get insurance money for the animal. No matter how many cult members there were, it would be pretty hard to lift a 1500 pound bull up 20 feet into the upper bows of a cottonwood tree.

■ ■ ■ ■ ■ ■ ■ ■

After hearing that story, I wondered about Sarah's horse, Rogue. What was he doing out of his pasture, racing blindly through the night into a cattle guard, where he perished? Were Rogue and Rebel being chased by a UFO, intent on mutilating them? Maybe the only thing that kept him from being mutilated was the rancher who happened upon Rogue shortly after he broke three legs in the cattle guard.

We were appreciative to know about the old timers' stories and felt what we were experiencing had been going on for some time, even for hundreds or thousands of years. The mutilation story was particularly chilling.

Then I wondered about the turkey vulture rookery, located in the Castlewood Canyon State Park 20 miles away-the largest rookery in the state. Did it have a connection to the mutilations in the area? I figured this large number of vultures needed plenty of carrion to sustain them. I called a park ranger and asked why the largest vulture rookery in Colorado was located in the canyon. He said there was a lot of roadkill in the area! I thought that was bullshit; this was a very rural area in the state's scheme of things. It seemed to me that roads south of Castlewood Canyon were few and far between. I had driven most of them looking for places to hunt for ducks with the dogs. I didn't notice an inordinate amount of roadkill, so what did these turkey vultures eat, perhaps leftovers from mutilated animals?

In the first months of our second year, most of my days and nights are spent in the studio. I get really good results with my work on fabric. Long hours are spent experimenting with diverse and exotic chemicals, pigment mixtures, and different fabrics. I vary heat-setting times to get the maximum saturation and light fastness of color on the various fabrics I use. The most difficult part of the process is mentally working through types of images I can effectively create within the limitations of my experimenting and research.

There is also the fact the studio can get TV and radio reception, and I make up for lost time in my thirst for outside information and visual stimulation. As in college, I find I work best when mildly distracted by the sounds of other human voices, music, or white noise. My left brain is distracted enough to leave the "driving" to my right brain. I do quite fine without my left brain's design criticism during the creative process. At just the right time, which can only be determined by oneself, I let my left brain out to critique my work-in-progress. The dance between the two brain halves is a delicate matter. But the dance is necessary to create work that is non-stylistic and will intellectually and visually stand the test of time.

Music is a great benefit to me, and often the color and rhythm of my work reflect the kind of music I play at the time I create a piece. I find over the years that I can subtly manipulate the work I create by using external stimulation, deadeners, distractions, or exciters to keep my left brain occupied. Late night talk shows are always good to design by. At the end of my years in the studio, had I been paying total attention, I could have qualified for honorary PhD degrees in psychology, sociology, and criminology.

On one of my night trips from the studio to the house, to take a break from my work, I notice that the closer I get to the house, the more anxious I am. I stop and look up at the night sky. There is no moon, and it occurs to me that when odd things happen, it is usually a moonless night.

As I scan the heavens, I am struck by a bright cluster of stars in the northwest sector of the night sky. I count seven stars. I have heard by now about the Seven Sisters, or the Pleiades. I have seen on the cover of the *Enquirer*, my only source of UFO information, it is believed that UFOs come from the Pleiades. I can't fathom how these people can travel such a great distance during their lifetime. But what all these space travelers do is beyond my grasp, and their motives are incomprehensible as well.

Earlier in the evening, it was still light and I forgot to take my flashlight with me to the studio. Is this why I feel edgy on my way up to the house, walking in the dark? The possibility of running into a snake, skunk, porcupine, or bear in the dark, always makes me nervous. But, tonight, the feeling is very different. For a short distance in my trek, I am overcome by a feeling of high anxiety, more than what the fear of stepping on a snake, or running into a bear would create. When I get to the house, the anxious feeling is gone.

On my way back to the studio I take a flashlight. Some distance down the drive, the light from my flashlight just disappears. I have not changed the angle of holding the flashlight, so I am momentarily confused as to how the beam just fades out. I keep walking and the light comes back up to full strength and is back to normal by the time I reach the studio. Perhaps the battery somehow goes on the fritz for a moment. When I make my trek back to the house to go to bed, the same thing happens at the same place in the driveway. I go to bed and blame the flashlight for the strange glitch, but I am suspicious that some unseen thing is responsible for the flashlight's strange behavior.

UP A TUBE | JULY 18, 1981

At 1:15 a.m. on the morning of July 18, Sarah and I wake to the loudest, most horrendous noises I have ever heard. We bolt straight up in bed and gape at each other, unable to muster a sound. There aren't words to be had. We hear a series of random explosions that lasts for three to four seconds. BOOM! BOOM! BOOM!

We don't know what is going on as the explosions continue. For the first time, I'm alarmed. I don't get out of bed to challenge the sounds. Before the booming stops, the explosions are joined by the sound of a tremendous low growl from a powerful motor of some sort starting up. The deep-throated and steady roar begins to diminish in volume and intensity as we hear it lift off above us and starts what seems to be an assent to where-we don't know.

It sounds like something is lifting off out of, or above, the living room. The tremendous thrust of the engine diminishes and abruptly changes in pitch. The number of pitch changes is four to five. With each change, the sound diminishes until the roar no longer exists. Suddenly all is deathly quiet.

My courage comes back. I jump out of bed, turn on the bedroom light, and run over to the hand railing separating the upper half of the living room from our bedroom. I expect to see a giant, gaping hole in the ceiling of the living room. I am flabbergasted; I see nothing, no holes, no smoke, no smoldering chunks of drywall on the floor, or splintered roof rafters. I am relieved but puzzled.

It occurs to me that the sound could have come from the courtyard. Grasses may be on fire and could spread to the surrounding tall grasses of the native terrain. I charge outside in my underwear, but there isn't any fire or smoke, nor do I hear anything. Mother Nature's sweet night breath and murmuring sounds had just been sucked up with whatever bore its way into the heavens. It is totally quiet; no sounds from crickets, night hawks, owls, frogs, toads, dogs, or coyotes. I don't smell any explosion residue.

The moonless night is dead calm, but beautiful, cool, sweet-smelling and nothing stirs. I stand outside on the deck looking for any irregularity in the immediate landscape. Then I hear it, the soft, fluid voice of water spraying out of our courtyard pop-up sprinkler heads onto the thirsty grass.

I am relieved that nothing has been destroyed or is burning. I go inside to see what time it is. I check my watch on the bedroom night stand; it is 1:18 a.m. in the morning.

I check the children's room; they are peacefully sleeping in their beds. I don't get it; how could the kids not have heard the deafening explosions and the tremendous roar of the rocket, or whatever it was. Sarah and I felt like we were going to get blown out of our bed. In the past, Scott woke me up in the night telling me he had heard noises that I did not. It is hard to believe that his young, attentive ears did not hear the sounds which nearly rocked us out of bed.

It's impossible for me to sleep; I am too excited and I go back out on the deck by the upstairs entry door. The pop-up sprinklers are gently watering the grass. I cannot believe the ufolks made so much noise lifting off. In the past, their hallmark had been stealth-based. I think, *Maybe we aren't technologically too far behind our visitors.* The roar of their engines sounded primitive compared to the low humming of the saucer that parked itself in front of the living room in the spring of last year. I am again encouraged, killing or capturing an entity is still within my grasp. I then think maybe they were interrupted by something, panicked, and blasted off instead of using a quieter propulsion system. The only thing different around the house this summer has been the recent change in the sprinkler times for the courtyard irrigation system.

※　※　※　※　※　※　※　※

It had been hotter and dryer than usual. A few days earlier, I switched the irrigation systems watering time from 4:00 p.m. to 1:00 a.m., more likely 1:10 a.m. I wanted to keep trans-evaporation of surface moisture down by watering at night.

The house sat on bedrock, a rather soft, light gray, slate like sedimentary rock. When I installed the sprinkler system the summer before, I could not dig a deep enough trench in the backyard to keep the sprinkler pipes from freezing in low spots. I put three-pound per square inch drain valves in every low spot in the irrigation system's pipeline. The whole system self-drained each time it shut down and quit sprinkling. Thus, it would never have water in the lines when it was not in use. I could activate the sprinkler system on Christmas day if I chose to because the lines wouldn't freeze up. When water first started coming into the pipeline, it drove out the air in the lines and made a noise like a hissing snake. The hissing sound from the sprinkler system could have spooked the ufolks, causing them to panic.

Perhaps the ETs had parked their craft and were just getting ready to come in the upstairs front door. The sprinkler system cycle began. Ten or more sprinkler heads popped up, the rush of air creating a cacophony of hissing noises that sounded like snakes. What a sight that must have been as the freaked out ufolks responded to the unexpected hissing of all those "snakes." Possibly, they were afraid of snakes; in particular rattlesnakes. Our visitors departed in emergency mode and literally blasted off, making a horrible racket.

I was smugly euphoric, for once, we had a defense system. I was sure they would return but not at the same time of night again. They were far too smart for the hissing pop-ups or water to stop them. Maybe I should have a powerful squirt gun to hunt them with instead of the twelve gauge! If I were right, the thought was so ironic that these most scientifically advanced creatures were afraid of water or snakes! On the other hand, maybe they purposely blew us out of bed as an in your face wake up call, suggesting they

Upstairs courtyard

could have me, or us, any time they wanted.

I preferred to believe they were frightened by the hissing sound of the sprinklers. The aliens' noisy rocket launch was unexpected. How could these brilliant people who allegedly come from the Pleiades have used such a primitive sounding propulsion system?

The next morning, I walked around the house, increasing the scope of my path at each completion of a circle. On my second pass, I found native field grass that had been blown down and into a subtle swirling pattern. The circular pattern was very small, perhaps five feet in diameter. The rotation pattern of the downed grasses was clockwise. The swirl mark in the grass was due north of the upstairs entry door, just outside the courtyard's curving wooden wall. The distance to the upstairs front door from that point was not more than 25 feet.

I continued looking around the area for anything unusual. I then detected a small, shiny mark on the grassy earth outside the swirled pattern. Scanning the circumference of the swirled native grass I noticed two more shiny marks. The three shiny marks formed a triangular pattern. This equilateral triangle did not seem as big as the one on the mesa the year before. The marks indicated to me that a tripod of some weight had sat down on this patch of tall prairie grass and the metal feet of its legs compressed the dirt to the point that it became shiny.

Maybe, whatever made these marks was a shuttle craft that landed there days or weeks earlier. I didn't think these prints were connected to the craft that blasted off and awakened us. If it had launched outside the courtyard, why didn't the children wake up, the prints were closer to the children's room than ours? But the sound of the craft taking off sounded like it was going up a tube, and this intrigued me. I was reminded of the wailing sounds of incoming V2 rockets plunging like daggers into the hallowed earth of war torn London during the last months of the Second World War. As the rockets plunged to the earth, their wailing sounds changed in pitch as they penetrated down through invisible densities of air. The craft I heard, made that kind of sound, but in reverse.

Was it the Doppler Effect as the craft shot out of the yard, or from atop the flat roof of the house and up an airless chamber? One would think the whole house would have vibrated; dishes, paintings, vases, and the like falling off the walls and counter tops. We felt no vibrations and there was no evidence of anything damaged inside or outside the house. The explosions and roar of the craft's engines were just another mystery for me to ponder for the rest of my life.

■   ■   ■   ■   ■   ■   ■   ■

On the weekend, there is a subdivision meeting and pig roast at the Hansen's home. Their home is at the same elevation as ours in the valley and is approximately one mile southeast of ours. The thought occurs to me to discretely ask as many neighbors as I can if they heard any unusual noises coming from our canyon earlier in the week. The cliffs behind the house are great acoustical reflectors and collectors of sound. On summer days we can hear our neighbors a quarter of a mile away to the south, arguing over their personal grievances against one another, very entertaining. They finally get a divorce and their soap opera ends.

I am convinced that because of how loud the blast off sound was, someone else must have heard it that night. It seems to me the noise from the craft would have been projected out and away from the cliffs, and into the valley to the southeast of us.

Most of the subdivision residents are at the meeting and pig roast. Everyone is very congenial and talkative. I make my rounds chatting individually with neighbors and then I work in the question, "Did you hear any unusual noises coming from our part of the neighborhood Tuesday night?" Everyone I talk to says, "No." I can't believe no one heard the tremendous explosions coming from our little canyon. As I work the party, I hear our new neighbor telling someone that he had a strange experience last Saturday. My ears perk up with interest, and I ooze in closer to hear what he has to say.

Our new neighbor has built a beautiful four-story, post-modern home that articulates its way up the side of the mesa in a most dynamic way. I am almost jealous; his new home is visually so interesting. Our home has sacrificed form for pure economic function.

He has a wife and daughter. The wife is an avid equestrian and they have a new barn for her horses. The barn is about two to three hundred feet east of their home. Our neighbor says, "Saturday, about mid-afternoon, I went down to feed the horses and when I came back from the barn it was dark and the moon was out!" He keeps on talking but I am not listening because I am trapped in my own thoughts. I know what happened to him, but I don't dare even mention it as a possibility.

I want to tell him what I think, but talking about UFOs or other-worldly topics is a recipe for intellectual and social disgrace. I keep my thoughts to myself. The next thing I hear, he and his family have moved to Colorado Springs.

I continue moving through the gathering asking the same question. When I get to Joe I strike pay dirt. Joe is the spiritual heart of the subdivision. He has lived here the longest and has a firm grasp of the area's history, county governance, and zoning ordinances. He is also the great mediator in the subdivision. Joe keeps the neighborhood from turning into a war zone with his calm, common sense methods to resolve disputes between opposing groups from getting into fisticuffs over the covenants. Joe was a courier during the cold war and is always alert to any changes in the natural, built, and social environments.

I quietly ask Joe the question.

He says, "No, but I did see something strange Tuesday night."

I leap to the next question, "What?"

Joe replies, "I saw a bright, whitish-red light come up from, or behind, your house.

It went straight up to above the mesa and then turned abruptly 90 degrees and went due west and out of sight. Judging by the light's trajectory, I think it might have gone down on top of the mesa."

"About what time was it when you saw the bright light?" I ask.

"I had just finished watching the late night movie and I checked my watch to see what time it was, it was 1:15 a.m. Then I went out on the north deck to smoke a cigarette. As I smoked, I looked north toward your house and that was when I saw the light come up from on top of or behind your house."

■   ■   ■   ■   ■   ■   ■   ■

I was internally ecstatic. For the first time since all these mysterious events began, I had someone who had seen something that corroborates almost exactly, to the minute, our experience that night. Joe should have heard the noise that we heard. That night was calm and the air was cool. I began to relive the blast off moment again to see if, in my mind's eye, I had missed anything that would be of help in deciphering the mystery.

Earlier in the day, before I talked to Joe, I thought I knew exactly where the craft had lifted off from, the roof of our house. Now I had my doubts. I thought about how and why the children weren't awakened by the noise. I tried to visualize a craft launching from where the tripod marks were outside the courtyard. It finally occurred to me that the craft might have had a noiseless booster to get it off the ground fast, and then the main thrusters could be ignited, the engine started, and the craft was full blown into flight up a vacuum tube.

Conceivably, the craft veered southwest as it lifted off the ground and ended up over our bedroom before it ignited its engines, creating such a noise as we had never heard before. The sound of the engine thrusts were evidently held within what seemed like a tube that kept the sound focused down on the roof above our heads. Thus, the children did not hear anything. The sound was encapsulated in a tube, directed straight down at our bedroom and nonexistent to their ears. But why were there no house vibrations? Maybe, the vacuum column, or hollow tube in front of the craft, could provide a pure frictionless environment to speed through space and time. Was this a wormhole they traveled through? If so, it was no wonder that when UFOs were seen, there was no sound associated with their movement through space.

■　■　■　■　■　■　■　■

Author's Note: On April 28, 2015 I become aware of a sighting of a huge UFO situated near the ground at O'Hara International airfield in Chicago. Numerous airport ground workers saw the hovering craft and called the tower to see if they saw it on their radar. The control tower answered in the negative, nothing on their radar. For some reason, the craft zoomed straight up through eight thousand feet of clouds and disappeared. The puzzling part was that the craft left a perfect hole up through the clouds. The clear cylindrical column through the clouds remained for a while after the craft disappeared. The control tower still did not detect the craft but the ground crews watched it disappear into the heavens. Had the workmen been directly under the craft, they probably would have experienced the sound of it.

■　■　■　■　■　■　■　■

Years later, after the subdivision party, I would come across the image of two small UFOs speeding through space. The crafts were depicted with cut away views showing human-looking pilots wearing robes like thirteenth century monks. The crafts and pilots flew in the background of *Christ's Crucifixion*, a gesso painting created by an unknown artist in 1350. The fresco was located above the altar at the Visoki Decani Monestary in Kosovo, Yugoslavia. The two, small, UFOs in the fresco looked like they were propelled by rocket power that generated projection-like flames behind them. Skeptics said the images were of the sun and moon, and not space craft. I say no. The inhabitant of the craft on the right is looking back at the individual flying the rocket on the left. Maybe the ufolks we heard were flying the same kind of small, rocket-powered craft depicted in this Kosovo monastery gesso.

I had always been suspicious of age-old stories about UFO-type vehicles, chariots, silver boats, magic carpets, *Vimanas*, silver shields, wheels within wheels, dragons, and serpents with wings, etc., that made great amounts of thunderous noise as they lifted off and flew. Now I began to believe the myths, that earlier cultures and artists visually described, about the noise and fire associated with alien craft launching into the heavens. Maybe our ancient ancestors were standing directly below the tube the noisy craft flew up or in.

I was excited to think Joe had seen what we had heard and that I was not going nuts. I was now curious about our neighbor's missing time story that he told at the subdivision party. To my knowledge at that time, most of my known abductions had always been accompanied or initiated by lights that subdued me. Our neighbor did not mention any lights. It was like he walked through an invisible doorway right into a different dimension, or world, in broad daylight. He then emerged hours later without a memory of what happened during that lost time.

For months prior to hearing our neighbor's missing time story, I had been wondering about some strange days in 1977-78. Shortly after we bought the land, I would come out to the property by myself. I cleared brush and yucca, stacked downed wood, and did what might be called an environmental assessment and clean up of the ten acre site. I logged the sun times, and its positions relative to the cliffs of the box canyon. I located magnetic and true south, and I noted wind directions, flora, fauna, colors and shapes of prominent land masses that would help with the design of the house we intended to build there.

One of the most exciting elements on the property was a beautiful little spring that tumbled out from under a large boulder. It flowed off the property to the large drainage ravine that headed southeast to the subdivision pond. The presence of the spring was one of the reasons we bought the property in the first place. I worried about a future war, and a source of fresh water, that did not rely on electricity to pump it out of the ground, would be a real bonus.

We had originally wanted to build an underground home with a southern exposure for passive solar heating during winter months. The county, however, did not have inspectors trained to make inspections during construction. Getting a loan on an underground house was even more problematic. We opted for a modern home that would be visually compatible with the horizontal sedimentary layers of the landmasses it would be nestled in, and the flat mesa top above. A modern home with lots of glass was also easily adapted into a stage three passive solar home.

After doing my assessment work, I determined I could dam the small spring and have a trout habitat that could help feed us if worse came to a worst case scenario. But the spring was very close to the boundary of the subdivision green belt, which I could not build a dam on. Plus, there were very large cedar trees that would have to be cut down. I could only construct a small impoundment on the land that was left between the spring and the property boundary. There was no room for an earthen dam. It would have to be a concrete wall almost incasing a large rock the water flowed under. I hated to construct

Me, pouring concrete for the dam

the wall so close to the rock, but I had no choice if I were going to stay off the green belt property and still build the pond.

My construction process was simple. I dug a trench and poured concrete footers for the dam. I let that dry, and constructed plywood forms for the wall of the dam. I bought ten bags of ready mix concrete at a hardware store on my way to the property each day I worked on the dam. I combined the dry cement with water from the spring in a trough I built. Once mixed, I shoveled that batch into the forms and gradually raised the height of the dam with successive pours.

Since hearing our neighbor's lost time story and having my less subtle experiences with the unknown, I started getting this nagging feeling something happened to me when I went out to hand mix and pour successive layers of concrete. It took me ten working days to finish the dam. What puzzled me was that when it was time to leave for home each day, I would always have three or four bags of unused dry concrete left.

At the time, I was 37 and in good physical shape. I had mixed lots of concrete in the past. I should have been able to mix and pour ten bags of dry concrete in two hours maximum. So what happened to those other hours? I didn't dwell on the topic then because missing time was not a conscious issue in my life, at least I never thought about it. I would just go home refreshed from a day away from my regular responsibilities.

I now think that sometimes when I went to the property to pour concrete, I was walking into another dimension like my neighbor must have done. Maybe ufolks can move this invisible gateway around to suit their needs. There is no telling what happened to me each time I went to the property. It seems to me that was why I did not get the pond's concrete dam poured in a timely manner. The project lasted weeks longer than it should have.

Sarah and the children are in Kansas City visiting her parents. For some reason I am sleeping in the southeast bedroom. I have been up late watching a video and have just laid down when I hear a faint humming sound. To my amazement, the oscillating sound increases in volume and intensity. Judging by the sound, it is descending from directly above me and coming fast.

Now the sound is stationary and right above my head. I lie there and listen intently for other noises. There are no lights outside the house that I detect, no creaking rafters. All of the sudden, awareness and curiosity plunge me into terror and fright of the unknown!

I think I know what the noise means, but I don't know what to expect. For me, the fear of the unknown is the most intense emotion associated with abduction. I can only compare the fear as similar to the fear one experiences when young and playing tag. Getting tagged isn't painful; the fear comes from the thought of someone catching you.

Once when Breana was 11, she played tag with friends and her brother in the second story hay loft of our South Park ranch's barn. In the heat of the moment and the fear of being tagged by her brother, she jumped out the second story window to the ground below. Fortunately, she was unhurt. That's the kind of fear I am feeling right now.

I wait while the humming persists in its stationary position. Finally, I get up my courage and turn on the bedroom light. Nothing happens. I then run from one room to the next and turn all the interior and exterior flood lights on. The house is lit up like a Christmas tree. I am an energy Nazi, but this night I go back to bed begrudgingly burning up kilowatts to protect me from-who knows what.

The sound is gone now, but I do not hear it go. I leave the lights on all night, knowing these people are after me and there is nothing I can do about it.

■ ■ ■ ■ ■ ■ ■ ■

The humming sound began about 1:15 a.m., almost exactly the same time as the big blast off we heard above our bedroom a week earlier. I didn't realize that there might be a time pattern to their coming and going. I could have used that information to my advantage and might have succeeded in ambushing our night visitors. 1:00 a.m. on moonless nights must be the key to hunting success. My theory that the sprinkler system kept them away the week before was debunked that night, or I was in the wrong bedroom.

"The first dance of a soul which does not
yet know itself is like dawn in the heavens;
it is the awakening of something radiant and unknown."

VICTOR HUGO

SEAN BARTOK

" *The most beautiful
things we can
experience is the
mysterious. It is the
source of all true
art and science.* "

ALBERT EINSTEIN

CHAPTER THREE | 1982

DOWNLOADED | FEBRUARY 18, 1982

I think I am peacefully lying on my back in our bedroom. I become uneasy, realizing I'm not exactly sure where I am. I cannot see my feet out in front of me, and don't feel the weight of my head, neck or shoulders. I don't feel the pillow under my head. I feel warm and relaxed. I sense there are living things around me, but I can only see ahead of me. The longer I am conscious, the more I realize that I'm not in my bedroom. The walls are luminous and curva-planear. Our bedroom is rectilinear, and the walls are solid satin white.

I go in and out of consciousness. The environment is foggy; slightly moist with no smells, vibrations, or noises that I can detect. The light in the room, or space I am in, is soft and luminous. Maybe that is why I think it is foggy. I feel like I'm looking through a film image created by a strange lighting system. The soft, white light seems to be coming from the wall itself. But through my hazy, gauzy view of reality, I'm not sure. I sense the presence of people coming toward me.

Though not fully conscious, I become aware of black and white and color images in front of me on the curving, luminous wall. I don't feel like I am being constrained, perhaps I just don't even try to move my eyes or head under these circumstances anymore. The images I see begin to slide by from top to bottom. They look like they are streaming down the wall like images on a smartphone. But this is 1982, and there aren't any smartphones that I know of. I liken the scene to 35mm slides being back projected and shown on a vertical, rather than a horizontal, axis. This kinetic technology is in use at this time for sophisticated slideshows, but they normally appear in a horizontal axis and take advantage of our binocular field of vision.

Soon, I recognize some of the images that are streaming by. The images are from a text book I use in my History of Design class. The images seem big, perhaps three by five feet, maybe bigger, but I can't be sure in my semi-groggy condition. I get this feeling that my mind is being downloaded.

As a visual artist, I am most interested in images of art, design, architecture, environments, color studies, symbols, signs, typography, etc.. I'm watching these kinds of images scroll by in front of me. I fixate on a fourteenth century woodcut of a black skull and crossbones printed on an acid green colored paper. I immediately recognize the print from my text book. The skull and crossbones design is an early label for an apothecary bottle filled with a poison of some sort.

When I pick up on the label and recognize it, the image freezes apparently so I can study it and digest its meaning. They seem to be silently coaxing me to think a specific way. I now seem to be fully conscious and definitely know there are biological entities somewhere in the area with me. I can sense their presence and keen interest in what images I prefer. I am not apprehensive or fearful of my captors. I sense their extreme curiosity, and they seem to have respect for me, a feeling I have not had from them before. I intuitively know they are my mentors, caring but very demanding. Maybe I am way off the mark on that assessment, only time will tell.

The images start streaming again. After some time, I see the ubiquitous image of General MacArthur wading ashore in the Philippines during the last months of World War II. The conquering hero returns to fulfill his promise, *I shall return*. That image stops and I look at it for some time.

The images are slowed down in accordance with the amount of time I want to look at them. My mind is fluid and I can think clearly and freely, but I cannot or choose not to move and can't roll my eyes around either. At first I think this must be some kind of Thematic Apperception Test. They are screwing with me to see my interests. With their capabilities, who knows what they can tell from my preferences for certain images, my GVSR, my EEG, my EKG. God knows what else they might be monitoring or manipulating. The images keep rolling by and then I see another black and white one that is very familiar.

I stop at this picture of a barren moon landscape with rolling craters smoothed by time and cosmic dust; the image stops as well. It is very confusing as to who's in charge of the speed with which these images stream by. But it stops and I study it. So far, only an idiot would not know what the message was; poison and zealous uncontrollable military generals will result in the earth being reduced into a lifeless planet. Stop senseless aggression or else the Earth will look like the moonscape I see before me.

I'm thinking they're singing to the choir unless I miss the point of this dog and pony show. Feeling completely at ease I wonder if I or they are in charge here in this laboratory. I believe these unseen ufolks could become really good beer drinking buddies.

Watching the images stream by, I think how easy it would be for them to tuck some of their own images and ideas into my mental and visual Rolodex and plant "seeds" that would bear fruit with their fingerprints on them later on in my life, or someone else's life. I understand how easy it would be to manipulate our future by planting ideas, formulas, and writing skills in the minds of more intelligent and creative people than me, as they download or, as the case may be, upload your mind. They don't need to walk among us, maybe they can't. All they need to do, by way of example, is to capture a physics professor and download his mind. Bingo! They know the best of what we are working on, and leave him with a little more information than what he started with. Suddenly, when the physicist least expects it, he/she has an "aha" experience and a new theory that advances his/her particular science is born.

The streaming images fade as I lapse back into unconsciousness. The next thing I know, I'm lying in my own bed, waking up from my night's "sleep." I don't feel any different than I do when waking almost every day of my life. However, after some nights that I have had a disturbing dream, I wake in an anxious state for no apparent reason. Sometimes I feel screwed over, or have a head or eye ache. I don't have a negative attitude toward those who I think have taken me in the night. As a matter of fact, I feel like they like me, and I am becoming more like one of them than who I am supposed to be. Perhaps the Stockholm Syndrome is changing my attitude about my identity, life, and purpose on earth.

* * * * * * * *

For days, I thought about what had happened that night. I didn't know why I remembered those images. Was I programmed to remember them in 1970, and did they want to communicate the idea that thermonuclear war can bring total destruction of the world? At the time, nuclear winter was not known to me, which makes their teaching all the more poignant. While the skull and crossbones usually meant death, they could have meant caution, beware, danger. The image of MacArthur returning to the Philippines could simply imply war or the defender of freedom. The last image of desolation indicated to me the consequences of war, death, and total destruction by overzealous warriors like MacArthur.

Between 1970 and 1973, I was obsessed with the plight of the environment, the human condition, political corruption, civil disobedience, hypocrisy, and nuclear war. In an Art Department exhibit, I created a series of very large transparent Kodalith film images of desolate outer space shots, blighted cityscapes from the air, maps of decaying cities, landscapes of cemeteries superimposed over an entire urban landscape, and hauntingly desolate lunar landscapes that could have a more earthly origin. Over those

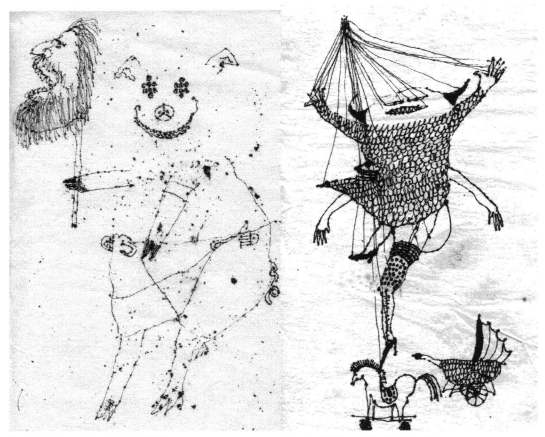

Doodle, "Guinea Pigs in Reality 101"   Doodle, "Lilith and the Priesthood"

Dying cityscape

images I superimposed incongruous, but relatable scenes that point to doom and destruction if we didn't stop destroying the environment and live peaceably with each other. One of the photographs I used in my collage was taken by U.S. astronauts in 1969 during their first lunar landing. Those black and white images focused on the barren moonscape.

My first interpretation of that desolate moonscape image shown to me by the ufolks, flip-flopped under a full moon near nightfall in April of 1986. I was driving at dusk from our new summer place toward our home in Plum Creek. The moonscape image I saw on the luminous wall of the craft may have had two distinct meanings: one, a warning of earthly destruction; the other, a precursor as to where we would be living in the years to come.

I was impressed by the ingenuity of my abductors and their ability to literally read my mind and see what I had been looking at while in the library and elsewhere. When not in my office or the classroom, I spent hundreds of hours in the university library every year. In my stays at the library it was not uncommon for me to go through eight to ten bound annual periodicals of magazines like: *Domus, Gerbrauchgraphik, Architectural Digest, Graphics, Progressive Architecture, Art News, Art in America,* etc., in an afternoon. Of course I didn't read articles; I scanned the images for the kind of content I was looking for or interested in. I could refer to these images if a project needed a full inventory of what had been done or created in the past on the topic. Most professional designers build on the shoulders of those who have gone before them.

Stylists blindly follow the dogma of a trendy "ism;" applying the same design elements to everything, be it a car or the cover of a magazine. To not know what has been done by other designers when solving two or three dimensional problems is unprofessional, irresponsible, and stupid. Now, I could only wonder if I were there at my own volition or on a reconnaissance mission that I did not understand or initiate myself. Was I nothing more than a visual vacuum cleaner, sucking up images of the best of my professional world from the past to the present?

To the educated and visually literate, art, design, and architecture are philosophy and represent a physical manifestation of a culture's highest thought processes, and ideals, that are related to current socioeconomic and political aspirations. To know that information coded in art, design, and architecture would be helpful to any visually intelligent observer of our cultural lifestyles.

By way of example, Hitler's architectural designs, associated rituals, signs, and symbols were part of a brainwashing campaign. This orchestrated campaign was designed to make the average German think they were not individuals but part of a community committed to the same socialistic ideals of Hitler's Thousand Year Reich, Aryan supremacy, and world domination. Hitler's architect, Albert Speers, translated Hitler's altered state of reality into physical form and created larger than life architecture that was consciously theatrical, didactic, and symbolic of Hitler's aspirations. All seemed to be well as long as his left brained generals kept the blitzkrieg lubricated with one conquest after another. Twenty six miles outside of Moscow, Hitler tried to become a left brained Field Marshal. Instead of taking Moscow, which he could have, sealing the fate of the Eastern front, he diverted most of his troops south to take the oil wells at Kiev. In my mind, that was his and Germany's undoing. Germany could no longer stand with Hitler's right lobe running the military show. His closest Nazi confidants were also mystical and partially under the influence of psychic, Maria Orsic, leader of the *Vril Gesellschaft* Group. The wheels just kept coming off the Nazi cart after his blunder not to take Moscow.

It seemed that with most socialistic governments, eugenics and euthanasia were implemented to clean up and streamline the culture. Then the dominant could champion over handicapped and undesirable individuals. Hitler performed eugenics on people who didn't have the "look" of the idealized Aryan German. Stalin, another great socialist, and probably a left brainer, performed eugenics on people's minds, not their bodies. Stalin allegedly was responsible for the deaths of 40 million of his own people because they "didn't think right." Hitler was reportedly responsible for 50 million deaths.

One only had to watch *Code of the Pyramids*, a 2009 TV documentary directed by Carmen Boulter, to understand why the ancient Egyptian civilization flourished as long as it did. The magnificent bas-relief stone carvings and painted murals of pharaohs and queens were instructional in nature. Pharaohs were depicted as left brained. Their symbol was the flail. They were concerned with history, linear time, science, dogma, rationality, and waking reality. Queens were depicted as right brained and were shown holding an ankh, or key to life and eternal life. Females were concerned with eternity, cycles of time, magic, altered states, art, music, and rituals.

The bas-relief of a pharaoh or queen was often shown with arms crossed over his or her chest and holding a flail in one hand and an ankh in the other. A staff cradled in between these right and left brained symbols, depicted the person as living in balance and harmony. The purpose of life was to live in true harmony through the balance of the left brain (male) and the right brain (female). Only then could true wisdom and insight be attained.

When the two qualities of the brain were out of balance, left brained societies replaced harmony with discord and destruction. The Egyptian stone bas-reliefs continually reminded the chosen to live in balance with their flail, ankh, and staff. Male and females were equals. A balanced brain insures intelligent, sensitive choices and longevity. The ultra-right brained *furer*, Hitler, had his Third Reich last only twelve years. The ancient Egyptian pharaohs' dynasties lasted three thousand years.

I thought the pharaohs would have been proud of Albert Einstein. After Einstein passed, an autopsy was performed. His brain was the subject of several neurological scientists' investigations. Supposedly, they expected to find more neurotransmitters in Einstein's brain than in the average person's, but that was not the case. Instead, they found more glial cells called astrocytes and oligodendrocytes. Theoretically, most scientists were not interested in those cells. The glial were thought to be just cells that glued the brain's more important neurons together. It was speculated at the time that the neurons did the real work associated with complex thought processes. Surprisingly, Einstein had more glial cells in the interior Parietal Lobe of his brain where imagery and complex thinking is said to take place.

I had often heard that the brain was like a muscle; if you didn't use it, it would atrophy. Einstein's imagery and math section of the Parietal Lobe of the brain would have gotten a good work out. Reviewing patents that were normally submitted in drawings, writing, and/or mathematical forms, would exercise both lobes of the brain. Perhaps years of reviewing right and left brained methods of communication fostered a tendency to think holistically and to develop original thoughts.

There were many stories about how Einstein came up with the Theory of Relativity. He said he had a dream that metaphorically pointed the way to the revelation. Some say Einstein imagined himself as a particle of light when he developed the theory. Others claim Einstein saw himself in a dream hurtling down a mountainside. He sped faster and faster until he looked to the sky and saw the stars were altered in appearance as he approached the speed of light. The Theory of Relativity, among other things, asserted that time travel was possible when energy and mass were equivalent and transmutable. Mainstream scientists said, "Hogwash," Einstein came up with the Theory of Relativity by using deductive reasoning based on the laws of physics.

It was my opinion that Albert thought as much in visual (right brained) terms as he did in mathematical (left brained) terms and eventually had a "Hemingwayesque" subliminal uprush while in a REM state of sleep. Maybe, wink wink, someone or something put a little something in Einstein's mental Rolodex one night, and after his "dream" he had an "aha" moment and out popped $E=mc^2$. I'm thinking that's what really happened.

■　■　■　■　■　■　■　■

For weeks and months after the slideshow experience, I became more convinced than ever that ufolks meant my family and me no harm. On the contrary, maybe they were actually trying to bring both lobes of our minds into balance using their incredible skills and technology to manipulate us physically and mentally into whole brain individuals.

Could it also be they were communicating their warning to as many contactees as possible? Those humans, such as a university professor, might then pass their knowledge on to many young minds. There was also the possibility that they were preparing some to survive a global apocalypse.

"Imagination is more important than knowledge.
Logic will get you from A to B.
Imagination will take you everywhere."

ALBERT EINSTEIN

4

*"The only real voyage
of discovery consists
not in seeking new
landscapes, but in
having new eyes."*

MARCEL PROUST

CHAPTER FOUR | 1983
LEO SPRINKLE | JANUARY, 1983

By the winter of 1983, I am at my wit's end, not sure if I am going crazy or are part of some kind of alien testing program. I begin to wonder what will become of me if I continue to keep my mouth shut about what seems to be happening to my family and me from primal forces and alien entities. Will I eventually go totally crazy? Am I dreaming or hallucinating? If I am right and we are being visited, are these visitors good or evil? I have to know.

I am at a friend's house and the Denver evening news comes on. The show features a vignette of a man named Leo Sprinkle who has organized the Rocky Mountain UFO Conference (RMUFOC). Leo talks to the interviewer in a friendly, matter-of-fact manner, and it turns out he counsels people who have, or think they had, a close encounter with a UFO or actual aliens. Leo is also the head of the Clinical Psychology Department at the University of Wyoming. I have never heard of Leo and his organization, but when the news program ends, I feel a sense of relief. I know I have to somehow get an appointment with him as soon as possible.

The next day I call Leo and get an appointment. I am excited, figuring he can hypnotize me and I can find out who is behind the bright lights, and identify those doing other unknown things to us in the night. I hope above all else, to get his opinion as to whether these strange events are imagined, or am I being abducted by aliens. I also desperately need to talk to someone who relates to my anxieties and will offer advice on how to keep from going insane.

Leo can see me near the end of the first week of January. The University of Wyoming is located in Laramie, a four to five hour drive from Plum Creek. I am to see Leo at nine a.m. I leave at four in the morning to compensate for potential weather changes and auto accidents.

As I drive down the driveway, a great sense of dread sweeps over me. I get the distinct feeling someone or something in the car is telling me not to go. I press on in the early morning through icy roads and blowing snow. Once in Castle Rock I turn north toward Denver. The negative feeling persists and I try to ignore it. I feel certain that something is in the car, but why does the entity not want me to see Leo Sprinkle? I can't think of any reason.

The roads are covered with patchy ice spots and are treacherous. My progress is slow. When I approach Thornton, in north Denver, the road becomes very foggy. I almost come to a crawl to avoid hitting the cars in front of me. The foreboding feeling and inclement weather seem to be teaming up against my wish to meet Leo. The fog finally lifts and I resume my northward journey to Cheyenne and I-80. I turn my car into the western winds and the clouds part. I am now speeding west on I-80 to Laramie.

The sun comes out and my pace accelerates. The sense of dread has lifted. Whatever was riding with me is no more. I speed west with great enthusiasm, bathed in sunshine. I look forward to getting some relief and understanding as to what has been happening to me.

As I careen down the hill overlooking the Laramie valley and the university, I get a bird's eye view of the campus. In the middle of the clutter of university buildings I see a huge, smooth-skinned hemisphere. Is it a modern Stupa? My enthusiasm soars. Perhaps this university is inhabited by forward-thinking professors who openly acknowledge the possible existence of other biological entities. Maybe they are showing their open mindedness with a space-aged UFO looking structure. Finding Leo among the monotonous, brick buildings smothered in gigantic overgrown spruce and fir trees is a daunting task, but at length I find his building.

Entering the foyer of his office is shocking at first, but soon I am amused. I have never seen so much controlled mayhem in my life. First semester will come to an end soon and the room is filled with frantic students clinging to the hope that Leo and his staff of counselors can absolve them for all their slacker activities resulting in failing grades.

The large room is like a MASH unit for desperate and psychotic students. Panic like I have never seen in my academic life is going on all around me. It is almost final week for the students and all the slackers are running for psychiatric cover and academic forgiveness. They are hoping for a reprieve to avoid their parents' wrath and being shipped back to the ranch.

The secretary is visibly frazzled, but manages to set me down in an oak chair by Leo's office door. Soon, Leo's door opens, he leans out and with a big smile says, "Hi, Sean."

Leo Sprinkle

The moment I see Leo, I feel a rush of hope, almost love, come over me.

I immediately know Leo can help me and will understand my plight. I am no different than the frantic students seeking help from him and his staff. I feel at home with this obviously brilliant, gutsy man. I closely follow Leo into his office. I am immediately taken back by a three and a half foot high, three dimensional interpretation of a reptilian-type alien he has standing by his office door. The realistic replica is scary and seems to come alive the longer I look at it.

Leo turns and we face each other. He is very tall, thin, and has a large head supporting a huge friendly smile. He looks really intelligent, dressed in a gray corduroy suit and vest with a brown tie. He wears a pair of silver rimmed glasses. As I study Leo, the thought crosses my mind, *Maybe he is an alien appointed to deal with mixed up earthlings like myself.*

Like old professor friends, we immediately begin talking shop. Then I start telling him of my experiences of strange dreams, lights around the house, bursts of light in my face, the vision of gnomes, the blast off, and the neighbor's experience of lost time and seeing lights around their home also.

Leo concludes, that indeed, I have been abducted by aliens. He then asks if I can think of anything in my past that had been perplexing, or seemed to be unsettling or out of place to me.

I can't believe it. I immediately recall events in my life that have always haunted me; ones that I have never talked about with anyone, nor thought about in depth. The memories are just there laying around near the surface of my mind. They immediately emerge when Leo asks his simple question. He evidently has the magic that releases memories I have kept bound up for so many years. Leo leans back in his chair and I begin reliving the strange accounts from my past.

TOE HOLD | SUMMER, 1949

When I am nine years old, I live with my family in a large subdivision in Kansas City, Kansas, called Quindero Homes. The subdivision is composed of large, single and two story wooden structures broken up into single, double, and triple bedroom apartments. The Homes, as they are called, were created to house workers who built B-17 or B-24 bombers and related aircraft and military hardware during the Second World War. The Homes sets between Tenth Street and Seventh Street in the north part of the city near the Fairfax Industrial District that stretched from the boundary of The Homes to the Missouri River. We have lived in The Homes since 1942. My father is a supervisor in the construction of B-17 bombers.

Over the years, Dad received seven pardons by President Roosevelt during World War II. His abilities were critical in producing the bombers for the war effort. We were very thankful he did not have to go to war.

After the war, The Homes becomes a baby factory. The tenants are in their twenties, home from the war, and the economy booms. The oppressive economic effects of the war give way to wonderful optimistic times. Everyone is busy making babies. There are two to three children in each apartment, and the streets are filled with kids riding their bicycles, tricycles, playing cowboys and Indians, jump rope, hopscotch, jacks, baseball, and a myriad of other pre-TV games. In the evenings, the children's laughter, screen doors slamming, mothers calling their children for dinner, dogs barking, and the sound of kids playing, linger until nine o'clock on spring and summer nights. Now these sounds have been replaced by the constant hum of window air conditioners.

We live at 1047 Manor Crest, a duplex near Tenth Street, and the most extreme northwest part of this sprawling, lower middle class subdivision. To the north of The Homes in this part of the subdivision, is a dense wooded area. It is composed of deciduous trees that resemble a tropical jungle, replete with massive wild grape vines and other dangling vegetative things. To me, the area is a vast, foreboding, mysterious, dangerous, and intriguing place. There are timber rattlers and copperheads waiting to bite the careless explorer.

By day, I live in the woods, hunting anything that moves with my trusty Red Ryder BB gun. I don't, however, penetrate the woods for more than half a mile. We are warned of homeless people living in the depths of the woods and that they did horrible things to children. At night, the woods resemble a black wall of tangled, oozing vegetation with strange bird and animal sounds coming from it.

There are hushed reports of peeping-Toms looking in the windows of apartments at night. Many men, including my father, work the night shift in the factories converted from building military products to cars and domestic wares. Mother is particularly concerned; the peeping-Toms are more likely to peep into homes where pretty women live. My mother and 13 year old sister fit that description.

Our windows have screens that are hinged at the top and latched with an inside hook at the bottom. Mother checks the screens each night to make sure they are locked down tight. This summer is hotter than usual, and only a few families have window air conditioners. Our family is not one of them. Sleeping with the windows closed at night is very uncomfortable and stifling in hot and humid Kansas City, Kansas.

On this night, my sister is away at a slumber party, and I am sleeping by myself in the bedroom we share. I have no idea how late it is, but I wake to the sound of the latch to the window screen moving, and then the unmistakable squeak of it being lifted up and opened. I freak out and pull the covers over my head. Soon, I hear something moving around the room and coming toward my bed. I try to scream for my parents, but I am frozen with fear. I expect to be stabbed to death at any moment, but as I lie under the hot covers with my eyes closed, I detect nothing.

All is quiet, and after what seems like hours, I feel a sharp, pinprick on my left foot's big toe! After that, I must have fainted, and I wake in my bed the next morning.

I check the window screen latch; it is locked. I am puzzled but relieved.

■ ■ ■ ■ ■ ■ ■ ■

The prowler didn't stab me to death as I feared. Nothing was stolen from our room. I didn't recall my parents mentioning anything missing from the house.

At nine years old I was embarrassed to tell my parents of my frightening experience. My father would have made fun of me for being a sacredly cat. I went on my merry way and never told my parents about that night. I knew that I had not imagined the noises I heard, but after all, the latch was locked, wasn't it? For some reason I did not look at my foot or big toe.

MATINEE MADNESS | SUMMER, 1951

One of the highlights of my young life is going to the movies. While TV is a reality by the time I am 11, the quality of productions is so poor, in my mind, that only the brain dead bothers to watch what is being served up each night. I prefer to read hunting and fishing magazines like *Field and Stream,* and *Outdoor Life,* or listen to mystery radio programs like *The Green Hornet, The Shadow*, and *Mark Trail.*

I am, however, an enthusiastic moviegoer and can hardly wait until Saturday afternoons when my neighborhood buddies and I go to the Gauntier Theater at Thirteenth Street and Quindero Boulevard. The Gauntier is over a mile and a half walk from The Homes, and the trek there with five to ten hyperactive friends is always a memorable event in itself.

Once at the theater, you either take your chances sitting in the middle rows of seats, or in the seating sections flanking the center rows of seats. The side rows were the realm of the horny teens, who with their errant mates, seldom come up for air to see what is happening on the silver screen. This hot house of horny teenagers is the backdrop to a much more insane group that sits in the center section of the theater. This section of the theater is for the teenagers who haven't received the "call of the wild" yet, don't have a girlfriend to neck with, and all other boys from twelve on down to seven year olds.

This pre-testosterone alley section of the theater is a seething mass of screaming, gum wrapper and water bomb-throwing, pre-teen and teenaged boys who do every antisocial thing our uptight fifties culture doesn't allow in public. In the darkness of the theater, things get exponentially worse. Every red-blooded young male attending the Saturday matinee is armed with something special to throw at the silver screen or into the *mêlée*, creating as much havoc as possible.

I am personally armed with seedless dry prunes, which I put in my mouth, allowing the saliva to breakdown the organic pulp and transform this diuretic wonder into a slimy, black, oozing luggie. A missile of this yuckiness is used sparingly. I prefer to launch it right after everyone settles down to watch the Looney Toons cartoon. Things get quiet. Then I can hear a scream after the gooey prune luggie is lobbed and plows into the back of an unsuspecting moviegoer's neck or head.

The movie we are about to watch is *The Thing*, directed by Christian Nyby, and starring Kenneth Tobey, Margaret Sheridan, and James Arness, who played "The Thing." A lot of us in the theater have seen every two-bit B horror movie ever produced to this date. We saw movies such as*: Giant Mutant Spider, Bride of Godzilla, Cat People, I Walked with a Zombie, The Devil Bat, The Mummy's Hand, Voodoo Man, The Creeper, The Curse of the Cat People, Bride of The Gorilla, Body Snatchers,* and on and on.

We are unshakeable, and quick to see through the amateurish attempts by producers to create viable monsters. Some monsters are close-ups of lizards we are supposed to think are horrible dragons, or dinosaurs. Other productions use *Plasticine* clay sculptures of monsters and animate them with jerky, awkward movements that reveal their cheap productions. Perhaps the worst animated monster is in the movie, *The Tarantula That Attacked Dallas.*

Today's monster will be different. The movie is about a flying saucer that crashes near the Arctic Circle. We have only vaguely heard of flying saucers, but we know of their existence due to movies like: *It Came from Outer Space, The Flying Saucer, The Thing from Another World, Invaders from Mars,* and *When Worlds Collide*. But these movies are so poorly produced that we cast them off like most of the other science fiction crap we endure.

One of the boys I hang out with has an uncle who works for Boeing Aircraft in Wichita. He says his uncle believes that flying saucers exist and that he saw a foo fighter during a bombing mission over Germany in 1945. He also says a flying saucer crashed near Roswell, New Mexico. His uncle's word is golden to me and my friends. We are believers, but our understanding of who flies the craft is sketchy. We think they are harmless little green men from Mars.

In the movie, a crippled UFO crashes on the Arctic ice shield and melts its way down into the clear ice. The craft is frozen there many feet below the surface. The UFO is found by a small number of scientists and American Air Force officials stationed nearby. They drill down through the ice to the craft and somehow retrieve the frozen pilot. They move the seven-foot alien encased in a block of ice back to one of their unheated Quonset huts. The creature is so ghastly looking that one scientist gets frightened and covers the block of ice with a blanket. Predictably, it is an electric blanket. Later, some nincompoop inadvertently turns on the power source to the electric blanket before going to bed.

During the night, the block of ice melts and out steps the seven-foot alien pilot. This ghastly, giant, vegetable alien is totally pissed and needs blood to survive. The alien also begins cloning himself and grows more vegetable aliens in the outpost's green house.

All the while, the outpost is under blizzard conditions. Snow and debris fly all over the place and stuff is flapping in the breeze; visibility is down to five feet. Huskies are mournfully howling, whimpering and being ripped apart and drained of their blood by The Thing. When there are no more huskies to kill and feed to the young, sprouting aliens in the green house flat beds, the alien begins feeding the sproutlings human blood for sustenance. All of this violence and tension is filmed in low light, blizzard conditions so it is impossible to see low budget *faux pas*. Jesus! What frightening, realistic, nightmarish mayhem!

At the height of all this chaos, the main generator is sabotaged by the alien; darkness ensues. The outpost's radio is no more. There are blood and guts, howling wind, dogs and shit flying around everywhere. Then the lights go out! Holy shit! My knuckles are white from gripping the seat's arm rest. After many scary moments, the last of the scientists and his predictably beautiful assistant, fend off this super tall, blood-thirsty alien organism at the last second before being murdered. They electrify The Thing with the finicky backup generator just as it closes in to kill the last of the surviving scientists and the beautiful girl. Whew! Shit!

My friends and I were breathless, riveted to our seats, and totally terrorized by the simple, low-budget movie that unfolded before us. Each scene generated tension and planted horrific thoughts in my mind by innuendo, rather than by direct example. I became one with the movie. I was emotionally swept along a river of terror and impending doom at a level I had never experienced before. The tall alien was never really seen up close and personal. His growling, frenetic, violent movements, blood splattered walls, dead dogs, twitching severed limbs, and a veiled sinister agenda planted scary seeds into my fertile, young mind. I was haunted for years by the simple plot and impressionistic scenes. To me, the movie was real, and I was frightened by what I saw.

I knew we all thought about the giant diabolical alien as we made our way back to The Homes that afternoon. We said very little. This was the first time we had been scared by what we saw and experienced. I now wonder how many other "home boys" experienced something coming through their window screen one summer night in 1949.

■　■　■　■　■　■　■　■

I didn't make any conscious linkage to a forgotten experience back when I was nine. So I didn't reference my brief experience of getting my toe pricked to my buddies. Had I talked about my experience, I would have been called a chicken. But now in Leo's office, I realized the movie may have struck a forgotten terrorized nerve that led directly to a sleeping subconscious memory.

That night, after seeing the movie, I became more and more anxious about going to sleep alone in my bedroom. My sister was again at a slumber party and not at home to protect me. I moved all my bedding under my parents' bed, and when night came I retired to my new abode. Even under their bed I was anxious. Today, psychiatrists would claim that I had been traumatized by the movie. My stay under their bed lasted one night and then I was ousted from my sanctuary.

For months, I was afraid at night as I had never been before. Why I was frightened by the movie, I will never know for sure, but I think the night my big toe was pricked, I might have been abducted and in the company of very tall aliens, like in the movie.

Me at 18 and a freshman in college

I'm 18 and a freshman at the University of Kansas studying graphic design. I don't want to be here, and I don't have any business studying art or design. I have a scholarship, but after taking the required Minnesota Multiple Personality Test, my aptitude favors research, not art.

Art is seventeenth on my list of unknown aptitudes, but my fate has been decided by my ophthalmologist and my parents. Since my accident and subsequent loss of most of the vision in my left eye by a misguided BB, my parents have been repeatedly told if I have a career it should be in a field that does not require much reading. Their reasoning is simple; excessive reading will put my good eye at risk and I might go completely blind sooner than later.

The doctors suggest a career in art or design because everyone knows artists just intuitively pull their work out of their asses, and that there is no reading involved in their training. My parents buy into this naive left brained idea, and from that point on, if I don't want to go to my high school classes, I just stay home, no questions asked. I have a golden excuse from home that trumps all the principal's rules and regulations. I don't take advantage of the situation because I like seeing my friends, and besides, home is boring.

■ ■ ■ ■ ■ ■ ■ ■

When I was ten, mother enrolled my sister, who was very artistic, and me in a summer Art and Art Appreciation course at the Nelson Atkins Gallery of Art in Kansas City, Missouri. That summer class was the closest thing I took, prior to college, to a legitimate art course. There were few art instruction courses to be taken in those days for middle class kids, so my early exposure was limited to what could be had in the public schools I attended.

My high school had one art course. I took it twice, but learned nothing as the teacher was talented but overwhelmed, absent-minded, and didn't have a curriculum plan. I was allowed to do whatever I wanted. I was very productive, but my work only reinforced bad technical habits that would be hard to break later at KU.

All the artwork I did was based on my real life experiences or what I had witnessed. The idea of creating artwork that came from my imagination never occurred to me. I was into realism, as I knew it to be and focused on developing various rendering techniques. For me, at this age, art was realism, technique, and a little content. Somehow I won a Gold Key award for my artwork in the Kansas City Scholastic Art Awards competition. The Art Institute of Kansas City then offered me a partial scholarship to attend their school. My parents said, "Nothing but queers, perverts, and freaks go to that school, and you're not going there."

My parents knew many people who had graduated from the University of Kansas and all were very successful in their fields. So off to KU I went after graduating from high school. Little did my parents or I know that the Design Department at KU was ranked second in the county for on-campus art schools by the National Association of Art Schools. And there were just as many queers, perverts, and freaks as at any art institute. I was way in over my head. Most of my university classmates had already taken a lot of quality art courses in and out of the United States.

■   ■   ■   ■   ■   ■   ■   ■

During my freshman year at KU I am lonely, depressed, and embarrassed at the quality of my art and design work in comparison to my classmates'. To even remain respectable, I have to redo each project at least three times before the work is good enough to submit to my professors. A professor threw one of my three dimensional designs in the waste basket during a class critique. How humiliating. Every night I work on my projects until midnight and beyond.

I am at best a C student in my six studio classes. To get a whiff of a decent job in the art world after graduation, you have to be in the top one percent of your class, or really good looking with big boobs. I don't have big boobs so…The thing I want most is a job so I can someday support my high school sweetheart and my hoped-for family. I know I'm wasting my time as a design major. My three academic classes are equally difficult for me. When I come home for Christmas vacation my freshman year, I am flunking two of the three Liberal Arts and Science classes.

I have been introduced to the reality of double and triple F grades on my written papers in English 101. One misspelled word in a 500-word in-class essay gets you an automatic D. A sentence fragment is an automatic F. I almost set a school record for the number of times I flunk English 101. I become so self-conscious of my poor writing skills that I am afraid to write home to my girlfriend for fear she will see what a dunce I am. I quit talking for fear of what kind of nonsensical dribble will roll off my tongue. My life is so stressful that I lose 15 pounds by Christmas break. My favorite song at this moment is the Kingston Trio's ballad, "Hang down Your Head Tom Dooley."

To my dismay, the Arts and Sciences College I am in, is rated tenth in the nation behind Stanford and the Ivy League schools. The fraternity I pledged to is the top academic chapter in the Social Fraternity system in the nation. Eighty actives have a combined B+ average. My Cs, Fs, and double and triple Fs are not appreciated. I am not a good pledge and habitually cannot measure up to the expectations of the actives. I always end up doing extra work on Friday nights and most weekends which keep me in Lawrence every weekend. I seldom get home to see my high school sweetheart whom I am deeply in love with.

In between graduating high school and attending KU as a freshman, I endure another botched eye operation and I look like shit. I am constantly reminded of my freaky looks by insensitive assholes. I think my first love, who is very beautiful, is having doubts about whether I will ever look good to her again. A person's looks is more than very important to her. She seldom writes me and I am deeply worried that I am losing her. I'm ashamed to write her, besides I don't have anything good to write about unless I describe the world of shit I'm living in. If my art professors aren't beating up on me, my academic professors are, and if they aren't, my classmates are during class critiques. When I get back from classes the fraternity actives give me hell and if they aren't, I'm beating up on myself for being so inept. I am in a world of hurt. But that was last year and things are worse now.

I am 19 and a sophomore. It has been a month since the college roommate of my first love writes and lets me know that my love is going out on me every night. I am not totally taken by surprise, but I am still heartbroken. I am to see her this weekend at home. I don't know how she can be so cruel to me. She is all I know and is the center of my very existence. Before her, I lived in a cold winter Brueghel snow scene. She has given meaning to my life and a reason to live. The thought of not having her for a wife has never crossed my mind. I just assume we will marry one day. But now all is over in a four line note from her freshman college roommate.

I do not go home to meet her for our weekend date, I am too heartsick. I don't know what to do or say. How will I deal with the problem of her cheating on me every night? The next Monday after that weekend I get a curt "goodbye" letter and my fraternity lovelier back, a token of my affection and commitment to her.

My emotions and I think our feelings are far more serious than a going steady necklace. I do not call or write her, after all, she has breached our trust, and I am the victim. The thought occurs to me that maybe I don't deserve her love. I get more depressed and do the unthinkable; I start writing poetry. One poem I write is particularly poignant for me at the moment:

Unicellular fantasies
Shrouded in text
Etched on my orbs
Like epitaphs
Ossification
Embryonic care
Decomposition
Who cares?

As the weeks wear on, I begin to reflect on our relationship. It becomes apparent she had been cheating on me during her senior year in high school while I was a freshman at KU. My sorrow is now tinged with embarrassment, regret, and anger. How could I have been so stupid and blind to what was happening to our relationship and our love? I keep hearing in my head the axiom, *If they cheat on you once they will do it again*. When her roommate first writes me, my love was cheating on me for a second year, not a second time. How incredulous, when she would go out with me, she was probably cheating on someone else who thought they were going steady. I mentally draw a line in the sand that my heart is not going to cross no matter how much it wants to.

My emotional self has ruled my life up to this point, and now my mind intervenes. Where my mind gets this crazy idea that cheating is immoral I don't know. But the idea is very strong and I act on it. Cheat on me and all trust is gone, and so am I. My heart is in agony, but my mind holds firm and controls my uncontrollable desire for her and a reunion. During that first week without her, I go out with a really nice girl. After three dates I know I can never replace my first love so easily. I drift back to my old self. I am no longer selfless, just still in love, and in great emotional agony. I double my work product to lessen my great sorrow and hang out with my fraternity brothers and drink heavily on the weekends.

Now, for some inexplicit reason I find myself speeding southeast toward Paola, Kansas late one Friday afternoon instead of drinking beer at the Wagon Wheel Bar with some of my fraternity brothers. I am acting on this irrational, sudden urge to go fishing at what could be called my "happy place." My happy place is a small farm pond on my grandpa and grandma's property near Paola.

I grew up there fishing and studying the habits of largemouth bass at this pond. I've had more happy times there than any place on earth. I am heading home for a reprieve from the sorrow that plagues me night and day. I haven't seen her for more than a month and all hopes of reconciliation seem to be over. I will not budge unless she calls or writes and says she is sorry for cheating on me. My mind keeps my heart locked up tight, but the tears that have filled my heart start overflowing and I begin to cry as I drive toward Paola.

I have not cried since I can remember: before breaking my arm, before dislocating my shoulder, before being shot in the eye, before having five operations, before being harangued by mean-spirited boys making fun of my handicap, and before my mind's decision to never see her again, no matter what. I am mourning the death of the most important relationship of my young life.

I am committing emotional suicide on my way down and am planning physical suicide at the pond. I want to die someplace I love. I am so distraught I have to stop the car twice to let the tears clear so I can see to find my way.

When I get to Grandma and Grandpa's it is very late in the afternoon and I am in a hurry to get to the pond to escape. I talk briefly to both of them and they can tell I am anxious to go fishing. I have not fished the old pond for several years, not since I had fallen in love, so my trek down to the pond in the valley below is a real sentimental journey.

I leave the house and walk the two-track road east toward the pond with my fishing pole and small tackle box. Inside I have my long, sharp, thin fillet knife. I know I can put my hands in the pond's cold November water, slash my wrists and end my sorrow; it will be easy and painless. That is my plan.

Walking past the big sycamore tree where Grandpa stored his truck and implements, I remember the comforting vision of him in years past. I was playing with my toy trucks and he was sharpening tools and working on his John Deere tractor.

The evening shadows are getting long now, the air is clear and the barn swallows are catching some of fall's last insect hatch. The sun's last rays of light make beautiful patterns of brightness through the ash trees' barren limbs; a calm serene evening.

I walk by the barn my sister and I played in and around for so many years. The smell of hay, old manure, and the sight of chickens scurrying away, brings back many more memories of happier times in my life. I can't help but to begin crying again.

Walking down the path by the cap rock, I recall the joy of finding my first fossil in an exposed shelf of limestone. It was a seashell from an ancient seafloor when Kansas and the Midwest was a gigantic inland sea. Grandma and Grandpa's house and barn are built on this old sea bed of limestone that is now a plateau that time and nature created. On either side of the plateau is a gentle basin made of rich earth. Grandpa farms this basin, raising corn, milo, wheat, and other crops to feed his livestock or to take to market.

Every sight, smell, and sound I experience is amplified in my heart as I walk down the two-track road to the pond. This walk is a sheer delight. I make my way down the gentle grade to the bottom of this shallow valley near the stream Grandpa had dammed up to make the pond. The dirt track that takes me to the pond is bound by a fenced-in, dense deciduous woods on the north and an open alfalfa field on the south.

How time has gotten away I don't know, but as I duck in between two strands of the barbed wire fence and enter into the woods, I realize how dark it is becoming. I hurry my pace through a patch of pawpaw trees and the sweet smell of fallen decaying pawpaw fruit. I go into a forest of eight to ten foot high horseweeds that are thick as hairs on a dog's back. I had never seen these dense stands of horseweed before, and realize the pond has been more or less abandoned. No cows graze its banks now. The pond's edges are overgrown, even the freeboard where I used to sit for hours watching large bass defend their spawning beds in the spring. I carefully make my way through the horseweeds and their abrasive hairy branches and stems. I think all copperheads and rattlesnakes would have hibernated by now but I pick my path carefully. I am afraid one might be out hunting a mouse, frog, or other last morsel before hibernating. I slowly work my way through the field of abrasive weeds to the edge of the pond.

Now it is almost dark. I quietly and carefully mash out with my feet a flat platform of ground free of horseweeds near the pond's edge. Adult bass can pick up sounds 100 feet away with their large, wide, black band that runs down the center of their sides. The larger the bass, the larger the stripe, the better the bass can detect and evade a predator. The freeboard of the pond and the deeper water is to the east of me. I can cast my lures toward the places along the freeboard where I think the largest fish will be found. I want to catch one last large bass in my life.

I quickly look in my tackle box and find a large top water lure called a jitterbug. This oval lure measures two inches long and at each end of the oval, dangle two sets of galvanized treble hooks. The oval shape is dark colored with yellow tiger stripes and a set of large eyes with black pupils. The lure replicates a frog, a mouse, a small bird, or anything that can get a bass's attention. The front of the lure has a concave oval, galvanized piece of metal that looks like the front of a bulldozer. This bulldozer form makes a great deal of noise and waves as it is jerked or pulled through the water. The sound often attracts large aggressive bass.

It is dark by the time I finish tying the lure on my eight-pound test line. I am without a flash light in my tackle box, so I use safety matches to see by. I wait for another ten minutes before I throw my first cast with the jitterbug lure. I want to make sure that if I have been detected by a big bass, it will drop its guard when its sonar does not pick up any more unusual vibrations coming through the water.

In ten minutes, the aura of the sun is gone and it is completely black; there is no moon. I wait until the stars begin to illuminate the dark night. It is 1959, I am in the country, and there are no city lights to mute the stars' luminosity. I can barely see the freeboard but it is there in front of me, 65 feet away. The night is without a breeze, the water is now a mirror reflecting each star in the Milky Way and beyond. Looking down at the inky black water is like looking up at the cosmos above, an incredible and surreal visual experience.

I study the water and do not see any tremors or "nervous water" that would belie the movements of a large hunting bass. As I look down at the water, I am surprised to see Sputnik silently making its way across the mirror like surface of the pond. I look up and there it is above me as well! To see Sputnik plowing across the heavens is one thing, to see it reflected in this Kansas pond is mind boggling. I am enthralled by what I am seeing and experiencing.

What a sight! Then the sorrow creeps back into my heart; I wish I were not here alone. I make my first cast toward the freeboard and an area that I think may hold a big fish. It is a funny right brained thing, but if you look at the target you want to hit and do not think about it and then cast, your mind-body relationship seems to connect with a perfect cast. The lure in this case hits so close to the bank of the freeboard that at first I think my jitterbug is beached, but it was within inches of the bank, perfect. If there is a large bass in the area it has heard the crash of the lure as it hits the water. This bass should be waiting for more information to tell it where the target is, and what it is.

Many terrestrials don't move right after they fall or inadvertently find themselves in the water-a very strange environment for them. They often freeze. Perhaps they are stunned or are trying to figure out what to do to negotiate this new stuff they are suspended in. I wait until I think all ripples from the lure have dissipated, and then I twitch the lure as though it is a living thing testing out the new environment it is mired in. I let the lure set and then give it three quick jerks. The jitterbug rushes toward me and makes waves, bubbles, gurgles, and a lot of noise as I make the lure seem to panic. I stop after three jerks. I should now have my quarry in an attack mode and lying under the lure at a 45 degree angle, waiting for the insect, frog, or whatever to move again. All predators are drawn to a fleeing prey; my big bass is the tiger of this freshwater world. I wait and tighten my line. Just as the ripples of my last move subside and the reflected cosmos in the pond stabilizes, I gently nudge the lure and make it bobble. Crap! Nothing. I feel nothing: no big strike, no great battle, no arcing rod and singing line, no magnificent leap with gills flaring, no water flying, no huge splash or the deep run of a heavy fish heading to safety. NOTHING!

That last simple movement should have provoked my big aggressive bass to strike. That last nudge was the tripwire to the strike, and I got nothing! I have played this patient game out a thousand times and I have always gotten a high percentage of strikes from aggressive, territorial bass. I'm puzzled, but maybe I have a large bass that is a little sluggish and needs to be taunted a little more. I wait and begin the process again.

I am now aware of and enthralled by the fact that my big ass jitterbug is metaphorically moving through the cosmos. The stars by this time of night are so bright that my lure is its own Sputnik. It is making its way across the inky watery pond's surface in an imaginary space among the beauty of the Milky Way that lies above. Suddenly, the Milky Way and the Cosmos disappear, and my lure is not visible. Without hesitation I look up and see with amazement a black void directly above me.

I am standing in the overgrown two-track road looking up toward the barn and house. It is broad daylight, about mid-morning. I am somewhat confused and swaying around. I don't know if I'm coming down from the house to go fishing or if I am going back to the house after fishing all night. I feel and see the sun is in the east, so it must be morning. I look around and notice there are pawpaw tree leaves that have blown over from the forest and are lying in random order on the path. The leaves have sparkling frost on their undersides and the tops of the grasses are moist from the nighttime frost melting. The earth smells rich and moist.

I notice I am holding my rod in my left hand and my small tackle box in my right. That is odd, so I reverse their order back to how I normally hold them and start up the gentle hill to the barn. My rod's fishing line still has the jitterbug lure on, cranked up to the tip of the rod. I am not thinking of anything.

I finally conclude that it is Saturday and I must have fished all night. I am very anxious, maybe to get back to school? I quickly walk up the two-track road to the house. I wonder why I am not wet and cold. I only have a light cotton shirt and shorts on, but I'm not concerned. I stop walking and smell my hands for the pungent scent of a large mouth bass. I smell nothing. I don't remember catching a fish, and if I had, the scent of it would be on my hands. I realize I did not catch a fish. I continue walking, and my thoughts are of getting back to school and going to the football game that starts at one o'clock. Last year, I only got to go to one game, and that was during Parents' Day when I did not have to do the extra work I normally would because of my poor performance in the fraternity pledge training program. The rest of the season I was doing extra work instead of attending games or going home to see my sweetheart.

My pace quickens and I am soon at the barn and then the house. Grandma and Grandpa greet me with cheery enthusiasm; they do not ask me why I didn't come up to sleep. They know what a fanatic I can be about fishing and I guess they, too, assume I have fished all night. I don't know if I did or not.

Grandma has a bed made for me and some leftovers from dinner. They ask if I caught anything and I say, "No." I can tell they are perplexed, I always catch fish. I don't go fishing, I go catching. I used to take a five gallon bucket with me and always brought large fish back to the house for them to see before I took the fish back to the pond and released them. Grandma makes me breakfast and we talk a while and then I leave.

As I drive away they are waving to me. The soft, fuzzy, yellowing image of them in my mind's eye, standing together on the back porch of the house waving goodbye to me in slow motion, will always be transfixed in my mind.

▣   ▣   ▣   ▣   ▣   ▣   ▣   ▣

My world would never be the same again. Within weeks, my beloved grandpa and mentor would die after having a massive heart attack while walking in the woods to the south of the house.

The farm was almost immediately sold to the neighbor across the road, and Grandma would be living in a small apartment in town. I never visited the farm or pond again. In two months' time, I lost almost all of the things that I loved and held so dear. Seven years later I found out I was not the only one who looked up above them to see a mysterious sight, and that my grandma was harboring an incredible secret.

▣   ▣   ▣   ▣   ▣   ▣   ▣   ▣

After leaving Grandpa and Grandma's farm, I drive home, not to Mom and Dad's, but to Lawrence. I am not filled with the same kind or depth of sorrow I had on the way down. For some reason, I'm beginning to think I dodged a big bullet. Marrying my sweetheart and then having her cheat on me, I probably would have killed her and her lover and ended up in jail for life. I have fallen off of one of Fragonard's most romantic swings and find myself in a Bosch-like world.

Paradoxically, I have this pleasant but persistent feeling that someone has told me an incredible secret that I am not to repeat. I am also fighting the feeling of being very special to someone. I'm dying to tell the secret but I don't know what it is! The unknown secret is a great one, and makes the core of my soul happy in an all-knowing way. I never remember what it is, but the feeling stays with me and ushers me through the difficult years ahead. The secret gives me hope, inner strength, and restless grit to succeed. I now feel driven and mentally prepared to make whatever sacrifices necessary to excel at whatever I choose to do. The incredible secret I harbor makes me feel special, but not arrogant, just extremely confident and needed.

I seldom think of my first love, remembering her is so painful that my mind does not let my heart go to that memory without making it pay an incredible emotional price. She so deceived me, and now I no longer trust myself to look for another love. I do not want to be hurt again. I transfer my libido's energy to working on my art and design studies. By my junior year, I am on the Dean's list every semester until graduation. My life resumes and I morph into a visual arts geek.

DESTINY? | 1963 TO 1966

Me at 25 and a graduate student

I am 25 and an Assistant Instructor in the Design Department at KU while working my way through school and getting my master's degree. I am beginning to feel good about myself, and I date occasionally, but I don't let anyone get too close to me. I love teaching and my students are doing excellent work. I discover that helping others is the best way to help myself heal.

I have this one student, however, who is habitually 15 minutes late to class. When in class, she often works on homework from her academic courses and then leaves early. I am not offended by her apparent disrespect; if she wants to flunk that's her business. I sometimes stand in the door smiling and keep her from leaving early. She does not appreciate my hints to stay in class. By the end of the semester we have a real game going, and I give her more attention in class than I should, but she has piqued my interest.

Turns out she doesn't want to be at KU, but her mother registered her with the university when she was five. She would rather be riding her horses, living at home, working in her father's grocery store, and dating one of the clerks. To appease her, her parents let her bring two horses to school along with her new sports car. She worked at her father's store and paid for her horses and car herself.

A year or so later in 1965, she appears again in my Saturday fall semester course titled, "Nature and Museum Drawing." The course is about learning how to do pen and ink wash drawings of natural elements that often inspire the creation of revolutionary man-made designs and architecture.

By way of example, the delicate lace-like wing structure of a dragonfly and Pierre Lugi Nervi's Ferro Cementos thin membrane vaulting roof structures have much in common. Louis Sullivan, the father of modern skyscraper design, is said to have based his work on the modular and radial growth of a pine cone. The study of nature as a potential genesis of advanced design concepts is very important to serious young designers who want to develop lateral thinking skills and practice the art of applied creativity.

I remember her and wonder if she will be any better in this class than the last, in which she got a C. To my surprise, she is very talented and works with proficiency, diligence, and great skill. She is as different this semester as she was the last. Now she only wears blue sweat shirts, turned inside out, Levi jeans with the cuffs rolled up, semi-dirty, white artsy fartsy tennis shoes, her hair pulled back in a ponytail, and no makeup. She is as pretty as anyone but stands out from the rest of the women who are always dressed to the teeth.

The class is small since no one likes Saturday classes. I get to know most of the 20 or so students in the class. It turns out she has her horses stabled out at Blue Mound, a prominent hill in an otherwise flatland southeast of Lawrence. Blue Mound is so steep and has a vertical rise high and long enough that it becomes the site of the first and last commercial ski run in Kansas. As soon as the class is over she goes there to ride her horses with her boyfriend and her best friend, Stephanie. She is very interesting to talk to, not vain or pretentious and has a wonderful sense of humor. She has a "hippie" philosophy that is refreshing to a serious, uptight, tight-assed, career-oriented graduate student.

After several Saturdays, she asks if I would like to go riding with her after class. I can tell she has no ulterior motives. She does not give a hoot about grades or me, and I'm sure she just thought I might like to experience riding a horse.

Experience is not the word for my first ride on her horse, Rebel. I ride bareback and follow her on her Arabian mount, Rogue. We gallop at a breakneck speed through the woods around Blue Mound. My only safety net while aboard her thoroughbred-cross, Rebel, is to grab a hunk of his thick mane, clamp my thighs tight behind his withers, hang on, and pray.

Then she takes me at a gallop cross country to a trail that goes up the north face of Blue Mound. As we get near the top, the grade is almost straight up. Rebel begins to lunge faster and faster until my frantic mind envisions him digging a trench in the soft, moist soil near the top of the mound. The grade is so steep that if he stops his forward momentum I think he will fall over backward. I am frightened. If I fall off Rebel's back and am drug under his thrashing iron shod hooves, I will be ground up in his frantic attempt to be first to the top.

I really don't fall off, but more like slide sideways off of his back and land on the ground just inches from his lunging hooves. As I flounder around beside him, I finally have the presence of mind to grab his reins. Now, in fear of being trampled, I scramble on all fours ahead of him, beating him by a nose, to the top. Wow! What a close call, I could have been ground into hamburger had I fallen under his powerful legs and sharp edges of the iron shoes.

We no sooner catch our breath once on top and away we go plunging down the gentler south face of Blue Mound. The grade down is not as steep, but now my butt begins sliding forward and down Rebel's svelte body and onto his bony withers, a very worrisome position to be in.

Hanging onto his mane does no good as it did when racing up the steeper north slope of the mound. I fear I am going to slide over Rebel's head and, once again, get trampled from head to toe by his hooves. Just as I think about reaching back and grabbing the base of his tail to keep on board we reach the bottom.

I frantically recoup my death grip with my thigh muscles behind his withers, grab a new handful of mane, and we speed off through the woods across a pasture and toward a large, deep pond. Sarah and Rogue, plunge head long into the pond and Rogue begins swimming toward the other shore. My "not to be outdone" herd-bound horse, Rebel, follows and also plunges into the deep water with great competitive zeal. I am in disbelief. He begins to swim, and as the water becomes deeper, Rebel's body disappears beneath me. I can only hang onto a hunk of mane and lie flat out on the water's surface as my mount swims below me with great, powerful, sweeps of his legs. As we approach shore and shallow water, Rebel's powerful neck, back, and heaving sides surface. I somehow manage to position myself behind his emerging withers and end up with my butt on board and my legs astride his body.

Without hesitation, we then race up the dam of the pond and on through a giant pasture. Mud, moss, pond water, twigs, and all sorts of field debris are flying around me as Rebel chases full tilt after Rogue. The two competitive horses race across the pasture at

Sarah talking to her horse, Rebel

reckless speeds and suddenly pull up rodeo style, and stop inches before going through a freshly-stretched, five-strand barbed wire fence.

Had I not had strong thighs to hold onto Rebel's sides, and both arms and hands interlocked and clasped around his huge neck, I would have been catapulted slingshot-style across the fence and into a thicket of thorny wild plum trees. Never to be seen again! As it is, I am flung off sideways and slide around his neck ending up facing his chest with my hands still clasped together and interlocked on the top side of his neck. I have spun around his neck like a cow bell on a leather strap. But I am alive. Thrilling!

It is clear that my student, Sarah, is a free spirit. She drives her sports car with the same vigor and careless abandon as she rides her horses. Sarah is unpredictable, a big risk-taker and fun to be with. By the way, Sarah grooms, pampers, loves, and talks to her horses. I instinctively know she can love someone else more than herself.

When the semester ends, I ask the Design Department Chairman if it would be appropriate for me to date one of my former students and she says, "Yes." When the new semester begins and Sarah is no longer in my classes, we start dating.

Almost all our dates center on riding her horses around Blue Mound. Sarah's best friend, Stephanie, keeps her horses there, too. Stephanie's father owns Blue Mound and spends his retirement time making trails through the woods for his daughter and friends to ride on. We ride those idyllic sun dappled trails through the deciduous woods day and night.

We usually end up cooking a big chunk of sirloin steak on a stick over an open fire. We eat it with our bare hands and wash the steak down with *Rose D'Anjou*, drinking from the bottle. We then cuddle in my sleeping bag under the Milky Way until her closing hours prompt a frantic drive back to the sorority house. Her girlfriend's parents also have a small romantic cabin along the Wakarusa River at the base of Blue Mound. When it is too cold to snuggle up in my sleeping bag under the Milky Way by the open fire, we end up in her friend's cabin playing board games by the fireplace and necking.

I receive my graduate degree from KU that spring and sign a contract to teach art and design at a university in Wisconsin starting in the fall of 1966. I also take a job as an art director in the Contemporary Department at Hallmark Cards in Kansas City, Missouri. I

Sarah and I at a party

only intend to stay there that summer until my teaching position at the university begins in the fall.

By August, Sarah and I are engaged and I do not want to get too far away from her. She has one year to go before getting her undergraduate degree at KU. About that time, the university in Wisconsin writes me and has arbitrarily added two more courses to my teaching load. The courses are in art history. They have evidently found out I had organized and taught the first art history curriculum at a college in Kansas City two summers earlier.

While I liked art history, my interests are in teaching studio courses. I also know former classmates who are now art directors in Chicago and I want to do freelance work with them when not teaching. The two more time-intensive art history courses dumped on me by the university would eliminate that plan. The change also makes me realize how insensitive and capricious the administration is. I break my contract with the university and stay at Hallmark.

Hallmark is very good to me, but I'm not a corporate person and I am unhappy there. I will, however, be close to Sarah and can keep the romance alive. I see her every weekend and send her flowers every Wednesday to keep her attention, affection, and love. We are married June 7, 1967, two days after she graduates.

* * * * * * * *

I was lucky to have married such a strong woman who had never flinched when facing the strange and challenging events that later occurred during our marriage. She had always been of good cheer and I only saw her angry a few times in our life together. I discovered, in the years to come, that if you were a visual artist and you wanted a lasting relationship, your spouse had better have a strong constitution, similar values, and lots of intestinal fortitude.

In 1988 another aspect of our romantic 1965 relationship emerged.

While Ethan was continuing to investigate the UFO phenomena occurring around our Plum Creek home, he asked Sarah if she had had any unusual experiences before 1980. Sarah said, "Yes," and preceded to tell him something I had never heard her mention before.

After the interview, he wrote in his report:

"In a 21 Nov. 1988 telephone conversation I asked the subject [Sarah] whether there had been anything in her life that seemed out of place prior to her experiences beginning in 1980. She responded saying there was something that she'd never mentioned because it seemed so ridiculous. She indicated that it could have been a dream. She envisions being along a dirt road and she was on the passenger side of a car. She went on to describe seeing a small cigar shape that passed slowly in front of her and looked like a horizontal rocket almost at eye level. It didn't make any sense to her because she doesn't recall anything before that or after it.

"She was just on a dirt road as a passenger, saw this small rocket which had no wings, was low in the sky and passing slowly in front of the car 'like a slow motion rocket', as she put it. I asked where she might have been at the time and was she with her family? She said she didn't know, that it seemed like she was with a guy. In asking her husband about it, he indicated it wasn't him. I asked about how old she was when this happened. She answered saying that she thought it had been when she was in college, maybe at about 20 years old. This would tend to indicate sometime around 1965. She further indicated that she knew it was her husband who was with her but that they weren't married at the time. She said the memory was just like a fleeting thing, that she had nothing leading up to it and had nothing after it. She felt that her then future husband was driving, that she was the passenger and that he doesn't have any recollection of this memory of hers. I questioned whether this might have occurred in Colorado. Initially, she assumed that it had. But then stated no, it couldn't have been because they had both gone to school in Kansas, and that it would have been in Kansas. She also stated her feeling that this had occurred in the fall."

Months later, Ethan wrote the following analysis after he had interviewed Sarah, Breana, Scott and me, off and on for many months. His analysis of Sarah's pre-Colorado rocket experience was as follows:

"I consider this report to be potentially a major experience because it is typical of the odd partial memories associated with certain types of UFO encounters as we understand them. The statement which the subject made about there being nothing leading up to this memory and nothing after it, is curious. It suggests there may be a period missing for which the subject is unable to account.

"Certainly the memory of an anomalous object slowly passing in front of the car is interesting. All of this raises questions. What might be responsible for such an unusual partial memory for which the subject feels there is a middle but apparently no beginning or ending she can account for? Why doesn't [Sarah] remember where she was and if her husband to be was with her as is her suggestion, why then doesn't he recall being there and seeing the same thing himself?

"If for the moment we assume a UFO encounter in this instance occurred in Kansas, then taking into account the other reports given by the subject, as well as reports from other members of the family occurring here in Colorado, it might then be argued that this phenomenon appears to be following either the subject, her husband, or perhaps both over time and distance. Hypothetically, if this were the case, it would tend to parallel numerous other accounts which are a part of the historical record of this subject.

"It is my opinion that the subject has honestly provided most all she can consciously recall about this memory. Because of the way in which it was characterized, I am inclined to think that much could be learned of the events surrounding this memory through the use of hypnosis, provided the subject were willing and someone was to become available. To date, she has expressed some anxiety about doing this and has indicated that if something more has happened she'd prefer not to know about it. Therefore, until more information becomes available I must classify this as a possible major experience."

I was totally unaware that Sarah had these unusual experiences when she was younger. Ethan's analysis of this one story was perplexing and reinforced the notion in my heart that some people are manipulated for unknown reasons other than to breed children who are parented by two abductees.

Considering the amount of time Sarah and I spent in the outdoors by ourselves prior to meeting, it seems highly possible that both of us had been abducted. Soon after we met, she saw the rocket slowly go by the front of the car while we were out on a county road in Kansas. I can only wonder if they made sure she met me, or I met her? Or were we subconsciously attracted to each other because of our common abduction experiences?

RUN, JIMMY, RUN! | WINTER, 1967

My new wife, Sarah, and I are double dating with my cousin Jimmy and his wife. We go to a movie and then stop at a nightclub and have a few drinks, dance, and talk. As we drink, Jimmy and I talk about our wonderful experiences with our grandparents on their farm near Paola. One remembrance leads to another and then Jimmy tells us this story.

He is young, maybe eight or nine, and is playing with his toy cars, trucks, and tractors in the dusty two-track road near the big sycamore tree, just as I often did when I was young. It is a sunny summer Kansas day, and all of the sudden he is playing in the shade. He looks up to see what is causing him to be shaded on this hot sunny afternoon. To his surprise he sees a large, metallic circular shape hovering above him! In the center of the metal shape is a bright red light. Jimmy just sits there in the dust and dirt, mesmerized by the light and the unexpected shiny metallic object over his head.

As he is looking up at the saucer, Grandma comes out on the screened-in porch and sticks her head out the door to check on him. According to Jimmy, she immediately sees him sitting on the ground with this flying saucer over his head. She screams in terror, "Run, Jimmy, Run!" At the moment he is getting up and starting to run, the saucer begins to wobble above him as though it is out of control. The craft then levels itself and suddenly streaks off towards the southeast.

The saucer barely gets away when three Navy Phantom Fighter jets scream overhead chasing after it. The planes are evidently from the Olathe Naval Air Base, not more than 25 miles away in Olathe, Kansas. Jimmy says from that time on, Grandma always kept her doors locked at night.

■　■　■　■　■　■　■　■

I was flabbergasted, what a fantastic story. I thought I knew Grandma, and yet I had never heard this story. We went home and I forgot the story for many years. After Grandpa Johnson died, Grandma moved to Paola and lived in an apartment. Sarah and I often drove from Kansas City to Paola and played cards with her. One day when we were alone with Grandma, we lamented Jimmy's suicide and how his death had impacted everyone in the family. For once I thought to ask her about Jimmy's UFO story. She said that what he told me was true and she was afraid to live there on the farm from that moment on. No wonder Grandma sold the farm so soon after Grandpa died. I bet the neighbor bought it for a song.

Jimmy committed suicide in 1968 and Grandma passed away in 1992.

FACE IN THE WINDOW | MARCH 17, 1970

I am 30 years old and teaching 3-D design, basic design, and drawing at a university in Denver. Sarah and I are living in a little house in the posh Cherry Creek area. Our rental home is very small, and when it rains I swear I smell the hint of chicken shit wafting through the humid air. I believe the house was once a farmer's outbuilding for his chickens.

Me at 30, January, 1970

Our abode is a one-gabled, ranch-style that runs north to south for 30 or so feet. On the north end of the house is a one car garage that runs west to east. On the south end of the house is another gabled area that juts out to the east. That area is the living/dining room. A bird's eye view of the house would look like one-half of a Navajo swastika. Glommed onto the central axis of the house is a small bedroom and bath. The house is set way back from the road at the end of a narrow lot. At night the house is barely visible, which probably suits the folks in this very upscale neighborhood in ritzy Cherry Creek. Behind the house to the east, are an open field and an upscale high-rise apartment complex.

The front of the house once had a screened-in porch that was converted into a sterile aluminum glassed-in porch. This addition has a slab floor and becomes my studio. I hate the cold, impersonal space, but I need an area to work and this space is the best available without renting additional room. The inside of the house is comfortable with all new carpet, drapes, paint, and old world furniture. We add what furniture we have lugged out from KC and the place becomes very cozy, except for the studio.

Sarah is working as a checker at the local King Soopers grocery store at night, and working on her master's degree in art education at the university during the day. On the weekends we are building a summer home with my parents along the banks of the Arkansas River near Buena Vista. In the years to follow, we will live in this home during the summer vacation months. Life is good and we are happy.

On this particularly beautiful morning, when I wake up I am very anxious for some unknown reason. I leave for my morning drawing class expecting the model to show up at nine. The class and I wait for ten minutes and then I go over the day's objectives and how we will proceed in reaching our goals.

After thirty minutes I know the model is not going to show. I say, "Let's resume our work in three point perspective drawings, so take ten minutes and go to your lockers and get your mechanical drawing supplies." I barely get the words out of my mouth when three female students raise their hand. I answer the first hand to raise. The student says, "I'll model!" The two other coeds offer to model as well. I very quickly realize I'm not in conservative Kansas anymore. I say, "I'm not sure you can, I'll go check with the office."

I don't care who models; once the nude takes the podium I am all business, and the body is the body; a marvelous machine that each art student needs to be well-versed in understanding. At this beginning level, drawing is more an intellectual activity to me than what the average person thinks it is. I know the students don't like to do perspective drawing, but I didn't realize what they would do to avoid the more mathematical, mechanical, and analytical process associated with perspective drawing.

By the time all the red tape is examined and the student is allowed to model, half the drawing session is over. I am frustrated by the hurried substandard drawings the students turn in at the end of the class. At 11:00 the class is over. I take drawings instead of taking roll. I normally grade the work between the end of this class and the beginning of my two o'clock 3-D Design course. Students get their drawing back with a written critique ASAP.

But today I have to leave and go pick up a piece of artwork. Days earlier, I got a call from a woman who said she wanted to donate an Andy Warhol to the Art Department. Andy is a big deal, and the work will be worth a lot of money. I suggest she brings the work to the School of Art office and give it to the chairman. She says, "No," and that she will only give the work to me personally. I am flattered, and the thought runs through my mind that if I bring back an Andy Warhol I'll be sitting pretty with the new chairman and dean. I say, "I'll come get the work as soon as my drawing class is over around 11:00." I should be at her house by 11:45. Visions of sugar plums are dancing in my head as I blindly drive in the direction of her house.

After much groping around northeast Denver, I find her home. I'm puzzled. Her home is a very middle class ranch house, nothing special to make you believe the owner would have such a valuable piece of art. I knock on her door and a woman in her mid-forties answers. She smiles and invites me in. I go in and again I am surprised to see a very common interior. The woman is ancient-looking to my 30-year-old eyes. We engage in cordial hellos and I thank her for the work and think she will come forth with it.

Instead she tells me she would like me to put my shoes under her bed. I'm not exactly sure what she means, but I'm getting the idea she's not giving up the Warhol without a contribution from me.

I try to sidestep her quiet, sexually-charged comment by saying, "May I see the piece?" I know immediately I have chosen my words unwisely. I'm squirming inside, with an open-ended question like that I'm not sure what she is going to show me. I remain sardonic and outwardly innocent of her sexually-charged comment. She disappears and brings a six-colored, posterized, silk screened image of a dozen eggs in a carton with the lid up, for my inspection. I am most impressed with the gall of this middle aged woman. The work looks like she created it in a YMCA Saturday artsy fartsy class. The work is technically well done, but it isn't a Warhol.

I pretend to study the work with apparent great concentration and professor-like critical aplomb. I am for a moment, at a loss for words. I maintain my decorum while she waits for my evaluation of the piece, and wonders whether my shoes will go under her bed or not. I slowly inveigle my way toward the door. I am a coward, and do not want to hurt her feelings.

I am happily married and know from firsthand experience that trust is the emotional glue that holds any relationship together. I tell her we already have a Warhol like hers, the art piece is wonderful, and she should insure it for at least twenty thousand dollars. She participates in the lie, and we both break off without losing our composure and self-respect. I drive back with no sugar plums in my cache and an ambivalent feeling for a woman whose emotional needs have not been met by me. I arrive back at school empty handed and just in time for my two o'clock 3-D design class.

I have somehow backed my way into doing the men's fashion illustrations for the Denver Dry Goods store. The job is temporary and the pay is nominal. I have never worked as a fashion illustrator, but the opportunity is here and I always like to see how well I can do in as many different venues as possible. KU had given me great mental and physical fundamental skills in art and I enjoy a new challenge.

After my two o'clock class, I bust my ass to get downtown through traffic to The Denver Dry Goods main store in the center of the city. Like most low-life visual artists, I park at the loading dock and go up the freight elevator to the fourth floor. The shittiest part of this floor has been especially reserved for the Advertising Department. It's staffed by a bizarre bunch of harried, testosterone-deprived males and overactive artistic, high-octane, estrogen-charged females. They are all running around like shithouse rats worrying about the result of yesterday's Maiden Form bra ad. It did not "lift and separate" like the morning fog.

I am sympathetic to these emotional roller coaster rides of sales statistics, but I'm here for one purpose, to pick up my weekly men's fashion illustration assignment. I have agreed to do these illustrations until a new illustrator can be found. So far, all is going well except the layout artist, a female, has not been happy because I don't follow her unimaginative layouts.

I do my own interpretations of the fashion or clothes given to me to illustrate. It's been a long disappointing day for me and I am not receptive to her complaints. She is not happy with me and I don't give a crap. I'm not paid enough to kiss anyone's butt in this office. In my mind, this is not a real office anyway. It is just small bullpens held together by a long, narrow, agonizing corridor which is always stifling hot and strewn with shitty graphite drawings on crumpled up bum wad tracing paper. The old idea, that if you treat artists like real people they will get indolent and slothful, resides in this wannabe "upscale" temple of fashion and decorum.

I'm taken back. The art director gives me an Oleg Cassini classic blue, pin-striped blazer and a pair of cordovan wing tipped men's shoes and a striped silk tie. Crap! I don't do shoes or ties! I think I'm a fuckin' artist! In my mind's eye, I can see the layout artist in her little hot, shitty booth laughing up her sleeve as I silently pick up the coat, shoes, and tie then head for the freight elevator.

I was mentally prepared to do one drawing, but three is going to push me. I have an important report due for the faculty meeting tomorrow and I am painfully slow when it comes to writing and typing. I rush home through heavy traffic, all the way, agonizing over my workload and what I am going to do that night. I try to pre-visualize how and what I will do with the clothing I have been given. I want to expedite the illustration production process and get this extra crap out of my hair. The illustrations are due by seven a.m. tomorrow, if they are to make the production run that day.

I get home by six o'clock. Sarah is preparing dinner, so I ready the studio and get my supplies out for illustrating. I rush through dinner and then we head to the kitchen to do the dishes. Our kitchen is a galley type, narrow, with counter space, oven, and refrigerator on the east side, sink and more counter space on the west side. On the east wall is a door leading out into a very small backyard. I never go out there unless I have to. When I am out there I get the strong feeling I am being watched.

We begin doing the dishes; Sarah washes and I dry. We are talking about the day's events, when I feel something rubbing on my right pant leg. I look down and see a short-haired, black cat rubbing on my leg and looking up at me with the biggest yellow-green eyes I have ever seen. I say, "Where did the cat come from?" I have not seen a cat in the neighborhood or around our house before. The thought flashes through my mind that Sarah might have adopted it. Surprisingly she replies, "I don't know." The cat is still rubbing my right leg back and forth with its head, neck, and body. I reach down and gently cradle the cat under its chest and pick it up. The cat is very cooperative and is intently staring at me and purring loudly. I open the kitchen back door and gently put it outside into the backyard. I shut the door and relock it.

We have learned to keep all our doors and windows locked. Our landlord has a son who is mentally challenged. On one occasion, while making love to Sarah on the living room floor, I looked up to see a pair of big, smelly, ugly tennis shoes with two legs attached to Kevin, the son, who was standing right above us.

From that point on, we religiously keep the doors and windows locked. We don't need any unnecessary surprises in our life. I continue to dry the evening's dishes, and before I know it, I feel the cat rubbing my leg again. I look down and it is staring up at me with its gigantic, hypnotic, yellow-green eyes. The cat looks at me with great intensity and hungry eyes, almost like it is longing for me, like I am a mouse, a lover, or something very desirable. Its stare is very unnerving. As I pick it up I am wondering, *How did this cat get in the house again?*

It is early spring and in Denver, the temperature can still be below freezing at night. The house is cozy warm; I do not feel any cold drafts coming from the living, dining, or bedroom. This time, when I put the cat out, I'm not quite so gentle and I shove it out the door with some force, hoping it gets the idea it is not wanted inside. I re-lock the door and then go to the living and dining rooms looking for a window that might be open. All the doors and windows are closed and locked.

The bedroom door is closed. I have about twelve cases of home brew chilling in the bedroom. The only moveable window is up to let cool air into the bedroom. The window screen, however, is latched down with a hook lock, and the screen is in good repair. I'm keeping the beer cool to prevent it from accidently exploding if it gets too warm and over ferments in the bottles. My first single batch of beer was great tasting, so now I am making three batches at once. I do not want any accidents to jeopardize the finishing of the freshly bottled beer.

I am puzzled as to how the cat is getting in, but for some reason not concerned. My big focus is on getting the illustrations done so I can write my report to the new Art Department chairman. I finish drying the dishes and go out the locked front door to the glassed-in porch. There inside the locked porch is the fucking black cat looking at me with its gigantic yellow-green eyes! A great surge of energy and frustration comes over me and I aggressively grab the cat with my right hand. It does not resist. I quickly unlock the porch door with my left hand, open it wide, and with great enthusiasm throw the black, big-eyed cat out into the night. I don't see any testicles as the cat hurdles head first, so I assume it is a female. I do hear the limbs of the big Blue Spruce tree in front of the porch rustle as the flying feline finds a new home among the bows of the tree.

I shut the porch door and re-lock it. I can't help but laugh. Maybe I should call NORAD in Colorado Springs and alert them to a low flying, black object heading west at supersonic speed. The interlude with the cat takes the edge off the anxiety over the three drawings I want to have finished by 7:30 p.m..

Then the thought occurs to me that all day, I have had nothing but problems with females; must be my lucky day. Sarah is the only female who hasn't given me any grief, but the night is young. At last, I can begin getting rid of the anxiety associated with knocking out the illustrations. For me, most anxiety associated with the creative process has to do with just getting incidentals out of the way so I can begin working.

It is cold in my studio porch, and I turn on the space heater that is by my feet under the drawing table. For me to execute this kind of drawing, it is important to sit straight and keep my muscles warm when drawing. Plus I don't want to freeze my butt off out on this cold porch. I have to move my feet continually to keep my pant cuffs from lighting up due to the nichrome wires' infernal heat.

I hang the Oleg Cassini coat up on the wall and look at it, and the layout sketch. Tonight I will follow the layout; there is not enough time to do anything else. I also sense I am pushing my luck with the layout artist. I construct the drawing of the male's anatomy in the position indicated in the layout.

It is my idea that the illustration should be just an impression of the Oleg Cassini blazer, not a photographic representation. This type of illustration fits into the retentive advertising strategy I think is appropriate to the quality of goods they sell. At this price point, as an illustrator, my job is to create a desire in the reader, based on the mood I set, not on how many gold buttons, or type of stitching the coat has. With this idea in mind, I illustrate the male figure in the Nicholide extended gesture style. I find that the Nicholide gestural drawing is the most natural and easy way to depict the human form. The looseness of the quickly drawn charcoal lines allows for an animated drawing that has its own life, and at the same time, screw ups can easily be glossed over in a flurry of energetic lines. This fact is important when your ass is to the wall. I do a quick preliminary drawing before I focus on the final illustration.

Oleg Cassini preliminary illustration

I'm smoking too much, and when I light up I already have another half smoked cigarette burning in my sandbag ash tray. I have become an anxious chain smoker. I keep telling myself to quit smoking, but I don't, even though I'm worried about my health.

I light up another cigarette, take a few drags, and finish the second illustration in a flash. I mount it to a one-ply illustration board and put a tissue cover over the drawing. A cover stock is added to protect the drawing from whatever it might encounter during the photo reproduction process. I then move onto the shoes and tie. Jesus, I would trade flagellation or scourging if I could get out of doing these. No such luck. I hold the shoe perpendicular to my point of view and draw it as a contour and then render it with all its lustrous highlights, easy as pie. Seeing the light at the end of the tunnel, I move onto the tie which is as easy to render as the shoes. I mount and wrap them for their trip to the repro room tomorrow. I'm done! It's 7:37 p.m. Great. Now I can turn my attention to writing my report for the new chairman.

I am wandering around in the kitchen; I feel really tired, anxious, and confused, my head aches. The kitchen's overhead dying, neon light gives off erratic buzzing sounds and rhythmic flashing that is very irritating. Looking at it and then at my watch, I realize it is 3:00 a.m.! I am charged with a great surge of adrenalin that electrifies me, and realize I do not recollect working on my report to the Art Department chairman. I'm screwed!

Besides being really tired, exhausted, and anxious, now I'm also depressed by the thought of not delivering my report on time. I normally don't miss deadlines of any sort. The chairman and I are both new to the university, and the rumor is he will clean house and get rid of as many old faculty as he can, replacing them with his own choices. Holy shit. I like it here in Colorado and Denver and I don't want to get a blemish on my early start with this man. I'm not tenured and I would be an easy mark.

How can it be so late? I think I finished the illustrations by 7:30 p.m. I go outside to my studio and all the lights are out. I turn them on and sure enough, the illustrations are neatly laying on my drawing board. Did I fall asleep? No, I couldn't fall asleep at my drawing table with the heater by my feet; my pant legs would catch on fire and I would have awakened. Well, whatever happened, I am too tired and screwed up to pull an all-nighter, but I am still anxious and innervated. I go back outside to my studio and look at the illustrations again to make absolutely sure I did them. They are still there. To hell with it, time to go to bed. Jesus, I'm so tired.

As I open the bedroom door I stop in my tracks. I am surprised, dumbstruck! Right in front of me, not ten feet away and looking through the window screen at me, is the ugliest son of a bitch I have ever seen in my life!

At first I don't know what to think. I am in shock and yet mesmerized and not sure what is looking back at me with such great interest. My mind is still foggy and I think this must be a joke some student is playing on me. Then I see the glint of a reflection off the deep set eyes of this ghastly person's face.

Instantly I know it isn't a student's two dimensional drawing mounted on a stick and stuck in front of the window for me to see. The head almost fills the small window frame. In the dim hall light, I can see that the structure of the head is like a three dimensional, oversized humanoid skeleton. It has huge eye sockets that are dark with only a glint to show a slick wet surface in the recesses of the dry skeletal frame. There is hardly a nose, only two vertical ridges, and small nostril openings that almost extend to what could be called a slit for a mouth. The cheek bones are exaggerated. The skin looks dry, and leathery. There is no hair to be seen, and the large head is not marked with the usual cranial ridges. Strangest of all, is that the lower jaw seems to have many vertical articulated tubes attached to it.

The tubes are reminiscent of flexible air hoses that scuba divers use. They appear to be an integral part of the head's and neck's anatomy. There seems to be about four such tubes; separate but attached to each other at what appears to be the base of a short neck. But it's hard to tell in the low light coming from the hallway. Then I think that the neck extends down below the window sill. I cannot tell how long it is. The face does not move.

I don't feel like I am in danger. I'm frozen in surprise and disbelief, but eventually I become filled with fascination and curiosity. I'm being stared at through the window screen with the same kind of intensity, curiosity, and lust as the cat did earlier in the evening. I keep looking at the unusual person while trying to collect myself out of the mental fog I'm in. I desperately try to analyze the structural components that make up this intense humanoid staring at me.

My view of the face does not last long enough for me to visually dissect its structure into fundamental forms. I teach beginning drawing in a very traditional way. Fundamental forms of cones, cylinders, spheres, tetrahedron, and cubes can be used to breakdown and understand the most complex of visual configurations. Spiritual drawing comes later. Once the complex configuration is broken down into its simpler forms, translating those forms into a pencil line drawing is easy.

Before I completely comprehend what I am looking at, the neck and face move down as though they are hydraulically driven; no lurches, no deviations, just a slow steady downward motion. The hideous face disappears below the window sill and is gone. I hesitate, and then lunge for the window and slam it down with great force and a big bang. Luckily glass doesn't fly all over the room from the heavy impact of the frame hitting the window sill.

Jesus! I tell myself what I just saw must be an omen. Yes, that's what it is, a fuckin' omen! God is warning me to stop smoking or I am going to die! Shit! I'm now wide awake and electrified. I'm going to die! I'm going to die! Shit I'm going to DIE!!!!

I make my way in the dim light through cases of volatile beer and go over to Sarah's side of the bed. She is sound asleep. How can that be? I frantically try to wake her up. Sarah does not budge. All the time, I'm rambling about the omen. She does not respond.

Finally, I bounce her up and down on the bed with such force that her body bounces a foot or so off the mattress. Only then does Sarah begin to rouse and she mumbles something. All the while I'm telling her how I just saw an omen from God! I'm going to die, God damn it, if I don't quit smoking! I need HELP!

I frantically go back through the cases of beer and out to my drawing table. Sure as hell, my once empty sandbag ash tray is totally filled with cigarette butts! Damn, I've got to somehow quit smoking. I'm wide awake, exhausted. I need sleep, but know I'll never get it without help. I take three aspirins, eat a peanut butter sandwich, drink a glass of milk, and collapse in our bed.

I deliver the illustrations on time and go to class. I assign a long drawing for the students to work on while I write the report I didn't do last night. By faculty meeting time, a very supportive secretary has typed and mimeographed my report for my colleagues, and I am home free. The chairman likes what I have written and he mentions that fact to my colleagues at the meeting. Some smile; some glare.

■　■　■　■　■　■　■　■

Meetings were testy events. The old, inbred faculty knew what was on the line and the schism between the Nolandesque hard-edged tape and paint work they had been perpetrating in class was now rubbing up against a more volatile individual, expressionist ideology that the chairman and I favored.

Early on in faculty meetings, sparks flew and at times I thought the meetings and all involved would spontaneously explode into flames, and a *mêlée*. Later on in the year, the ego claws were sheathed and meetings became a laborious intellectual tug of war. I felt like I was watching the chairman try to pound a square wooden block into a circular hole with a twelve pound sledge hammer. The chairman and I were on the same page philosophically, and so for the moment, my job seemed secure.

■　■　■　■　■　■　■　■

At the meeting, while the chairman hammers away at the old inbred faculty to change their ways, I absent-mindedly doodle on the side of the director's mimeographed agenda. To me, doodles can be messages from the subconscious. They illuminate a world where there can be great clarity of vision that speaks the truth and begs the conscious mind to consider their coded messages.

Generally my doodles in these meetings are abstract compositions, a kind of visual dialogue where you play with each line, shape, and space to see how and what the line or shape speaks back to me. For me, the abstract doodle is a symbiotic, iconic dance between expression and intellect like concrete poetry is to sound, word, and cognition.

Today is different; I doodle the head of a very ugly person who is similar to, but not as disturbing as, the one I saw at 3 a.m. this morning in the window. When I realize what I have done, I stop, and go back to doodling my old abstractions. The face I sketch is still fascinating and yet unsettling to me. It reminds me too much of what I saw earlier. I do not tell anyone about my sighting of the person in the window. No one would believe me.

Doodle, "Face in the Window"

Years ago, when I was an undergraduate in design school, I briefly dated a girl from Wichita, Kansas; the big silver buckle in the Midwest's Bible belt. Things between us were going great until she confided in me that Jesus had come into her bedroom one night. To believe in Jesus was a good thing, to say you saw

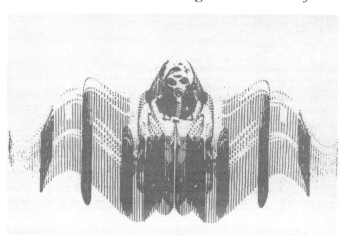

Recruiting postcard

him in your room was more than I could swallow. All the whistles and alarm bells went off in my mind. She had to be a bona fide nut case. I never dated her again, as I thought she must have a screw loose or a disease I didn't want to catch. I knew enough at that moment to keep my unusual thoughts and experiences to myself.

Doodle, "X-ray view with mutilated horse head"

I quit smoking for three hellish days. Then like any confessed sinner, who is not immediately smote down by God, I resume my bad habit as if nothing had happened.

Later that same week, I am designing a postcard for the Art Department to send out to recruit prospective students. I design the upper torso of a strange-looking person wearing a gas mask with breathing tubes coming from it, similar to the creature I saw in the window. The threatening figure has wings, suggesting flight. I have the design printed in black on silver. The chairman wisely rejects it.

I should have been fired; the postcard design has nothing to do with the Art Department's educational mission, just my momentary subliminal obsession. What was I thinking? Perhaps I am subconsciously recreating a modern vision of a

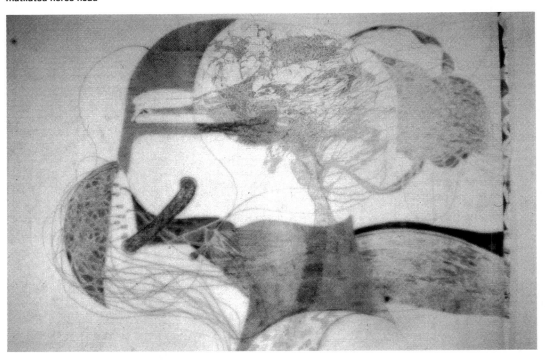

Drawing of profile with wires, tubes, and cut away view of the brain for Biannual show

Fravashi, the symbol of the Zoroastrian faith and a guardian angel.

Hard pressed and without specific direction, I submit a black and white photo image of animated star patterns frozen in space at warp speed. The stars are seen from a one-point perspective and create a strong linear pattern depicting great interstellar speed. The image of implied space travel in the cosmos has no rational relationship to what the Art Department is philosophically about in 1970. I think I took a little trip with the ugly bastard in the window that night and the experience resurfaced in graphic form. Ironically the director accepts the work.

My fixation with space travel, stars, and faces with breathing tubes ends up with another laborious drawing that is juried into a Denver Art Museum Biannual show. The futuristic profile of a person wearing a mask shows wires going here and there, and a cutaway view of the person's brain.

Compare doodle, "Wired"- 1970 to portrait, "Jackie Kennedy and John John"- 1969

I do many spontaneous x-ray vision drawings showing bones, internal organs, people with animal heads, and the like. I have never done this type of drawing before. Other drawings that I now do, depict people with arms and body appendages sliced up like sausages and their bodies connected to wires and tubes. I have no idea what precisely prompted the images, but I know I generally draw images from my experiences.

Along with the accepted Biannual artwork, is a multimedia piece depicting a trapezoidal, metallic, minimalist, futuristic skyscraper lodged at an angle into a barren, moon-like landscape. Other surreal drawings I create depict people with many wires coming out of their heads as though they are under the spell of the computer or machine. Some doodles depict children without major parts of their bodies but are still alive via tubes and wires attached to them.

These doodles are a far cry from an illustration I did of Jackie Kennedy Onassis and John John for the People to People Ambassador from Ecuador. I created that drawing a year before moving to Denver in 1969.

■ ■ ■ ■ ■ ■ ■ ■

Author note: In 2012, I read online the accounts of UFO abductees who claim to have seen live people in jars of fluid with missing body parts and tubes attached to their bodies.

■ ■ ■ ■ ■ ■ ■ ■

Another one of my subconscious doodles depicts babies coming out of an artificial

Doodle, "Sage with Cloned Children"

vagina and delivered via a conveyor belt. The mass produced cloned humanoid babies are overseen by an ominous tall figure with a beard. The ancient one may be a subconscious reference to the giants I saw in my flashback while walking up a mesa in February of 1980.

Maybe the doodles are also a subconscious reference to something I might have seen that night after I was abducted from the porch in March of 1970. Was I shown, by my abductors, hybrid children being produced on a production line basis? Or is the simple drawing my mind's distillation of that complex and frightening process reduced to forms I can visually articulate and understand? Could this be an epiphany like Einstein running down a mountain or appearing as a particle of light? I'm not comparing myself to Einstein. I am alluding to the possibility that we reduce overwhelming images, thoughts, and events to a simplified form we can later mull over, interpret, and understand in our waking state.

In the months to follow, my work is consciously focused on satirical film images protesting the destruction of the natural environment. My ink drawings depict man's inhumanity to man through war and the nurturing of children to become killing machines. I also show through ink drawings my disgust with any form of civil disobedience that smells of anarchy. I create experimental poster designs that promote the peaceful use of space by all mankind.

Something has happened to me and my thought processes. I have always loved and coveted the natural world, but my work to save the environment becomes an obsession.

Giant movable foam blocks, participatory piece

I also begin to think the root cause of our insensitivity to the care and wellbeing of the natural world is based on our worship of left brained motives and objectives. I have this crazy idea that contemporary art is no longer part of the average person's life. So I begin working on large participatory art projects designed to engage the public in creating art. Am I unwittingly attempting to increase the number of glial cells in left brainers' minds?

On a participatory project for the Denver Art Museum I use large geometric building blocks made of soft foam rubber. Participants can stack these blocks in a myriad of different ways and create new interior and exterior three dimensional spaces.

With another project, I convince a company to donate two miles of plastic pipe to

Participatory pipe sculpture

create participatory sculptural forms in conjunction with the Denver Symphony Orchestra (DSO). My work is to complement and advertise the DSO's on-campus participatory events involving students and the public. The Symphony plays the participants' musical compositions. University music majors are also allowed to play in and with the DSO. The interactions between the DSO, students, and the public are unprecedented and inspirational.

The pipes I use are 20' long and come in one-half, three-fourths and one inch diameters. My students and I paint most of the pieces of pipe colors that contrast with the green environment they are going to appear in around the university campus. The theme is music, so we want the pipes, when slipped over four foot by one-half inch rebar driven into the ground, to sway in the breeze and create visual rhythms and sounds as the air goes through them. When participants arrange and cluster the pipes in fields of a hundred or more, the sound made from the pipes swaying in the breeze, is melodious and provocative. Some pipes have holes in their ends, allowing the pipes to whistle when strong winds blow through them. One participant creates a rhythmic ground piece that is a metaphor for polyphonic sounds frozen in time and space. For years after the participatory event was over, I would see clusters of the painted pipes sticking up in the air in front yards around the area.

People subconsciously bring their own symbolic logic and life references to the constructions they make, thus giving new creative insights, meaning, and visual context to the assembly. For many participants the process results in developing a new point of view and creative use of found and industrial materials. Others can gain an appreciation of conceptual art and constructivism. For some, the process is senseless and, at best, just mindless physical therapy.

■   ■   ■   ■   ■   ■   ■   ■

Author's Note: 46 years after I saw the face in the window, Ethan, asked me if I would draw a picture of the face I saw that night in 1970. The face on the postcard and my written description jogged the old memory, and after many attempts, I thought the drawing depicted a good facsimile of the person I saw in the window.

Recent drawing of the face in the window

What came out of the trip down memory lane was a garden variety reptilian ET. At the time, in 1970, ET images were not as ubiquitous as they are today. After I extracted my ufolk from the past, I could see why I went cuckoo and confused the face in the window as a death mask and an omen.

I found the differences and similarities between the doodle and the focused drawing done 46 years later very interesting. My subconscious was really fascinated with the tubes and their probable purposes.

The theme reoccurs in many of my doodles from that time suggesting my preoccupation with artificial life support systems I knew nothing about but must have seen that night during my abduction in 1970.

The whole time I am talking about my remembrances of strange events, Leo Sprinkle is quiet and listens intently. When I finish, I ask him what he thinks. He says I am a sane person and that I have probably been abducted many times in my life by ufolks. I am not surprised now that I have told Leo the events prior to 1980. But I am surprised I did not remember those powerful episodes and did not link them up to what has been happening since 1980.

I'm puzzled though how my mind has selectively forgotten the past strange events that can be so important to me now and in the future. I am relieved that Leo confirms my belief that I am not having dreams but flashbacks of real events that have recently, or in the past, happened to me. I am in disbelief, but in my heart I know what Leo is saying must be true. My dreams have been so intense and seemed so real. But who are these strange people coming and going in and out of my life?

I now want to be hypnotized. I want to see who is taking me in the night and is behind the lights that blind and anesthetize me in my flashbacks. I cannot believe gnomes are responsible for taking me in the dead of night. Before I can muster the courage to ask to be hypnotized, Leo suggests that we take a break and go to lunch. He says he needs some time to digest all that I have told him.

We leave Leo's office and walk to the Faculty Club for lunch. As we look for a place to sit and eat, two tall, stately, well-dressed men come into the room. Leo introduces me to them; they are high ranking administrators of the university. They are cordial, but I see their pupils dilate then narrow and I know their greetings belie their real feelings for Leo. He is jovial, cordial, and respectful to, what I believe, are two undeclared adversaries who obviously don't condone his high profile UFO research activities. Leo is getting a lot of international press for his beliefs and popular Rocky Mountain UFO (RMUFO) Conference. Perhaps he is a real threat to these administrators' closed-minded thinking.

We sit down; they sit at an adjacent table. Occasionally they look at us as we eat, talk shop, and mull over my stories. They look at me and Leo like we are cockroaches that should be crushed under their Jack Boot heals. Leo is totally oblivious to their disrespectful body language that I believe shows their true feelings for him.

■   ■   ■   ■   ■   ■   ■   ■

Good illustrators are masters of the art of reading and depicting body language. It is estimated that 94% of what we know comes to us through our visual precepts. Using the human form as a vehicle to communicate concrete and abstract ideas is a prerequisite to being a good illustrator. That is what separates Norman Rockwell from his peers.

My interest in reading body language started at a very young age. During World War II, when gas was rationed and travel restricted, my parents used to drive from The Homes two miles south to Minnesota Avenue in Kansas City, Kansas. Dad would park our '39 Chevy coup in front of the Katz drug store, the most popular store in downtown. We would sit there for hours eating popcorn, drinking tap water out of fruit jars, and watching people go in and out of the large front doors of the store-old time reality TV.

As we watched people, we openly tried to guess what kind of person we were looking at. Was the person narcissistic, kind, nasty, loving, caring, or grouchy? We would guess what they bought, what they did for a living, were they smart or ignorant, poor or rich, and so on. How they dressed was also a clue as to what they did and what their social status, sense of fashion, sense of self, and cultural awareness was. No detail of the person's being was overlooked. The free pre-TV entertainment was like play, but very important to two young visual artists sitting in the back seat of the Chevy coup.

My artistic sister and I developed our interest and skill in reading the body language of strangers at this early age. Later, we moved on to reading the body language of friends, relatives, even our dogs and cats. We were involved in a casual Thematic Apperception Test juried by the collective logic and personal life experiences of the whole family. Much of what I learned about reading body language began in front of that Katz drug store back in the 1940s.

■   ■   ■   ■   ■   ■   ■   ■

I think Leo could be in professional trouble with his "superiors". He must not suspect, or Leo has such inner strength he rises above the ignorance of these redneck administrators. I can tell, however, that if these two typify the intellect of the administrators at the university, the writing is on the wall for Leo and his career. After meeting these two narrow minded jerks, he would be wise to leave or lucky to be bought out and move on to a more fertile intellectual environment. We finish lunch and go back to Leo's office.

During lunch, I work up the courage and ask Leo to hypnotize me so we can find out what these extraterrestrials look like, what they are doing to me, and for what purpose. Leo agrees to hypnotize me; I am charged with hope. Leo has hypnotized many abductees and probably already knows what is going on and who is behind the abductions. He treats me as though this is his first time hypnotizing a contactee, and is anxious to find out what may be trapped in my subconscious mind.

Leo has me lie down on an adjustable psychiatric couch that is too short. I am all scrunched up and uncomfortable, but I am too in awe of Leo to complain. He has me relax and picture myself in a pleasant, restful environment. Leo then begins his relaxation therapy and hypnotizing ritual. No matter how he tries, I cannot relax enough to "let go" and become hypnotized. Finally, Leo states I must be too insulated for him to hypnotize. Leo says, "Perhaps I can read you." I am not familiar with the nomenclature he uses and have no idea what he means. I remain in a prone position, while Leo sits in his chair and puts his right hand up near his temple and cradles his head in his hand. He shuts his eyes and bows his head slightly.

I can sense that he is hypnotizing himself! I am amazed as he silently sits in his chair. The idea of self-hypnosis is strange to me, but I am open to the thought if Leo says he can do it and he can read me.

After a short time he begins to talk. He starts out with, "Great, great sorrow," and then continues. And as he does I am totally shocked and mesmerized. He is reading me and revealing my most personal inner secrets, not universal human wants, needs, and coincidental facts that would typify anyone. Then he starts telling me stories that relate to what he describes as other lives I have lived which parallel my current life. As Leo continues through two former past lives, there is a knock at his door.

Leo comes out of his trance and says, "Come in." His secretary sticks her head in the doorway and says, "There is a student threatening to commit suicide over at the dorms! Leo, you need to go over there as soon as possible." Leo excuses himself and rushes out of his office. I stay lying on my back on his couch.

Leo is gone for quite a while and in that time I relive the stories I have told him. I cannot believe how I didn't link up the events of the pinprick in my big toe, the night at my grandfather's pond, the face at the window, Jimmy's experience and the new events since 1980.

A new picture of my life begins to emerge. I have evidently been visited and sometimes been under their influence and review since I was at least nine years old. Maybe I was contacted even earlier when I reverently began saying my evening prayers. Perhaps at the young age of five, I was so frightened by their unusual appearance that my only possible defense was to say my prayers.

I now realize that the black cat with the big yellow-green eyes and the face in the window were one and the same creature. The Native Americans would call the entity, a *shape shifter*.

I think my night at Grandfather's pond was no coincidence and I didn't fish after I looked up into the black void. I believe Jimmy's story and now wonder what happened to me that night at the pond during those lost fourteen hours. When Jimmy told me his UFO story, I did not remember to connect his experience with my lost time at the pond and the black void above me. Where had I been? Was I kept from slashing my wrists or was it pure coincidence? Whoever erased my memory that night was very thorough.

The revelation that I may have been saved from committing suicide by my abductors makes me think my family and I are probably not in danger unless I break some unknown covenant with them. Could I have made a contract I am not consciously aware of? Might that contract have particulars in a breach category, such as "punishment?"

I also realize that the focus of my art and thinking has changed dramatically since seeing the strange face in the window in 1970. Am I a conduit for the aliens' concerns about humanity? I am no longer drawing whimsical doodles of people doing simple things such as promenading, dancing, thinking, and metaphorically representing spring as I often did in the 1960s. My art is now focused on man's inhumanity to man. I am working on pen and ink anti-war drawings and posters.

I begin to realize the strong memories, or flashbacks, seem to be spaced out at ten year intervals, except for all the abductions after 1980.

Now I feel like some animal that has been tagged by a curious, benevolent, and manipulative zoologist. Maybe they use some internal tagging device to recapture me every ten years to review my progress from previous injections, modifications, and/or tests performed on me. Perhaps I am just like one of the plants that The Thing was culturing in the movie that scared the bejesus out of me when I was 11 years old.

Who is to benefit from these abductions, tests, and experiments? Am I a Petri dish carrying some form of chemical, virus, or whatever to be taken from me every ten years? Am I intellectual entertainment for some brilliant people performing biological tests on me to benefit their own needs and future purposes? What is reality for me when I am on my earthly plain or theirs? With each new revelation a different, more complex conundrum emerges to add more mystery to my waking life.

Drawing, "Dancers", 1966   Drawing, "Spring", 1966

Anti-war posters, 1970

I am beginning to have this totally irrational idea that when I was returned to myself in the living room in 1980 and became so confused by the fragmented images coalescing into the vision of a wolf and rabbit, that my body might have never left the room, only my higher self or soul was taken. For several months after that February 1980 experience, my head felt like something was missing. I was not as intellectually or physically whole as I once was. At the return from that abduction, had my higher self or soul been returned to my physical body like someone re-inserting a memory card back into a digital camera? Was that why my return was so much different than from previous abductions when I just woke up the next morning or found myself wandering around on Grandpa's two-track road?

After a physically uncomfortable, introspective hour or so lying on Leo's couch, he returns. He has talked a student out of committing suicide, all is well. It is late and I can tell he has more students to deal with and I should leave. Before leaving, I ask him what he thinks I should do about my predicament.

Leo says, "Go up on top of the mesa and meditate. In your meditations tell the entities that you have put away your guns and that you want to meet them. Tell the ETs you do not want them to frighten you by showing up as you round a corner in the house or any other surprise meeting."

I immediately do not like the idea of meditating on the mesa at night. There are bears, cougars, snakes, and who knows what else running around at night up there. I would need a gun if I went at night, and that would not work. I have never sat down and consciously meditated in my life and I'm not exactly sure how to do it.

I don't tell Leo that I'm not going up on the mesa and meditate, especially at night. I'll just meditate or silently repeat the same message wherever I am and do it repeatedly until something happens or I give up. I really don't think anything will happen. I'll try to do what Leo says, but not by meditating on top of the mesa. Leo is harried so we say our goodbyes and I thank him. Leo wishes me, good luck. I leave about 5:00 p.m. for home.

THE MANTRA | JANUARY 16, 1983

As I drive home, I mentally repeat the mantra created from Leo's suggestions: *I have put away all my guns. I want to meet you. I don't want to hurt you. Please do not frighten me when you come.*

I'm driving on the interstate and can drive and meditate at the same time. Finally, I realize I can move the mantra to the top and back of my head and also think about the meeting with Leo. My trip home is uneventful except my mind is mulling over what has been revealed to me by my recall of past events. I religiously repeat the mantra all the way home, arriving about nine at night. Sarah and the kids are in bed asleep.

I quietly put the .38 snub nosed revolver on the top shelf of our clothes closet. I take the shells out of the twelve gauge and take them downstairs to the mechanical room, put the three twelve gauge shells on the header of the unfinished mechanical room door, and the shotgun to the side of the door. The empty gun is out of sight, as well as the shells, but easy to access if I need them in a hurry. The knife stashed near the .38 is put back in my fishing tackle box. I have complied with all the conditions of my mantra.

I am really charged up and don't want to go to bed. I begin heat-setting a large banner on my four by eight foot ironing board in the family room, with the drapes open, giving another signal that I am receptive to their visiting me. In the winter I usually close the upstairs window coverings to conserve energy. Heat-setting the colors into the fabric has now become a mindless activity. As I work, I consciously repeat the mantra over and over as I intuitively go about my business. About three o'clock the next morning I call it quits and go to bed. I get up about 10:00 a.m. and begin heat-setting again, repeating the mantra.

It is the weekend and everyone is home. The day is a beautiful, sunny winter day with the temperature in the 50s. As I work, I am auditorily conscious of the children going in and out of the house. Sarah and Breana are downstairs preparing for lunch. Their constant mother-daughter soft chatter is comforting to me as I work and meditate.

I have always thought that when you are really one with your artwork you are in an altered meditative state. For me, time seems to stand still when I work. I feel very comfortable and one with what I am doing and thinking.

Scott is out on the west upstairs deck playing. He is running his miniature cars back and forth on the two by ten inch deck handrail. Out of the corner of my ears I hear him contently playing in the warm January sunshine. Sometime later, I pick up on the fact that I no longer hear Scott playing on the deck. I assume he has moved to the patio downstairs, but feel he is close by.

All the time I work, I am repeating over and over my mantra. About two o'clock, I hear Scott come in the downstairs' living room sliding glass door.

He runs over to his mother in the kitchen and excitedly says, "Mommy, Mommy, there's a live skeleton out in the tree!"

"Scott, what did you say?"

He repeats himself, "There's a skeleton out in the tree, but it's alive!"

Sarah says "Scott, it is probably a bird of some sort."

"No, Mommy, it is a skeleton sitting in the tree, but it's alive!"

I am upstairs overlooking the downstairs living room and I listen to Sarah's logical argument.

She says, "Did it have feathers?"

"NO, Mommy it is not a bird!"

Sarah and Scott go round and round over what it could be, an owl perhaps. He says "no," and for several minutes, Scott emphatically makes his case that there is a live skeleton sitting out on a limb in a tree west of the house.

Finally, in great frustration, I hear Scott coming up the spiral staircase, and then I watch him out of the corner of my eye run into his bedroom. His room is close to the family room I am working in. He quietly thrashes around looking for something in his room. After five or so minutes, Scott runs to me with one of my *Encyclopedia Britannia* reference books. He has the book cracked open to a particular page.

He runs up to me and says, "Daddy, this is what the live skeleton out in the tree looks like."

He shoves the book in my face. It is open to a page on human anatomy with a human skeleton shown in a standing position. It only takes a second for me to make the connection, and all the sudden I say to myself, *OH, My God! There is an alien out in the tree!*

Sarah must have had the same intuitive thought because by the time I rush downstairs, with Scott right behind me, Sarah and Breana are running from the kitchen to join us as we are going out the living room door. We are all really excited, but a little nervous as to what will happen if the thing is still sitting in the tree.

We rush to the big Ponderosa Pine tree that is 150 feet or so due northwest of where Scott was playing on the deck. We slow down as we approach. We look at the limb that Scott says the live skeleton was sitting on. We are crestfallen; there is no living skeleton sitting on the limb. Scott is also disappointed and continues arguing his case.

Scott is not prone to fabricating stories and since he isn't loaded up with the kind of crap the kids watch on Saturday morning TV, he has no reference point to invent a prototypical cartoon "monster." Scott's reference point is from an *Encyclopedia Britannica*. In short, I completely believe him as he goes over pointing out exactly where and how the creature was sitting on the limb. The limb almost becomes consecrated as a holy site to me. I want to touch the place where the entity had sat to edify its existence. As we walk back to the house, we ask Scott how he saw the live skeleton.

Scott says he was out on the west bedroom deck playing with his cars. Scott points to

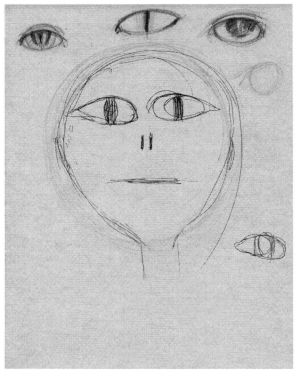
Scott's drawing of "molly eyes" with my eye examples

the deck where he had been playing. From there he saw something out of the corner of his eye, a "white thing." He looked in the direction of the white thing and saw the skeleton in the tree.

"I jumped over the handrail to the ground and walked out to the pine tree where the skeleton was."

Scott continues, "I walked up to where it was sitting. Its bottom was on the limb, its legs dangling down and its hands were holding onto the limb. Its body was bent over with its head down like it was sad."

"And then, Daddy, as I looked at it, it raised its head up to look at me, and it was scary, it had 'molly eyes'!"

I can feel the disappointment, fear, and excitement in his voice as he speaks. We do not judge him or his story. We reassure him that we believe him. Sarah and I are secretly puzzled by his statement about the skeleton having "molly eyes." We look all around and scan the trees in the area for the entity; we see nothing out of the ordinary.

After a few minutes I say, "Let's go inside and draw what you saw."

I think we can get a better idea as to what he saw while it is fresh in his mind, and at the same time find out what "molly eyes" are. I then knew the people he saw leaving his and Breana's room in 1980 were not the same ones. I think Scott would have said it looked like the ones leaving his room that night.

I get pencil and paper and we sit down at the kitchen table so he can draw a picture of what he saw and the "molly eyes." Scott's first drawing is a formula happy face, an archetypal line drawing that all children his age create, a frontal view of the head with eyes nose and mouth. There were no other details.

It's time to dig a little deeper. I sketch some prototypical eyes, then a head, neck, a few quick pencil strokes for a mouth and nose. I leave the eye area open for him to fill in, since that is the issue in question. Scott fills in the eyes with vertical slits for the pupils. Bingo! We now know what "molly eyes" are.

Molly is the name of our family cat and she has yellow eyes with vertical slits for pupils that can be opened wide to see in low light conditions. This type of eye would be appropriate for our night visitors and their natural environment! No wonder our visitors come at night, the daylight must be very painful for their sensitive eyes. And with no eyelashes to shade its eyes, the alien was looking down at the ground when Scott walked up to it; less sunlight to torture its sensitive eyes. I think maybe that is why, when cattle and horses are mutilated, the eyes, eye lids, and lashes are often taken for use in creating hybrid ETs that can see in the sunlight.

Perhaps the purebred ufolks are like fish and must regulate their life to low or no sunlight conditions. Fish go deeper in the water as the intensity of the sun increases. Often they seek shelter in shaded areas to protect their eyes and avoid predators. Some people may think aliens have solid black eyes, but I think the black is a dark covering over the ufolks' eyes much like sunglasses.

It occurs to me these people have to live in dark places to protect their eyes. No wonder they are light in color. Maybe they live in caves, in the depths of the oceans, on the dark side of the moon, or under the polar caps. They must live somewhere where the light is low in intensity and it is cool or cold. So far, most of our visitors come during cool to cold months of the year. I know Scott is not lying or making up the story.

I am mildly euphoric, knowing what the entities, which we decide to call *star people,* look like. That name is not new, Native Americans living in the Southwest refer to alien visitors as star people, a term most appropriate since they are believed to come from the heavens or stars.

We ask him to give a more detailed description of the eyes of the star person.

Again Scott repeats, "The eyes of the star person were scary." He says the part of the eye that should be white was yellow, what should be brown or blue was purple, and the vertical slit was blue not black like our round pupil.

We ask Scott to make a more detailed drawing of what he saw. As we continue to press Scott for more information he says, "The skeleton had an upside down nest on the

Scott's drawing showing a large head, small body, tree limb and nest.

limb next to it."

I sketch a bird nest and ask him if that is what it looked like. He gave me a tentative "yes" and then he draws the star person's nest on his picture. I know I am in the ball park but the nest may not be as literal as the one I draw.

This longer drawing is a mind blower. No wonder Scott said, "It was scary". He draws what is most important to him, the eyes. The eyes look intense, hypnotic, and angry. Could this drawing represent the last thing he remembers before he was anesthetized and maybe taken?

Scott is less interested in the body and creates it almost as a stick figure. The stick figure is on a limb and beside it is a dark nest. Scott illustrates it as a circular shape with sketchy lines representing twigs.

Scott is understandably using the only conceptual models of what must have been some sort of transportation device used by the star person to travel in or on top of. A bird's nest that adults conceive of is a hemisphere with a concave interior comprised of twigs, saliva, cob webs, mud, grasses, etc..

Star people are reductionists in their design philosophy as seen in their craft, clothing, clones, physical structure, etc., I assume there were no protrusions coming from the hemisphere. I believe it was a smooth-surfaced, metallic form inside and out. I may be way off the mark, but Scott might not have the vocabulary to describe what he saw, so he uses terms and forms he has knowledge of.

■　■　■　■　■　■　■　■

Suppose Scott's verbal description of the upside down nest was accurate, and it was constructed of what appeared to be twigs or limbs and not metallic on the outside. The nest could have had a metallic structure with twigs, limbs, leaves, and other textures applied to its surface so it became camouflaged under certain conditions.

A small star person could hide under the nest in full view while on top of the barren mesa during the day. Maybe the textured hemisphere covered a hole in the ground or the mouth of a small cave, camouflaging it from view by people or airplanes. It could appear to be a nest high up in a tree. From the ground, it could appear to be a growth in the tree, such as mistletoe, or a large nest of an eagle or hawk. It could become invisible in the dense forest canopy that existed in the area. If any of these ideas were accurate, aliens could even be hiding in the caves of our canyon region and behind our house.

I recalled in my research, the Hopi legend of the "Ant People and Snake People." According to the Hopi, the world had gone through several cycles of life and death, and we are living in the fourth world.

The original first world was destroyed by fire. At that time, the peaceful benevolent ant people living in caves gathered the chosen Hopi and took them underground to their mysterious subterranean habitat. The Hopi were safe from the fire raging above. The ant people shared their food and water with the Hopi to keep them from perishing. The sky god, Sotuknang, destroyed the first world above. The Hopi people waited for the earth to cool before they ventured above to the second world. As they waited, the ant people taught the Hopi how to gather food and keep cool in the summer and how to stay warm in the winter. They were taught how to live in peace with each other and to obey the Plan of Creation. The ant people saved the Hopi from the holocaust and sure annihilation.

Was what we called a star person really a terrestrial the Hopi called an ant person? Maybe an ant person lived in the caves behind the house? The caves might penetrate the rock formations for hundreds of miles. Were the star people hiding in the trees in the forest near our home in their upside down nest that could be right side up?

We didn't think to ask how big the upside down nest was. We jumped to conclusions and assumed that it was big enough for a three and a half foot tall gray or white alien to sit in. We didn't know whether the star person rode inside or on top the hemispheric form.

I remembered the frescos painted on the rocks at the Palace of Sigiriya in Sri Lanka. The images were of ladies in the court of King Kassapa. One of the King's nymphs appeared to be floating around in a rather nebulous concave form. To me, at the time, it looked like a big dish, but perhaps Scott couldn't think of the word *dish* and said *nest* since it was on a tree limb.

Images of people riding on flying carpets and *Vimanas* had been around for centuries and made the idea of the nymph flying or floating around in a concave shape okay with me. In the Botticelli painting, *The Birth of Venus*, Venus is seen riding into shore in the bottom half of a giant sea shell. Even more relevant to Scott's experience was the Vincenzo Foppa painting, *The Adoration of the Child with St. Benedict and Angels,* painted in 1480. In the sky behind the Madonna and child is a glowing bird nest shape in the sky. There was much to think about that day in January 1983, far more than we could digest at the time.

■　■　■　■　■　■　■　■

We are all excited and highly animated as we talk about the star person in the tree that Scott saw this afternoon. Getting back to work is hard but I do, and Scott, Breana, and Sarah resume their activities.

As I settle back down to heat-setting, my excitement is dampened by an ominous thought, *How many people could ride in the upside down bird's nest?* I was nine when I had the pinprick in my toe and I think my first experience with the star people. Is history repeating itself right in front of my eyes? Do these people follow generations of the same families around as I had heard? The thought is unsettling. Am I here with my family in this little canyon because I want to be, or are there other forces affecting our decisions that I am unaware of?

Have I learned nothing from my trip to Leo's? Then I recall the night at my grandparents' pond. No experienced fisherman in their right mind would have used top water lures at night in November. The big bass I was after was way down deep in the thermocline sleeping, not up on top cruising for terrestrials. There were no terrestrials out that night. I was a hell of a fisherman, and I knew as well as the best fishermen what bass behavioral patterns were. Yet there I was that cold November night, using a top water plug with the apparent thought I could catch a big bass cruising just below the surface the way it might have done a month or so earlier. Insane! And why was I down there anyway? I thought it was to do myself in, but possibly I was called. Maybe we don't have any more choice to be where we are than I had that night at the pond. Perhaps they knew how I had decided to rid myself of my great sorrow and intervened.

I continue to heat-set that afternoon and silently keep repeating my mantra. Sarah takes the kids to pick up Paul, one of Scott's friends, in a subdivision some miles away. I am unaware of her leaving, or later, that Paul is even there that evening playing in Scott's and Breana's bedroom.

Suddenly the boys wash out of the bedroom in a deluge of excitement. A torrent of surprise and high anxiety sweeps over me as well. Their eyes are bulging out and Scott excitedly says, "There's a star person looking in our window!!!"

A great surge of electricity goes through me and I jump up. We all rush back into their bedroom. There's nothing looking into the room from the outside. Both of the boys are really excited and point to where Scott saw the star person. They point up to the glass top of the bayed out sliding glass door. The ET was evidently on top of the roof leaning down over the parapet and holding itself steady on the glass top. The star person was looking into the room and at the kids playing inside. It was viewing them from above!

Son of a bitch! I can't believe it; this star person is really obsessed and persistent. Inside I am freaking out! Scott says, "Daddy, aren't you going out to see what it is doing?" Oh shit! It's dark outside and my courage just flew out the window. I can't take my gun or I'll chance breaking the integrity of my mantra. There are no words to describe my desire to go outside. But my great fear of going out in the dark without a weapon to defend myself if things got hostile, keeps me in the house. Subconsciously, I fear that I will be met with another great blast of white light and just disappear.

I say, "No." The boys look up at me and I can tell they must think I'm a coward. At that moment I would agree with them. I break my cardinal rule of being the aggressor and confronting whatever causes an incident around the house.

Banner, "Fear of the Unknown"

Detail of Banner, "Fear of the Unknown"

My other mantra is: "No God, know fear–know God, no fear." I wish this mantra would have come to mind. I know I would have gone out the door. I try to smooth things over, calm the boys down and then pull the drapes. I shut out the night and my fear of the unknown.

I don't remember what happens after that, other than I go back to the safe process of heat-setting. The boys go back to playing in the bedroom. I think I quit meditating or mentally repeating my mantra, but I'm not sure. Paul stays overnight, and to my knowledge nothing more happens this night.

When I pull the drapes shut, the act is probably a negative signal to the star people that our relationship is back to square one. I leave the guns where they are for a while and later move the .38 back in between the mattress and the box springs of the bed. One would think this day would be a significant event in our lives, but I don't recall discussing Scott's sighting and his description much after it happened.

The next day, I create a quick expressionistic banner that depicts me rushing away from a star person who is looking into the house from the top of the patio glass door. I think this banner adequately describes the children's and my excitement, fear, chaos, and anxious reaction to our star person's peeping activities.

Perhaps the creation process of designing the banner defuses the reality of the star person's visit and makes it a two dimensional abstraction encapsulated in fabric. The existence of the banner makes it possible to live with the star person's appearance and my guilt for not going out that night to befriend it.

※　※　※　※　※　※　※　※

I didn't make the connection between my meditating and the sudden daytime and nighttime appearance of Scott's star person until I began writing this memoir in 2012. I didn't recognize at the time that Scott was the messenger used to diffuse my sense of fear in meeting the star person. Or was it strictly coincidence and it was Scott's time to be abducted? He was nine years old.

What a rush, when I realized I could have made a connection back then with an entity from another dimension or planet. If I had a lot of faith in my meditation abilities I might have made the association and would have called Leo to tell him what happened and ask for advice.

I didn't recall if Scott ever talked about the sighting and his unusual experience again. However, I could swear I vaguely remembered him saying he saw the same kind of lights on the mesa from his bedroom later that night that Sarah described seeing in 1980 when a craft launched or disappeared off the mesa. He must have seen the lights through the glass covering on top of the patio door where the star person had been watching Paul and him play.

I could only regret that I didn't think to turn on the porch light and go outside that night. How stupid of me. I might have met Joseph Smith's Moroni! At the time, turning on the porch light was not an option in my thinking. My lifelong inherent fear of the night and what might happen to me was all I considered. How my early observations rang hollow when I thought back to 1980, and lamented, "Why don't they just knock on the door and we'll invite them in for a talk?"

I got my early wish and maybe an answer to my meditation. When I thought of that moment I became irritated with myself. I should have known nothing was going to happen to me or us that hadn't already happened. We had nothing to lose and so much to gain.

I thought of all the great civilizations: the Sumerians, Egyptians, Mayans, Incas, East and West Indians, the Greeks, and so on. They attributed their advanced learning and development to those various gods who descended from the heavens and helped them. I could only wonder what kind of knowledge the star people might have passed on to me and my family.

Maybe a beginning dialogue could have resulted between ufolks and our government. Of course, earlier leaders of civilizations didn't chase after aliens with jets armed to the teeth with rockets. Nor did they try to shoot ETs out of the sky as we had so many times as documented on February 28, 1942 in *The Battle of Los Angeles*.

The eagerness of this star person to meet with us or let us know of its presence was an affirmation that I secretly held; not all aliens are here to harm us. I believed some were our ancestors and they were us coming back from the future. Star people came to get the necessary ancestral stem cells, sperm, and ovum to reproduce and survive whatever cataclysmic event they might be facing on another ethereal plane or dimension. In exchange, ETs could be slowly bringing contactees up to speed, so subsequent offspring would be better prepared to survive and populate the future with a stronger, more intelligent human.

Perhaps after world governments developed weapons that were potentially lethal enough to kill aliens or destroy their craft, the star people began to contact individuals instead of government leaders. I thought there was no escape once you were contacted. The ufolks could/would follow us wherever we moved. They had taken me from a high density baby factory in Kansas City, Kansas: a pond in Paola, Kansas, the heart of an upscale Denver residential community, and I think many times in Plum Creek Valley.

THE NICE ALIEN | FEBRUARY, 1983

The excitement of the star person's visit is pasted on my prefrontal lobes with rabbit skin glue and will always be with me. The rest of the family appears to have forgotten the experience in the hectic comings and goings of our daily school year routine.

Living in the country, Sarah spends two and a half hours commuting which compresses the family-time down to nothing on week nights. Those evenings are frantic times as we get ready for the many demands of: the kids' homework, their emotional

Breana's drawing, "The Nice Alien"

health, clothes for tomorrow, care of the animals, Sarah's grading and lesson plans, and me developing my work and preparing for the next day's classes. During the school year I gladly become the house husband and cook, clean, wash, dry, and perform almost all the household chores on my days "off". On days I have classes, I juggle my schedule so I can be home ahead of Sarah and the children. I try to have dinner ready, and the house picked up by the time they arrive around 6:00 p.m.

Not long after our visit from the star person, Breana brings home a crayon drawing she has done in her first grade class. There are two subtitles to the drawing. In the upper left hand corner written in cursive is: "The nice Alien, sitting on the doorstep scare[d] of the new world." In the lower right hand corner in printed form is written: "The lon[e]ly and scared Alien."

At first I am amazed at her interpretation of the event and her graphic empathy for the star person who she drew with three toes on each foot and three fingers on each hand. I am, however, not sure if she was interpreting the night I wouldn't go out on the porch or if she had some unknown contact with our wannabe friend. She illustrates the star person sitting forlornly on the front porch of a house. We are puzzled because normally a child will draw the house he/she lives in. But her drawing shows a gabled, shingled roof; our house has a flat roof. We do not realize at the time that her drawing of the house looks almost exactly like the old ranch house we first see, and buy, three years later, in 1986.

Scott said the star person looked sad before it lifted its head up and he saw it had "Molly eyes." That is the way Breana draws it, except the star person is sitting out on the porch. Was it waiting for me?

I often wondered what Breana's teacher thought about her "Nice Alien" drawing. Breana was naturally expressive in many ways and didn't hesitate to create her own music on the piano, or her flute. She was given to spontaneous outbursts of singing and always eager to dance to her favorite music. Breana expressed herself verbally by writing stories and illustrating them with very intuitive drawings. In both fifth and sixth grades, she wrote and illustrated the outstanding story in her grade level. One of her books seemed so insightful that I know she knew much more than any of us about the Wolf Clan shaman spirit that I suspected lived around and occasionally in the house.

KOKOPELLI? | APRIL, 1983

The studio/barn becomes my regular habitat during my days off and every night. Often, I work way beyond the eleven o'clock hour, and when deadlines are pressing, I can pull two all-nighters in a row without my work showing any ill effects. I love the studio and my work is showing it in many ways. I have hustled up several clients that need banners and sometimes collateral design services. But it is my banners that spearhead my ability to now compete again in regional and national fine art and graphic design competitions. I have developed unusual techniques and procedures to generate my work

It is late one night and I am working in the studio on a new banner design. I'm getting tired and begin to think about going to the house for the night. Suddenly out of nowhere I hear the melodic sound of a flute playing outside the studio's west window! All the hair on my neck stands on end, and I'm alarmed, puzzled, and concerned for my safety. It is one or two o'clock in the morning and someone is not far outside my window playing a flute! What the f...? Only a fruitcake psycho would be outside in rattlesnake country wandering around in the dark playing a flute. In a twelve alarm panic, I quickly lock the doors to the outside and turn on all the outside flood lights. I then turn the inside lights and radio off and grab the only weapon I can think of, my 42 inch metal T-square.

When I turn on the outside lights, the melodic sound of the flute stops. I am adrenaline charged with fright and ready for whatever wants to come into my space.

While the T-square does not have a sharp edge, I still would be a formable fighter with it anyway. I am very athletic and do not fear anything unless it's someone with a gun.

I stand at the ready by the door that leads to the barn area. This door is my most vulnerable point of entry. The outside lights illuminate the west entry door so I can see if anyone approaches. It's a solid core door, and by the time someone smashes through it I will be on them slashing at the cervical area of their neck. I wait and wait for whoever is outside to show himself.

I only hear the horses in the foaling stall that adjoins the north wall of the studio. We share my inside north wall, and though insulated, I can still hear our mare and her new foal. Sarah's newly purchased Appaloosa mare, Rose, and her half Arabian colt are very active and there is a lot of movement and kicking on the stall walls.

After a long thirty minutes or so, I think there will be no assault on me. I turn on the interior lights, put my T-square next to my drawing table, and continue working on the banner. I decide not to go outside until the sun comes up, when I can see any threat to me. I get my second emotional adrenaline charged wind and have no difficulty continuing on with my work until morning.

About seven o'clock in the morning I leave for the house where I plan on sleeping until three or four into the afternoon, and then begin designing again. As I walk west up the drive, I meet Sarah coming down to the barn to feed the horses and rabbits. We greet.

"What's going on down at Charlotte's?" she says.

I turn and look east to see two sheriff's patrol cars across the street from the entry to our driveway.

"I don't know," I say. "I haven't seen or heard anything after I turned on the outside lights earlier in the morning."

"I think I'll go see why all the cops are there," Sarah replies.

I go to bed and quickly fall fast asleep. About four o'clock I get up, shower, and see Sarah downstairs. She is eager to tell me what happened at Charlotte's house.

It seems Charlotte also has a mare and a new colt of almost identical age as ours in her barn's foaling stall. Her barn is east across the road from us, but not more than four hundred feet from our barn. Her mare was taken out of its stall, away from her colt, and moved to the driveway between a large cabin cruiser and a four horse trailer. There the mare was killed and mutilated. Unlike the bull that was said to have been found in the top of a cottonwood tree, I hear, later that day, a neighbor say, alien mutilation not cult ritual.

Charlotte was not at home last night. Before she left she nailed the door to the stall shut as she had done for the previous three nights. Each night, however, the nails were removed in an apparent attempt to access the mare. Charlotte had to re-nail the door closed each morning to make sure the stall was secure. The stall door showed the nails were removed again last night when the mare was mutilated. Charlotte had also filled three 500 gallon stock tanks with fresh well water for her horses pastured outside the barn corrals. All the water tanks were empty when the sheriff got there. The foal and the other horses in the pasture apparently were not physically harmed.

■   ■   ■   ■   ■   ■   ■   ■

Not much was made of the incident and to my knowledge; the mutilation didn't make it into the local newspaper. Strange, but I didn't remember thinking about the mutilation in the days and years to follow. I didn't worry about our animals and I didn't recall Sarah talking about the incident either. It was just something that happened, and was soon forgotten.

On two occasions, the little spring pond on our property turned up empty. Our pond was filled with water that had thousands of duck weeds floating on the surface. The spring had never stopped running in the seventeen years we lived there. Assuming the aliens drained Charlotte's tanks of water, I could only wonder why they preferred well and spring water over nearby Plum Creek and subdivision pond water.

Who was playing the flute outside the studio window that night? We had no immediate neighbors who could have just stopped by to walk around in snake country at night and serenade me. The house next door was for sale and had been vacant for over a year. The nearest house with residents was a quarter of a mile north of the studio.

Perhaps the flute player had alerted me to stay inside and be wary, which I did. I was totally convinced that the star people were benevolent and we were quite safe. After the mutilation of Charlotte's horse I wasn't sure what to think about our relationship with these entities. I also wondered if I had not been in the studio with all the lights on would they have taken our mare and mutilated her? Did someone, a chickadee spirit, or friendly star person, warn me to stay put that night? Maybe there are more, different kinds of aliens running around than we realize. Some are benevolent, some are not. My understanding is that no other livestock in the area were mutilated that night.

I concluded that if Charlotte's foaling stall door had been tampered with the previous three nights, then her horse was targeted. Our horse stall door was kept shut with an unlocked stall latch. It would have been easier to take our mare instead.

I had been in a testy relationship with Charlotte's boyfriend and her hired hand for some time. We were fighting over the covenants that were designed to protect the subdivision from the overgrazing of the native grasses by Charlotte's and other lot owners' horses. These people had no respect for the environment.

When I first started jogging on the subdivision road, Charlotte and her boyfriend sicced their Doberman on me to vent their anger for my resolute position of protecting the natural environment in the subdivision. Fortunately, Huggy nailed the Doberman days later and almost killed him. After that, they no longer turned their dog loose on me. Many years later, a neighbor told me that Charlotte's boyfriend almost killed Huggy in the process of separating him and their Doberman. In 1989, Breana would tell a MUFON investigator that the star people liked Huggy and Charma.

After the Huggy incident, I carried a three foot club or my .38 in a Bianca holster when I jogged. The Doberman no longer charged out Charlotte's kitchen door after me, but her hired hand followed at my heels in his one-ton flatbed truck as I jogged the secluded subdivision road. He always had this shit-eating grin on his face when he menacingly passed me in his truck. I didn't let him and his antics intimidate me from jogging when I wanted.

We went back to our regular daily schedule and that night with the flute player melted away in our memory with most of the other strange events that had happened to us over the years. The missing water in Charlotte's stock tanks was a strong clue that would become significant to me, an Aquarius water bearer, who would end up in South Park, Colorado many years later. I didn't get the significance of duck weed or spring water at the time.

NATIVE INSTINCTS | APRIL 20, 1983

hen not creating banners, I am working with fine art experiments on fabric. The artwork that I create is non-objective compositions resembling moving subterranean geologic formations.

I get the idea from some late night talk show host that the earth

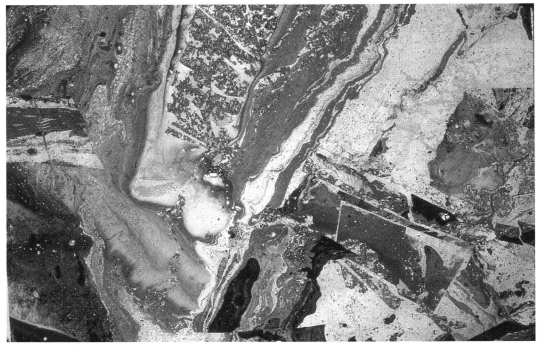
Painting, "Subterranean Flow"

is going to change poles and everything is going to go to shit, or fly out into space. Somewhere I read that scientists have found buried Woolly Mammoths in the North Pole region with undigested buttercups in their stomachs, some with fresh grasses in their mouths. Why did those Woolly Mammoths have fresh flowers and grasses in their frozen mouths and stomachs?

When I checked into the concept, I found that geologists deduce that the world reverses its polar field every 200 thousand years or so, and we are overdue for a change of venue.

So now my experimental work has a new emphasis, and I am cranking out rock formations on fabric that are transforming themselves from sedimentary to metamorphic rocks by the ton, so to speak. I am really good at rocks, but they lack a traditional focus unless you are a geologist.

For some unknown reason, I begin including Indian petroglyphics and pictographs on the imaginary rock surfaces. Soon, my new passion is collecting and xeroxing Indian icons that speak to me. My research material is found at the university, and public

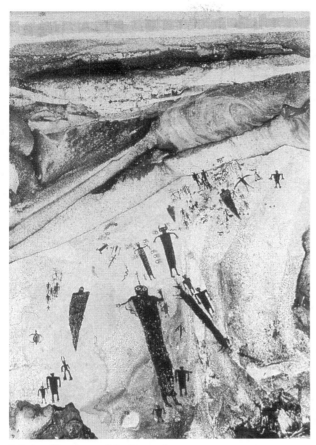

Painting, "Language of the Canyon"

libraries in the region.

I love what I'm doing, collecting and learning about Native Americans through their artwork and related history. I am expanding my research interests into Native American Winter Count and Ledger Book drawings. Before long, I have collected a hundred pounds of Xerox and Kodalith film images in my research morgue that I use in conjunction with my non-objective rock art.

I am right ahead of the coming pictographic art trend in Santa Fe. But my interest and obsession for Native American drawings goes far deeper than embellishing make-believe rocks. I am becoming somewhat of an expert when it comes to early man's mark making, and children's drawings, which many adult Plains Indians drawings resembled. As a visual artist, I am able to see more in the Plains Indians drawings on rocks, bison hides, shields, teepees and ledger pads than some anthropologists.

■   ■   ■   ■   ■   ■   ■   ■

In 1966, my Master's thesis at KU was on children's book illustration. I based my research work on the premise that "when I was a child I spoke as a child" and I added "and drew and commutated my ideas as a child." I studied children from the psychological, physiological, perceptual, cognitive, and mental concept formation points of view. What I found was a whole new world of visual communication formulas that children and beginning drawers all use. I concluded that most children's books weren't particularly illustrated for children to understand, but for the adults who bought them. Imagine that!

Helga Eng's ground breaking book, *The Psychology of Children's Drawings*, studied the psychological interpretations of children's drawings and proposed that we all went through the same stages of intellectual and mental motor skill development as manifested in our drawing skills at specific ages. The upshot was that Native Americans from centuries ago, went through the same mental, motor, perceptual, and cognitive stages of development and drawing skills that most modern children go through from birth to twenty years of age in every culture.

One could learn to read and understand these universal stages of drawing development in Winter Counts and Ledger Books. Those drawings gave valuable insights into Native Americans' daily social and religious life. When one knew the basic language, their drawings could be appreciated on a whole other aesthetic and socio-intellectual level.

While I loved what the Native Americans created in all forms of art, I looked for drawings of deities and spirits that could tell me more than I already knew about the ethereal entities running around our house. I concluded what was here in the canyon now was here hundreds of years ago. I sensed that somewhere I would find what I needed to verify my feelings on the topic of Native American spirits and UFOs.

I looked for drawings that visually validated who the spirits were and what the Native Americans thought about them: which spirits depicted were good, and which were bad. Once I knew that, I would research how to cope with the spirits' presence.

In the book, *Visions of the People, a Pictorial History of Plains Indian Life,* by Evan Maurer, I discover an 1850 Crow Absaroke war shield cover. The shield cover depicted a bison being lifted up in the air by zig zag lines that were coming from a large dark shape. The bison's tongue was sticking out of its mouth and it was bellowing in fear. Urine was being excreted, in terror or pain, to the ground below. The urine went down to the edge of the shield and off the picture plane.

The circular shield cover clearly depicted the abduction of a bison by a shape that was a UFO. In the book, it was alleged to be a storm cloud. Storm clouds drawn by most Native Americans usually had a scalloped or bumpy top. This cloud was a smooth shape that partially hugged the top perimeter of the circular shield. Had the brave, who created the shield, made the dark shape totally hug the perimeter of the shield, his drawing

War Shield cover drawing with bison being abducted

would have not carried so much information. However, the dark shape curved away from the edge of the circular perimeter of the shield at a different angle on both right and left edges and said, *boomerang shape*, not *cloud*.

Beginning drawers will often tip the picture plane and depict some things from a frontal view; other objects are shown from a different perspective. This form of artistic representation is called spatial displacement. Cezanne, the painter, used this convention in his mature work and provided the inspiration for Picasso's and Braque's development of Analytical Cubism. Ancient Egyptians used similar conventions to depict the human form.

The dark shape abducting the bison was a boomerang shaped craft as seen from below. Maybe it was shaped like the UFO craft seen over Phoenix Arizona in 1997 by hundreds of people. The orthoscopic form of the bison was seen from the profile and was easily identified. Red, dry brush marks (not shown in drawing) surrounded the bison in the negative space of the war shield cover. These brush strokes could represent the blood that would be mysteriously taken from the animal by the abductors or the magical dark shape above. These red strokes symbolically represented a process and animated the loss of blood by the bison. When the carcass was dropped to the ground there would be no blood left. This artist was animating a mysterious process and therefore adding more powerful symbolism to his shield.

His protective shield might take your blood as well, and protect his. The shield was alive with symbolism and truly sacred to the Indian brave. Anthropologists said the red brush strokes represented rain or hail coming down from the cloud. I made a structural drawing of the shield to simplify the visual elements that made up the shield's symbolism and message to enemy warriors.

War shield covers used by Native Americans were big medicine. Power images depicted on them were revered as strong medicine that would protect the owner in battle. What could have been a stronger icon and medicine to have on your shield than a UFO abducting a 1500 pound animal, and mutilating it? Depicting a dark cloud with red rain or hail drops on a warrior's shield was hardly what I would call protective when in battle.

I believe that UFOs were abducting and harvesting bison. Native Americans observed them in the process and revered the power, mystery, and visual magic associated with them and the abduction phenomena. When most of the wild bison were slaughtered by white man to rid the west of Native Americans, the aliens then substituted domestic cattle for bison. Now they still hunt in the same areas of the U.S. that once supported vast herds of bison. Part of that area is affectionately called the Paranormal Highway by believers in UFOs.

Another of my most beneficial resource books was Thomas Mail's *The Mystic Warriors of the Plains*. The book contained a drawing by the author, of a warrior from the Bear Clan. The drawing showed a warrior with the hide of a bear draped over his back. The head of the bear was on top of the warrior's head and stuck out way beyond the head of the wearer. The rest of the pelt draped down the back of the warrior's thorax, abdomen, pelvic, lower extremities, and trailed off onto the ground.

The profile drawing of the Bear Clan warrior or shaman was almost identical to what the spirit wore the night Charma was thrown up against the east wall of the house. It is my opinion that the spirit I saw was a Wolf Clan, not a Bear Clan warrior. The profile was not as bulky and suggested to me wolf not bear. All I saw was the light brown color of the pelt. Why the human form of the spirit was not visible, still puzzled me.

I also thought that it was a Wolf Clan shaman, and not a Bear Clan, because Breana wrote a booklet called *Wolf's Eye* when she was in the fifth grade. Breana raised rabbits from the time she was five or so, and they were her first love and she took great care of them. Cinnamon, her favorite rabbit lived for seven years before dying of natural causes. When I read her book I was shocked to know that she let the wolves in her booklet eat her prized bunnies! Breana was somewhat of a psychic and I believed she was aware of the Wolf Clan shaman and Indian spiritual presence in the house and elsewhere in our environment. The idea of a wolf also tied into my experience of seeing, in my mind's eye, the wolf and rabbit on the first night in our new home

I'm getting ready to go to the university, and just before I leave I feed the dogs a morning meal. Today I have a special treat for them. I boiled some chicken leg quarters early this morning and put the meat I stripped off the chicken bones into their regular dry dog food along with the chicken broth. I put their bowls out near the door on the south side of the house by the kitchen. Both dogs are hungry, can smell the chicken, and come rushing up. They jump in and begin eating heartily.

For some inexplicit reason, they look up from their bowls at the same time, turn their heads and look west, toward the spring pond and the ravine. In unison, Huggy and Charma quit eating and dash away at full speed across the yard and down the path that leads to the ravine. They appear to be excited and are racing each other. I watch them disappear down the path and then I go inside the house and continue dressing and getting ready for classes.

As I go about my business, I can't believe how Huggy and Charma just quit eating a great meal I spent a lot of time on. It's as if they have been called by someone who has something better than the meal they were starting to eat.

We had a light snow last night so the thought occurs to me that I can follow their paw prints to where they might be. About 20 minutes have passed since they ran down the path; I easily follow their trail. Huggy's and Charma's tracks go down into the ravine, and then go around and around the large broad leaf cottonwood tree growing in the bottom of it. Their paw prints make so many circular trips around the tree that there is only bare brown earth showing.

* * * * * * * *

When I saw the circular path around the base of the cottonwood tree I was taken back. It immediately reminded me of the Plains Indians' Sacred Sun Dance ceremony performed around a designated sacred cottonwood tree. If a tree wasn't available near the camp, they used a large cottonwood limb or sapling that they would mount into the ground at a special site. To many Plains Indians, the cottonwood tree was sacred as a conduit for their prayers to travel through and ascend to the Great Spirit above.

In June or July some Plains Indian tribes would perform the Sun Dance Ceremony.

Drawings of Sun Dance pledge and my abduction at the pond in 1959

The tribe danced around the sacred tree, sapling, or transplanted limb for days, sending their messages to the Great Spirit through praying, chanting, dancing, singing, and beating of the drums. This induced a condition called *entrainment,* which captured the dancers' minds and allowed them easy mental passage into an altered state of consciousness. In this state, the people could access ancestral spirits, and send messages and prayers to the Great Spirit.

At one point during the three to four days of dancing, male tribal volunteer pledges came forward. Each was tethered to two rawhide straps attached to bones that had been inserted under his breast muscle. The other end of the two tethers was tied high up to a large tree limb or trunk of the cottonwood tree. The volunteer pledges then leaned their upper torso back, pulling against the rawhide straps in an attempt to rip the tethered bones through their breast muscles and skin.

The braves said prayers to the Great Spirit and their painful sacrifice was made to insure the health and welfare of the tribe during the coming year. As they performed the sacrificial ceremony they stared at the sun and blew an eagle bone whistle to help them endure the pain and escape to an altered state of consciousness. The pledges' altered state allowed for heightened mystic communication with the Great Spirit. They asked for special favors to enhance their bravery in battle and skills in hunting.

Once a volunteer pledge had pulled the tethered bones through his breast muscles and skin, the brave was taken by a priest to a special tent to recuperate. Pledges who had endured the Sun Dance were held in high esteem by their tribal members.

Realistic drawings I had seen of a UFO abduction event reminded me of the Sun Dance pledges trying to pull the tethered bones through their breast muscles. I did a quick drawing of a pledge pulling against the bows of a cottonwood tree, and one of my abduction at the pond in 1959 for comparison.

Perhaps the Sun Dance pledges and ancestors were really emulating a classic abduction scene they had witnessed or experienced during their lives. If the ufolks were abducting bison, it would seem logical they would also abduct people. The life changing abduction event could be the basis for the most important ceremony of the Plains Indians, the Sun Dance. Maybe the Sun Dancers were attempting to get in touch with the Great Spirit that resided in the brilliant "sun" (shiny UFO) above them.

The pledges might have been saying prayers and communicating their wish to be helped by the Great Spirit in the shining circular disk. Their painful sacrifice proved their commitment to the gods within the craft. When conceived as a whole three to four-day event, the tribal Sun Dance might be a mass altered state of consciousness for the entire tribe in an attempt to communicate with the Great Spirit or star person.

Possibly, that was what I did when I meditated earlier in the year. If a tribe could communicate to gods in their altered state, perhaps I did as well when I meditated. Sun Dance worshipers might have been asking for help in finding bison herds, protection from competing tribes, and other life saving/giving information.

Conversely, could the Sun Dance have been a sacrifice to keep UFOs from abducting fellow tribal members or bison? The symbolism of the Native American tribe dancing around in a circular path could have been referencing the classic UFO shape or rotating lights on alien crafts. Could they have been referencing circular burn marks on grasses or circular imprints in the snow? The analogy of the abductees and pledges looking at the brilliant sun in the July sky and being bound by the rawhide thongs tied above to the sacred tree was obvious to me. The sun was the brilliant light of the UFO. The tethered pledge was the abductee being beamed up to the "sun" or craft.

■   ■   ■   ■   ■   ■   ■   ■

As I stand here looking down at the base of the cottonwood tree in the ravine and the dogs' paw print path around it, I am surprised by what insightful thoughts

Banner, "Blue Gann Dancer"

I am having. It appears to me that our Wolf Clan shaman, who was probably guarding this sacred healing ground when we first moved into our house, has made friends with Charma and Huggy. The dogs' behavior seems to indicate they are now his loyal tribal members. The spirit may have them performing the Sun Dance ritual around this sacred tree as Arapahoe and Apache Indians might have done in the past.

Charma's and Huggy's paw prints then leave the tree area and go into the Gamble Oak trees beyond the south side of the ravine. I do not see any other prints near or around the tree. Later, I find Huggy's choker chain not far from the base of the tree. How could it have come off and why?

I wish I would have had the time to follow their tracks into the forest to see where our Wolf Clan spirit took his loyal tribal members. I cannot understand how the spirit called the dogs to the tree, but they seemed to be more than eager to follow his lead. To our knowledge, the spirit never throws Charma against the walls of the house again, and our Wolf Clan spirit has not bothered us physically. But I think he has influenced me and the work I am doing.

The first large banner design I create is of an Apache Blue Gann dancer. My great interest in Native American pictographs and petroglyphics gives me pause for reflection. The spirit may have also influenced me and the family in many more ways that only time will reveal to us.

▨ ▨ ▨ ▨ ▨ ▨ ▨ ▨

Many historians wrote that the Sun Dance was brought to the Plains Indians about two thousand years ago by the White Buffalo Calf Woman. There were as many variations on the story as there were tellers. I preferred this one because it reminded me of an incident Breana had when she was a teenager.

According to this legend, the combined Arapahoe/Apache tribe who were starving to death due to the lack of sufficient game to hunt held a council meeting. They convened to discuss what to do since there were no buffalo herds to hunt. During the meeting a brilliant fire or light descended from a dark cloud and came to rest in front of the tribal council elders.

Then the brilliant orb of light opened and out stepped a beautiful maiden clothed in a white doeskin dress. She presented the council with the sacred Chanupa (Pipe) and the Seven Sacred Ceremonies that almost all Plains Indians perform to maintain their sacred ways. The ceremonies she gave them were:

The Gift of the Chanupa or Sacred Pipe;
The Keeping of the Soul;
Inipi, The Rite of Purification;
Hanblecheyapi, Crying For a Vision;
Wiwanyag Wichipi, The Sun Dance;
Hunkapi, The Making of Relations;
Ishna Ta Awi Cha Lowan, Preparing a Girl for Womanhood.

White Buffalo Calf Woman stayed with the Arapaho/Apache people for 14 days, and taught them how to use the sacred Chanupa to carry their prayers to the Great Spirit. She also taught them the meaning of, and how to perform, the Seven Sacred Ceremonies that would ensure the favor of the Great Spirit and the people's continued harmonious relationship with Mother Earth. I am reminded of Moses coming down from the mountain that was shrouded in a glowing dark cloud. It is alleged that when he came down carrying the stones inscribed with the Ten Commandments he was glowing and his hair had turned white. Had he received his instructions from ufolks?

As White Buffalo Calf Woman prepared to leave the tribe, she lay down, rolled over, and turned into a white buffalo calf. She walked some distance and rolled again, turning into a red buffalo calf. She repeated this process three more times, each time turning into a different color buffalo calf (black, brown, and yellow). She promised to return and bring eternal peace and happiness to the Native Americans once a white buffalo calf was born. She then rolled again and turned back into the beautiful maiden and ascended to the heavens inside the brilliant fire or light she descended in.

Shortly after she ascended in the brilliant orb to the dark cloud above, a great herd of buffalo appeared nearby providing the tribe with sustenance. After reviewing the Seven Sacred Rites in Black Elk's book, *The Sacred Ways of a Lakota*, I realized how much more civilized the Native Americans Plains Indians were than the pioneers who replaced them.

When I left for school that morning I felt reassured Huggy and Charma would be around the house when I returned home. The two dogs had always been left to their own devices when we weren't home since we didn't have any leash laws. So over the years, I knew they had a mentor to keep them out of trouble and close to home.

"SIR" SEAN | MAY 6, 1983

While working in the studio late one night I get a bright idea as to how I can speed up the heat-setting process of dyes on fabric. I develop the idea into a physical reality and soon I'm in business. I can now heat-set colors on fabric in minutes instead of hours. A new world opens up for me. Sometime later, my banner work is being exhibited in a gallery in Aspen. The owner of a local upscale boutique buys one of my banners to create a dress.

I am amused and flattered, but I don't have a clue about the fashion industry or fashion design. The owner of the boutique gives me the idea as to how I can utilize what I do in a new context.

I think about what I will do as a fashion designer. After a week or so I decide to create surface designs that can be used in conjunction with a simple sheath dress or kaftan. A friend hooks me up with a seamstress who can do the structural design and sew my work into wearable art.

The Native American influence is evident. I call my first design a banner dress. I

First banner robe dress   Southwest gown/cape

then do a gown/cape based on a simple Southwest Native American design.

I create a collection of fashions based on Indian motifs and my work is shown in a Native American fashion show sponsored by the Denver Art Museum. Now I have a positive experience in this venue. I jump into the surface design and fashion world with both feet. I have a method of designing unique surface designs, a seamstress to help me, and the energy and enthusiasm to make sure I achieve most of my goals. And what art form could be more participatory than art to wear? Of course, art is in the eye of the beholder, and I've seen a lot of shit passing for art in this new venue.

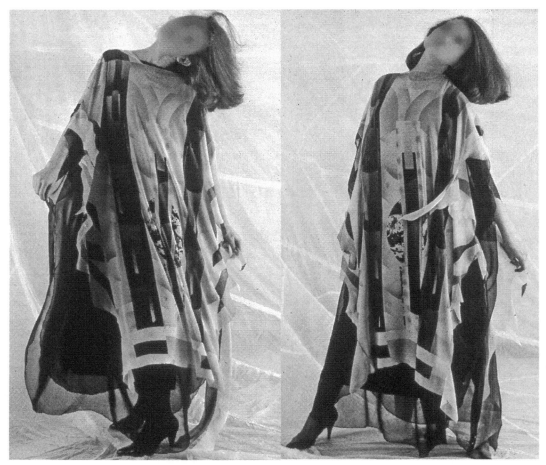

"H" shawl gown

It is 1983, and women aren't wearing, in my mind, fabrics that flatter their natural grace and beauty. I chose the exotic ephemeral material, chiffon, to do my surface design on. Chiffon also allows me to build a gown or dress in layers, which adds more visual variety, movement, and structural dynamics to the whole piece.

▪   ▪   ▪   ▪   ▪   ▪   ▪   ▪

Designing gowns, robes, shawls, kimonos, and kaftans was totally foreign to my experience and lifestyle. Whenever possible, I was outdoors working, fishing, hiking, boating, etc.. I rarely dressed up, and Sarah had no interest in high fashion. The last time I saw her in a formal gown was when we were married in 1967.

In 1989, one of Scott's friends, who came over to play, told me he saw two people he had never seen before, walking down the bathroom hallway. The people were wearing robes that were very fluid and flowed behind them as they walked. His view only lasted a second or so. When the strange people approached the entry to the west bedroom, they disappeared into thin air. I recall my first flashback walking with the tall ones around me wearing robes. I now believe my reason for designing gowns and long flowing cover-ups for swimwear was partially due to the ancient ones I had been around and later seen in my flashbacks.

EMPATHY AND IDEAS | JULY, 1983

In the summer of 1983, Sarah and I go to the Rocky Mountain Unidentified Flying Object Conference (RMUFOC) for the first time. We do not know what to expect, but we want to find out what others think about their experiences with UFOs and aliens. The issue for these conferees is not whether ETs exist or not, but where do they come from, what do they want, and how can we communicate with them?

Leo Sprinkle organizes the event each year, and the conference is held on the University of Wyoming campus in Laramie. The conference covers these topics as well as many lectures and workshops on other-worldly metaphysical topics. We are like babes in the woods and really don't have a clue about most of the metaphysical themes presented and discussed at the conference.

Conferees talk about: Planet X, the Pleiades, strange named galaxies, channeling, the Ananaki, the Egyptian god Isis, Kukulkan, the Feathered Serpent, Vishnu, Sanskrit texts, the third eye, higher self, hypnosis, past life regression, self-hypnosis, propulsion systems, Roswell, etc.. We discover the scope of the UFO phenomena goes way beyond anything we imagined. The conference opens up a whole new world of bizarre ideas for us to think about and consider. We don't know how we fit into the star people's lives and motives but for once we are with other like minds. Their positive and supportive response to us and our stories is reassuring.

During the conference, I take part in a past life regression workshop with several other conferees. I am put into a light hypnotic state, and asked about the future. I predict that by 2027, the only people alive on the planet will be living in caves or underground. When told what I had predicted under hypnosis, I'm puzzled. Where did that kind of idea come from? I have been consciously worrying about nuclear war and the environment, but near total annihilation of the human species has never entered my mind.

Then, another conferee begins screaming and sobbing during his regression session while under hypnosis. He says he is being crucified and the crows are pecking his eyes out and the dogs are eating his feet. It takes several people to comfort him. I am shocked by what conferees blurt out under hypnosis. I can't wait for the workshop to end, so I leave early. I am alarmed by what might ooze out, or on to me if I stayed any longer.

⁂ ⁂ ⁂ ⁂ ⁂ ⁂ ⁂ ⁂

Why did I even think about 2027, that was 44 years away, and I was living in the present, doing the best I could to just survive and keep my sanity. I could not imagine why my subconscious came up with this idea. Was it put in my head by Bucky Fuller in the 1960s, or on February 18, 1982 when I saw the images on the wall, or more recently when I was again with the star people? I didn't believe in gnomes that were shown to me by my subconscious, so why should I have believed in this scary prediction my subconscious dredged up.

Maybe this prognostication was the reason I was so obsessed with building an underground house in a sheltered environment with pure water running nearby. When I couldn't build underground I opted for a bermed, stage three, passive solar home with a super-efficient fireplace that squeezed every BTU possible out of each ounce of wood.

The notion of men-in-black terrorizing people who said they had UFO experiences was brought to our attention at the conference. I was unmoved and the conferees' fears seemed misplaced. As we left Laramie for home, I noticed a large black sedan with dark tinted windows some distance behind us. It piqued my interest and then a flash of fear went through me. I kept the black sedan in my sight and mind. When we reached Cheyenne and turned off from I-80 onto I-25 and headed south towards Denver, the black sedan followed. I sped up, and the black sedan kept pace, staying the same distance behind us. We sped up again; they sped up, again. We slowed down: they slowed down. After 30 miles of this dance, it was time to say, *goodbye*. We were in our Jaguar XJ6L sedan. I put the pedal to the metal and…poof! No more men-in-black behind us.

After we return from RMUFOC, several people we met there or who had heard of us, wanted to come and investigate the property. At first we consented, and a member of the Westminster UFO Society came out to look around. Bruce seemed very knowledgeable and was articulate. He stayed for dinner that evening and told us about "ley lines" and how UFOs were often seen near these energy lines that traverse the earth's surface. It was his opinion that our house was on one or a series of ley lines. We knew very little about the topic, but considered it a possibility since other credible people spoke of ley lines and their existence.

Over dinner, Bruce talked freely about his experiences with UFOs. We were all ears. He alleged that he and three other people were abducted in the middle of Kansas. He didn't say how, but there was missing time and they found themselves out on a gravel road in the Kansas boondocks when they became conscious again.

He went through this long involved story of how they got back to I-70. Then he started talking about a star that played hide and seek behind the moon; all his mail was being stolen by UFOs; his check to his landlord had been lost in the mail which was being tampered with by the aliens; and how miserable the cops treated him because of his belief in UFOs. Finally he left and we could see why the general public found it so hard to believe the stories that came from an "investigator." Had we not had any experiences ourselves, we would have considered him to be absolutely crazy.

We decided not to have any more "investigators" out who did not have a national reputation in the field.

Luckily we made that a policy, for in quick succession, we had all sorts of people who wanted to come out and investigate our home ground. One guy was a dowsing expert who could supposedly identify ley lines and the spaceships from which these entities were coming from. He was to accomplish this identification process by dowsing the sky instead of Mother Earth. Others wanted to hold séances, hold sweat lodge ceremonies, and examine our electrical boxes. Phone calls came from everywhere, and there were as many theories about our happenstance as there were callers and "investigators."

The only investigator who penetrated our defenses that year was Frank M. from California. He called us from Longmont, saying he was on his way to L.A. and would like to have a look around. I was in the middle of a design project so I told him it was OK to come, but he would be on his own. Frank looked over the property and says, "Yep, ley lines!" How he could tell there were ley lines here I never knew, but he went on his way and he wasn't a problem.

What was always amazing about those people was their belief that because they came out to see us, something strange would happen while they were here. I was sure that when we told stories that had transpired over many years, people conceived of them happening in only a week or two! Soon, we distanced ourselves from all investigators for fear they might leak stories to the press or tell tales that would scare the children.

After the conference we also learned about the Metropolitan UFO Society in Denver. They met once a month. We went to one of their meetings and found more support for our belief that star people were benevolent. For several years, we gave the group a yearly update during their December meeting. The Society's members were always courteous, very interesting, and had many suggestions on how to understand what was happening around our home. Most of these people channeled information from celestial entities. We appreciated their support but I secretly didn't believe many of their bizarre stories or methodologies. We were stodgy conservatives compared to their far out ideas. None of them ever asked to come out and investigate our house and property. We were thankful for their respect.

Nothing unusual, like an animal being mutilated, or an ET in the tree happens in our part of the subdivision the rest of the summer of 1983. We hear noises around the house and secondhand stories about our neighbor to the north. It is alleged that occasionally when our neighbor drives home from work late at night and crosses over the ravine's culvert, his car head lights dim to almost nothing. When he gets to the other side of the culvert, his head lights come back to full strength. How similar his experiences are to mine with the flashlight in 1981 and again in the spring of this year.

One spring night, as I walk down to the studio, my flashlight again mysteriously dims down to nothing as it had in 1981. After passing that undefined point, the light comes back up. Later that night, I go back to the house and get another flashlight and walk back down to the studio. I hold both flashlights at the same height and direction. As I reach a certain spot, both flashlights dim at the same time and then after I pass by the spot, both lights come up to full strength. Weird. It appears that something just absorbs the beams of light. Whatever this thing is has to be transparent or I would have seen it, but the identity of the "light snatcher" remains a mystery.

Another light mystery occurred late one summer evening. A neighbor friend, Ann, is walking down the road with Sarah and Breana at dusk. As they approach the culvert bridge going north, there is a flash of brilliant yellow-orange light that comes from behind them. The light is so bright and low to the ground, that they can see their long shadows directly on the road ahead. They quickly turn around in unison, thinking a car is approaching from behind. But as they turn around, they are surprised to see nothing at all; no car, no light. Their shadows disappear and it is dark again

◼ ◼ ◼ ◼ ◼ ◼ ◼ ◼

The place in the drive where my flashlights dimmed is about 350 feet from the culvert bridge. Was it possible that some invisible force could absorb the energy from my neighbor's car battery as he passed over the culvert bridge, thus dimming his lights? Perhaps the entity regenerated itself, and could move around grabbing energy wherever it could. When it was fully charged and excited, it gave off a burst of yellow-orange light like Sarah, Ann, and Breana saw as they approached the culvert? Could the entity draw energy from people?

Wasn't it the mythological Grendal who brought darkness wherever he traveled? Maybe Grendal wasn't a mythological creature. Was it an alien entity or a super magnetic spot absorbing my light? I couldn't help thinking about our neighbor's time loss and how he might have walked into another dimension. Possibly, the phenomena were related.

Years later, a black bear was killed not far from the culvert bridge. The Colorado Division of Wildlife collected the bear's carcass. The forearms were ripped out of their sockets and the bear died of shock. There was no evidence a car hit the bear. I thought the bear got tangled up with whatever lived in the ravine or culvert and was killed.

"Art is the marriage of the conscious and unconscious."

JEAN COLTEAU

*"The greatest
obstacle to discovery
is not ignorance.
It is the illusion of
knowledge."*

DANIEL J. BOORSTEIN

CHAPTER FIVE | 1984

INTO THE NIGHT | JANUARY 13, 1984

Almost a year has passed since Scott saw the star person in the pine tree west of the house. I have not consciously meditated since then and the year in between was relatively uneventful. We buy a large TV satellite dish. Now, like most people, we stay inside and watch TV during the cold winter months. I have installed a really great looking, efficient, contemporary, airtight wood stove in the family room. With a little wood we can heat the upstairs and make the family room cozy on cold winter nights.

We all enjoy the radiant warmth, and on this Friday night, January 13, everyone but me is sound asleep on the couch or the floor of the family room. At approximately 9:30 p.m. I look out the upstairs entry door. A very fine, dry snow is falling, the type of very cold weather snow that typically blows in from the north. This kind of snow can fill our lower driveway with drifts three to four feet deep.

I'm wide awake, bored, and decide to drive our Bronco SUV up and down the driveway to keep a path open to the main road 800 feet away. I put on my heavy duty snow suit, grab a bottle of beer from the refrigerator, and go outside. The snow storm is almost over, the wind is down, and only fine champagne snow flits erratically through the frigid night air. The night is black as pitch, but I can see. The new six inches of white snow illuminates the ground ahead of me.

The temperature is about ten degrees above zero. I get in the Bronco and turn the ignition key. Nothing happens; no clicking, no interior lights, nothing. The battery is absolutely dead. Odd, the battery is a new 72-month Die Hard. I drove the Bronco to Denver on Wednesday and the battery worked perfectly. I check the battery connections. They are on tight and connected at both ends. I turn the ignition key again and again, but the Bronco will not start.

By now, the snow storm is completely over and I don't feel ready to go to bed. I decide to go down to the studio and continue working on a fabric design. I cannot help but notice and appreciate how serene and beautiful the night is. On my way to the studio, I kick the snow up in front of me as I walk along. The night is so quiet, I can hear the new snow I kick up ahead of me settling back down in hushed silence to the snow covered earth.

BITTEN? | JANUARY 14, 1984

Saturday I wake up about 8:00 a.m.; however, I cannot get out of bed. I am sicker than I have ever been before in my life and for no apparent reason. I'm nauseated and my whole body aches. A spot on my left wrist feels like it is on fire. The intermittent sharp pains that shoot to my wrist bone from the wound are excruciatingly painful. To my surprise, the area that hurts so badly is marked by a deep, bluish-red, rough-edged, rectangular shape on the side of my left wrist. The wound is partially over an artery.

The wound measures about an inch long by an inch wide. It is reddish-blue in the center and spreads to a darker red on the outside edges. On closer inspection, running down the center of the wound are a series of four darker bluish-red marks that are approximately one-fourth inch by one-fourth inch with one-fourth inch spaces between them. The bluish-red marks in the center look like they were made by rectangular mechanical teeth. The teeth must have been shaped like dull square chisels. The surface of the area is dry and crusty and reminds me of an incredible hickey. The wound isn't puffy or filled with body fluids. I have no inclination to bandage it, nor do I think about seeing our family physician. What would I tell him; I was bitten by an alien?

I eat breakfast in bed for the first time in my life. I promptly throw up. The rest of the day I lie in bed, vacillating between fits of extreme pain, confusion, anxiety,

Note: The following photographs in Chapter 5 have not been touched up or altered and contain dust and scratches.

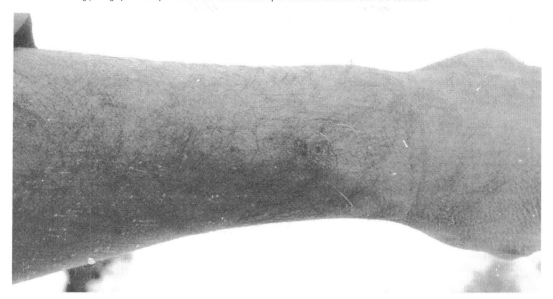

Photograph of wound on my left wrist

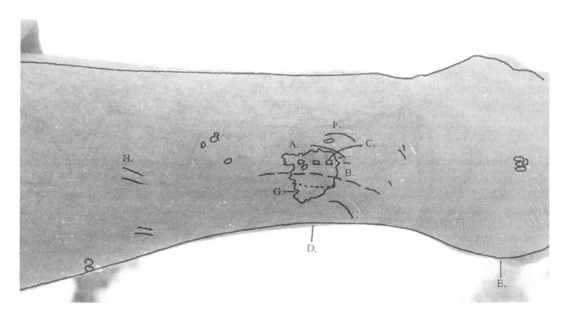

Photograph of wound on my left wrist with overlay: A. bite or suction mark over or around an artery. **B.** Artery. **C.** teeth or clamp marks inside the wound. **D.** My arm. **E.** My hand. **F.** White arm hair. **G.** Rough boundary of wound area. **H.** Dust particles on original negative.

nausea, drowsiness, and a fitful sleep. During the time I am in a waking state, I try to remember how the wound on my wrist got there. It wasn't on my wrist when I left the house Friday night. I can't remember anything beyond starting for the studio to work on a fabric design. Sarah can't remember my coming to bed and I can't remember coming to bed either. Usually, I wake her when returning from the studio. What happened between 9:45 p.m. January 13th and 8:00 a.m. January 14th is a mystery.

During one of my half sleeping states, I have a disturbing, but very vivid dream. I become aware that I am sitting in a large one-piece, banana-type bucket seat. The back of the seat in front of me is much like a commercial airline seat but devoid of any pockets or change of material surfaces or textures. It is so high I can't begin to see over it.

As the veil of confusion in my mind begins to lift, I realize to my amazement that the seats are enormous. I am like a 5 year old child sitting in a gigantic adult seat. My legs stick straight out in front of me and I don't know what would happen if I lean all the way back in the chair. So I sit erect in an uncomfortable position in this gigantic seat. Who are these people whose butts fit on the seat with their back resting on the back of the seat and their feet touching the floor?

I begin to have the distinct impression that I am not to look around but to stare at the back of the seat in front of me. However, I can also sense there are other people in the area with me. After a time, and with difficulty, I slowly turn my head a miniscule to the right and roll my eyes as far around as I can in that direction. In the foggy, luminous atmosphere I can make out portholes on the adjacent wall that are maybe ten feet away. I sense there is a row of people across the aisle sitting next to these portholes. I strain to roll my eyes a little further to the right so I can see more of where I am.

Groggy and confused, I can tell little except that the most immediate person to my right looks human, but he also looks odd, strange. Maybe I am in such a mental fog that anyone would have looked strange to me. For one thing, this gigantic person sitting near a porthole fits in the oversized seat. The features are humanoid, but somehow animalistic. It must be a male due to the amount of facial hair.

About this time, he rolls his large eyes around in my direction. They are gigantic and I swear his eyes extend around his head farther than on a normal human. Our eyes meet for a millisecond. His dark eyes acknowledge my existence. He does not move but gives me this slightly malevolent, all-knowing smile that puzzles and frightens me. I can

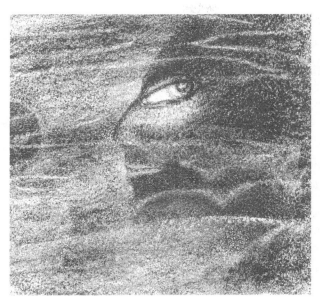
Drawing of strange person on the ship

tell by his expression we are not equals. A blush of dread washes through me. For some reason, I know they have gone to a lot of trouble getting me and they aren't taking me on a joy ride.

The person across the aisle from me seems to be dressed in dark clothing and his facial features look Middle Eastern. He reminds me of men I have seen on bas-relief stone walls of the early Sumerian civilization. I can swear most of his face is covered with short, fine, dark reddish-brown hairs like an animal. The short hair seems like it is packed down flat on the contours of his face. However, with my foggy perceptions, everything goes in and out of focus.

I only have a fraction of a second to see and sense what I think I see, when "WHACK!" I am brought to full attention by a sharp painful gouge to my right kidney. I feel like I have been hit hard with the metallic head of a riding crop. Intuitively knowing these gigantic people will not tolerate disobedient acts on my part, I quickly roll my eyes back to staring at the seat in front of me. Then I drift off into an anxious never-never land and the seat ahead of me melts from my conscious view.

Suddenly I wake up. In my confused state I become momentarily, wildly ecstatic! I feel like I want to cry with joy when I realize I'm in my bed, not on an alien craft with giant strange-looking people. What a relief! This dream is like other dreams; too real, too intense, and foreign to my life style; bizarre, but never to be forgotten. Life goes foggy again and I lapse back into an uncomfortable, fitful sleep, but at least I'm in my bed.

All day Saturday the children mostly stay inside and play or help Sarah cook pastries. The dogs go outside only for brief periods of time. The temperatures outside remain in the low teens. For the first time in my life, the mysterious sickness keeps me in bed until four or five o'clock this afternoon. Sarah and Breana cook a special dinner of chicken and dumplings for my 90 year old Grandmother Johnson. She is living in an apartment in Castle Rock. This evening, we eat dinner with her, but we are back home and ready for bed by 8:30 p.m.. I am still sick, but the sickness is beginning to leave as mysteriously as it arrived. My wrist is still throbbing and painful.

Before I go to bed, I take my nightly tour of the house and check all the doors to make sure they're locked. They are secure. I have barely gotten to bed when Breana comes running in.

"Daddy, Daddy, I heard a noise down in the kitchen!" she whispers excitedly.

"I just came back from the kitchen and there is nothing down there and the doors are locked," I tell her.

I want to go recheck, but I'm still sick and tired. Besides, I have just come from downstairs. I can't imagine someone coming into the house moments after I have toured the area.

On the other hand, I don't want to thwart her diligence in reporting noises, so I say, "What did you hear?"

"I heard three thuds and some scurrying around," she says.

"What did the thuds sound like?" I ask.

"Like when someone drops wood logs on the floor."

I know exactly what that sounds like and I say, "Well, Breana I didn't hear anything, so everything is okay. Why don't you go back to bed?"

She fiddles around with the bed covers and then with desperate reluctance, she goes back to her bedroom. I'm puzzled because she had heard noises and I didn't. How could I miss such loud and distinct sounds?

JACOB'S LADDER | JANUARY 15, 1984

On Sunday morning, we have our traditional breakfast. I feel 100% better. The sun is out, but the temperature stays in the low teens. After breakfast, the kids put on their snowsuits and go outside. No sooner has Breana gone outside than she returns to the kitchen door yelling about strange tracks in the snow. Breana is well versed in identifying the tracks of all the animals that live in our little canyon. I know she must have discovered something unusual to draw it to our attention. The dogs are called in to keep them from destroying the strange tracks with their paw prints. There is great intellectual anticipation and emotional electricity in the air as we file out the kitchen door to see what Breana has found. I am excited. For four years we have hoped for some sort of physical evidence to substantiate the

Circle Photo 1: Strange tracks in the snow

Circle Photo 1 with overlay: Strange tracks with overlay showing two sets of footprints near the center of the circle. One set of footprints appeared to be twice as big as the smaller set. **A.** Large set of prints. **B.** Small set of prints.

existence of the entities that have caused all the strange events occurring around the house and to us.

I tell Sarah to bring the camera and I step out of the kitchen and head east. The first of three strange tracks was straight ahead of me (Circle Photo 1).

What I see is a beautiful circle that, at once, becomes a shrine to me and a symbol, expressed in snow, of the ephemeral, mysterious existence of our visitors. When the snow melts, all we think we have as evidence of alien visitation will be gone. "Now you see me, now you don't." There isn't much doubt about who made the circles in the snow, star people. We have no idea as to how they made the circles, but we know the circles weren't made by pranksters.

Walking toward the circle, we are excited to see what I think are two different sets of human-looking footprints in the center of the circle. We are mesmerized as to what we are looking at and who belongs to the foot prints. I also see what appears to be one footprint outside the circle; otherwise there are no footprints that indicate someone just walks out of the center of the circle. It appears the inscribed circle in the snow had to be made by something rotating around an invisible core or from something above. The path in the snow that defines the circle seemed to have been pushed by something going in a clockwise direction.

When I walk up to the circle I just have to touch it (Circle Photo 2). Whoever or whatever made the circle represents the thought processes of someone from a different, planet, galaxy, or dimension. The ground below and around the circle is now also sacred to me, and I feel insignificant as I gaze down at the track in the snow. Now that I am close-up, I notice the circle seems to be made by a thin-walled cylinder that rotated around in a clockwise direction. My belief the circle was made by a cylindrical force field is a guess or a subconscious thought based on a previous personal experience. I cannot conceive of anything else that could create a similar circle around a set of footprints without affecting the objects inside the circle. The wall of this imaginary cylindrical force field appears and disappears as the terrain and depth of the snow varies. The scale of the circular path is revealed by my image next to it. I am 5'10" and weigh 170 pounds.

I reach down and put my hand out to roughly measure the width of the tracks. It varies from seven and one-half inches to nine and one-half inches, depending on the lay of the land, and depth of the snow (Circle Photo 3). The ten to fifteen degree

Circle Photo 2: Scale of my body to the circle.

Circle Photo 2 with overlay: I stood 5' 10" tall. **A.** The track of a circular beam with a clockwise rotation. The vibrating beam wall measured from 3/4" to 1" in diameter, making a hand width of approximately 7 ½". The vibration of the craft distorted the 7 ½" diameter circle. **B.** Mysterious spray of snow kicked up by the footprints forming in the center of the circle.

Fahrenheit snow is consistent in its grain and density and appears to be lightly brushed by the rotating force field. The edges of the circle seem to indicate that the rotation of the field moved at a steady rate of speed. Where the snow is deepest, the speed of the rotating force field spewed the snow beyond the nine and one-half inch track and gives away the speed and direction of the force field rotation.

The longer I look at the tracks of the circle, the more I'm convinced I am looking at the effects of a force field of some kind. Attempting to give the circle a sense of physical scale, I lay down my 36 inch ruler inside the circle.

Later, I get a light rope and Sarah and I stretch it across the diameter of the circle. It measures seven foot, three inches from outside edge to outside edge. In measuring the circle with the light rope, it leaves a track across the circle which adds some confusion when analyzing the photographs.

The footprints in the center are the most enigmatic aspect of the circle (Circle Photo 4). The larger prints appear to be twice the length of the smaller prints. No footprints are found from someone walking out of the center of the circle as you would expect. The people who made the footprints just disappear into thin air. It seems logical that they had come down from above, considering the events that have occurred around the house. There is no evidence to suggest people walked up to a point and were taken up into space. What happened to the owners of the footprints is a mystery.

God, I hate to disturb the circle but I need to photograph the footprints in the center (Circle Photo 5). The snow would eventually melt, and the sooner I photograph the footprints the better the physical evidence will be. Once I get closer to the footprints, I see that the owner of the larger footprints appeared to remain stationery, while the owner of the smaller prints moved around a lot. Then I conclude there are two sets of small footprints in the center with the owner of the larger footprints. Possibly, the two smaller people were adjusting something in the center of the circle or supporting the stationary person who did not move. The longer I study the footprints, the more I think the owner of the larger prints and both sets of smaller prints just floated out of the circle headed north. They didn't walk out; they floated out, but how?

Their feet produced drag marks that were broad at first, and as the people elevated, less of the foot was touching the snow, and thus a thinner track was created as they rose above the surface of the snow. The drag marks in the snow pointed north, perhaps to

Circle Photo 3: My hand over the beam down track.

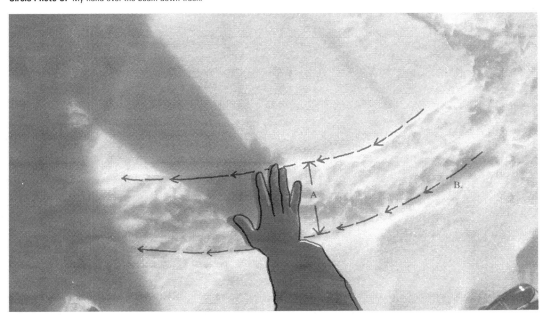

Circle Photo 3 with overlay: A. My hand gave scale to the beam down track in the snow. The beam down track was from 7 1/2" to 9 1/2" wide. **B.** Soft edges of the rotating beam down force field in the snow.

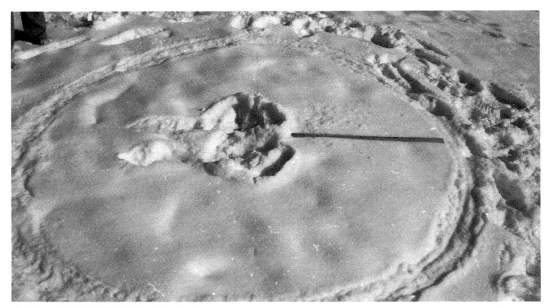

Circle Photo 4: Interior of the circle and the footprints.

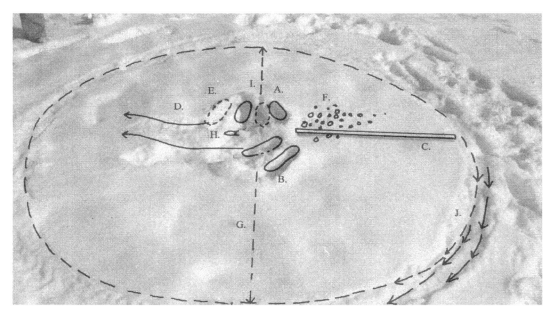

Circle Photo 4 with overlay: A. 4 1/2 " footprints. **B.** 10 1/2" footprints. **C.** 36" ruler. **D.** Drag marks in the snow headed toward the driveway and the house. **E.** Overlapping small footprints showing a lot of movement or the footprints of a second star person. **F.** Splash of snow from near the footprints. **G.** 7'3" diameter of the circle. **H.** 1" hole in the center of the circle. **I.** Mark made by string line while measuring the circle. **J.** Beam width rotating clockwise and vibrating.

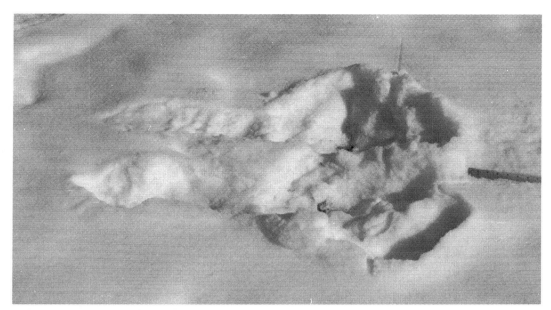

Circle Photo 5: Close up of the interior of the circle.

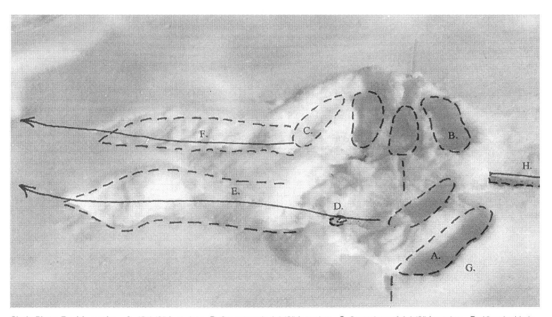

Circle Photo 5 with overlay: A. 10 1/2" footprints. **B.** Star person's 4 1/2" footprints. **C.** Second set of 4 1/2" footprints. **D.** 1" melted hole and center of 7'3" circle. **E.** Direction of A's path out of the circle. **F.** Direction of C's footprint out of the circle guiding A to the driveway and the house. **G.** Edge of footprint formed around my 10 ½" foot. **H.** Tip of 36" ruler. **I.** Mark made by string line stretched across the circle to measure its diameter.

the upstairs of the house. The other set of small footprints indicates the entity must have elevated straight up in the air. What was this airborne person doing?

An uneasy thought creeps over me; maybe the larger footprints are mine. What if I were the person in the circle? It might have taken two small star people to move me back to my bedroom. Perhaps I was being returned after the ride on a ship with portholes that my flashback brought to my attention on Saturday morning. Maybe, if it were me, I was immobilized and that is why my prints did not move around in the circle.

It is my opinion that one star person lifted me up from behind and the second one guided me out of the circle toward the house (Circle Photo 6; drawing). The second star person made the single step outside the circle as it launched itself up into the air. Both guided me toward the house and back to bed.

As I was lifted up, my limp body let my feet dangle down and leave the drag mark in the snow on my side of the circle. I think the other drag mark in the snow was made by the star person guiding me toward my bed. As he aided me in moving out of the circle, he dragged his left foot, creating the drag mark that parallels mine as we moved toward the house. I think his right foot created the footprint on the outside of the circle. I believe he used this foot to provide the necessary leverage to launch us into the air and out of the circle. Other than that small footprint, I find no other small footprints in between the circle and the house. The three of us were evidently airborne once we were outside the circle.

This very unusual small footprint outside of the circle, is in direct line with the drag marks in the snow heading north (Circle Photo 7). The foot that made the print came straight down into the snow. The star person had a stride of over five feet. That length of stride is a pretty neat trick for a star person who is probably three and a half foot tall and has short legs.

Even stranger than the drag marks, was the way the ten to fifteen degree Fahrenheit snow responded to the foot entering the snow outside the circle. The foot entering the snow threw snow out like slush splashing out and away from the foot's impact. It has been my experience that a dry, light, fluffy snow would not respond to a foot's impact on it in that manner. Did the owner have hot feet or what?

Stepping into the circle wearing my Moon Boots I take close up photographs (Circle Photo 8). I know I'm partially screwing up the only evidence proving the existence of

Circle Photo 6: Drawing of me being flown out of the center of the circle

Circle Photo 6 with overlay: I believe I was flown to my bedroom in the fashion depicted in the drawing. I also believe the marks in the snow bear witness to this theory.

Circle Photo 7: The star person's first footstep outside of the circle into the cold snow.

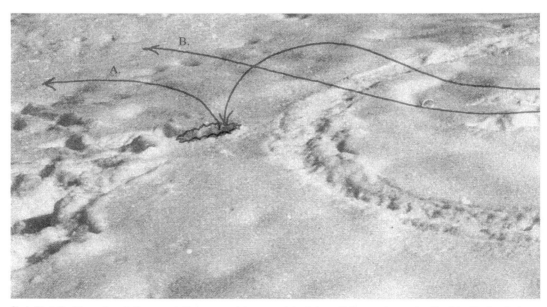

Circle Photo7 with overlay: A. Star person's first step out of the center of the circle to aid the second person in taking B (me) back to the house and my bed. The first footprint out of the circle appeared to splash down into the cold snow that was 5 to 10 degrees Fahrenheit. The footprint was headed north and exactly parallel to the direction of the drag marks out of the center of the circle. **B.** My flight path out of the circle.

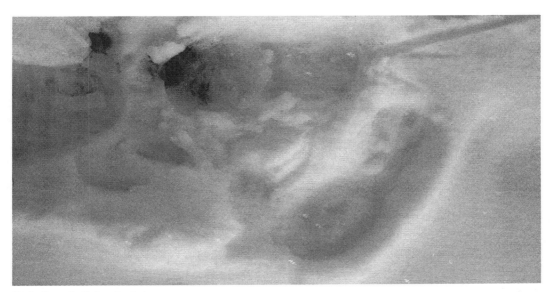

Circle Photo 8: My footprints in the snow.

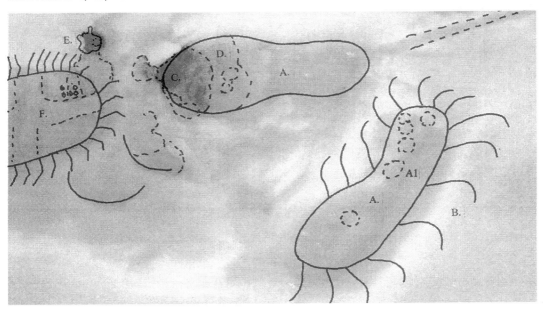

Circle Photo 8 with overlay: A. My 10 ½" footprint in the center of the circle. **A1.** Strange hemispheric protrusions and indentations on the bottom of the smooth footprint. **B.** Smooth walled prints suggested to me that I was materialized on the spot. The snow seemed to form around my foot. **C.** Toe of my footprint (with bootie on?) showed how hot the area around the center of the circle was. **D.** Melt line expanding away from the center of the circle. **E.** Hot hole in the center of the circle. Four years later, Geiger Counter readings registered .10 milliroentgens of radiation per hour at approximately this spot in the yard. **F.** My Moon Boot print created straight edges pressed into the snow, near the hot spot that was still hot 24-48 hours later when this photo was taken on Sunday, January 15, 1984.

small people coming and going on our property and that they have extraordinary capabilities.

Once inside the circle, the first thing I do is measure the impression of the small set of footprints. These small prints measured four and one-half inches in length. The large set of prints measures ten and one-half inches, the exact size of my bare foot. The arches and shape of the footprint are a mirror image of my feet. I'm excited, circumspect, and a bit fearful, but now 99% sure I stand looking at my own prints. Now I'm a slightly horrified witness to the last part of my abduction experience I think started on January 13th.

■   ■   ■   ■   ■   ■   ■   ■

I knew my footprints were made Friday night or during the early morning of Saturday, the 14th. I was right in my belief I stood looking at my own prints for a number of reasons. I could not remember coming to bed that night after I headed down to work in the studio. Sarah could not remember my coming to bed, either. I normally would wake her when I came back from working. I remembered that the Bronco would not start, even though it had a new battery. I had this horribly painful wound on my wrist. How I got it, I did not know. And then there was the strange sickness that kept me in bed most of Saturday. Of course, there was the bizarre dream of being on a ship that had portholes instead of square windows. And then there was the humungous, dark, malevolent-looking person sitting across the aisle flashing me an all-knowing grin. My snowsuit and Moon Boots were not put back in the hall closet as I would have done coming back from the studio. Instead, they were put in our bedroom closet not far from our bed.

The countless flashbacks I had over the past four years and the star person in the tree that Scott had seen made me realize that I was abducted on Friday night or early Saturday morning. I was looking at my past inside that circle.

Looking at my footprints in the snow with small alien footprints near my own was mind boggling and emotionally numbing. The ETs had evidently taken my Moon Boots off or they would have made the prints in the circle instead of the smooth soled footprints. What was once an abstraction in my reality is now concrete fact in my mind; I was abducted! I didn't feel blessed, cursed, or anything else that I recall. I was just relieved to know for sure that I hadn't been dreaming all this shit up.

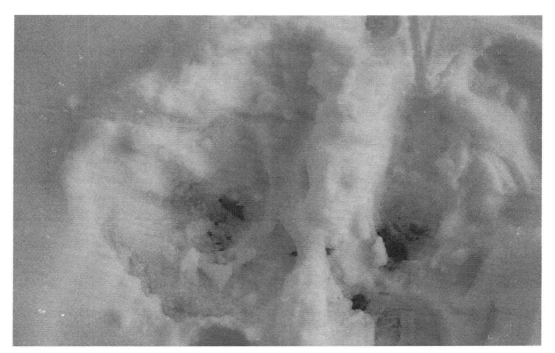

Circle Photo 9: The star person's footprints in the center of the circle

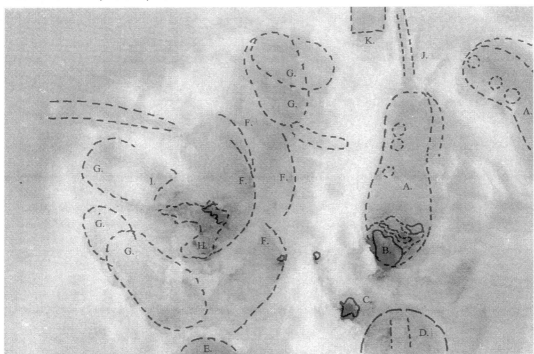

Circle Photo 9 with overlay: A. My 10 ½" footprint with strange protrusions on the sole. **B.** Melted snow near my left foot toes, notice the heel of that same foot was cool and set high on cold snow, not the ground. **C.** Center of circle showing snow melted and heat spreading away from the center point. **D.** Moon Boot print, compare to edges of my 10 ½" footprint that wasn't pressed into the snow. **E.** Heel of star person's footprint. **F.** Star person's footprint inside the circle near G. **G.** Muted footprints. **H.** Warm area on star person's side of the circle. **I.** Warm area extended many inches from the center hole to this point. **J.** String line mark in snow. **K.** End of 36" ruler.

Off and on over the years, I studied the photographs taken that day. The following were some of my observations and theories.

I noticed my footprints had abnormal protrusions (Circle Photo 8). I knew I didn't have protrusions or indentations on the bottom of my feet. I must have been wearing some kind of bootie over my feet to keep me warm and they came with protrusions and indentations. Had I not been wearing some light weight bootie or sock, my toes would have left their prints in the snow. If my bare foot had come straight down into five inches of soft snow, the protrusion of my ankle bones would be visible. There were no such protrusions showing.

I began looking at my right footprint in the snow. The toe of my foot covering showed that the ground was warm there and when it touched the snow my weight went all the way down to the grassy, leaf-covered ground below (Circle Photo 9). The area had to be hot or warm as my toe was on the ground and my heel was elevated inches above in the snow. Why was my toe on hot ground and my heel up above on cold snow? My left footprint showed no difference in elevation between toe and heel.

I saw an ominous hole in the snow that seemed to be the center and hottest point within the circle. Whatever made the hole melted the snow all the way to the ground and the heat radiated out from there. When my weight was put on the hot spot, it compressed and melted the snow revealing grasses and leaves.

Why was this area so hot? I began to visualize a shaft of microwave that was beamed down from a craft above. The thin-walled force field radiated and rotated around this hot center core or shaft of energy.

The more I looked at the photographs of my prints, the more obvious it became that I did not come down a pole, nor was I lowered to this spot. The snow appeared to grow around my feet (Circle Photo 10). There was not a straight up and down wall of snow around my foot as it should have been if I had stepped down on the snow. The snow just peeled up and away from the outside edge of the base of my foot.

When I stepped into the circle wearing my Moon Boots (Circle Photo 8), the snow was compressed down and the edges were clear and distinct; not soft, pushed up and peeled away from the foot like the prints in the center. Where my big toe was, inside my Moon Boot, the snow was compressed down to the ground. The ground in that area was still warm around the center hole more than 24 hours later. How bizarre, my footprints

Circle Photo 10: Star person's footprint showing drag mark and leaping out of the circle

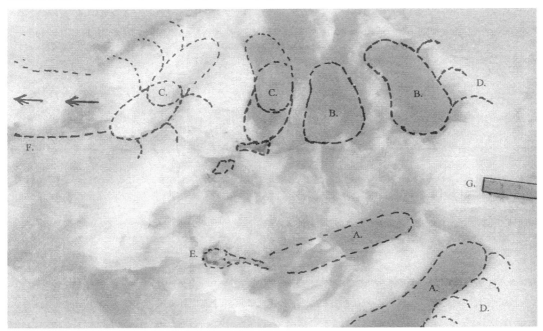

Circle Photo 10 with overlay: **A.** My 10 ½" footprint. **B.** Star person number one. **C.** Star person number two. **D.** Soft edges of B's footprint suggested star person was materialized on the spot. **E.** Center of circle and warm area around it. **F.** Flow pattern of star person C sliding out of the circle towards the driveway and the house, and making drag marks in the snow that were parallel to those made by my feet A as I would eventually be guided through the air and to the house. **G.** End of the 36" ruler. Refer back to Circle Photo 7 for my visual description of this event.

in the circle made Friday night or Saturday morning, came face to face with my Moon Boot prints made on Sunday.

Even stranger was the idea I had that as the force field rotated, reconstructing me and my "beam mates" on the spot. My thought was that we were materialized from our feet to the top of our heads. I was looking at a graphic representation of myself being materialized. Right next to my Moon Boot print was the hot spot that measured one inch in diameter. Five years later, two radiation experts scanned the area with their Geiger counters and found the area where the circle had been, was giving off more radiation than the rest of the yard.

To the right of my Moon Boot prints were two boot impressions evidently made by one of my companions. I thought that star person was moving around the core before it helped me out of the circle.

After further studying the center of the circle photos, I came to more conclusions. The sharp edges of the four and one-half inch footprints indicated a rigid boot or shoe that was totally different from my soft edged footprint. The small prints did not have a tread or small protrusions or indentions as my footprint did. I somehow thought those booties I wore allowed me to fly or levitate off the ground. Perhaps the Egyptians and Incas used similar devices to move huge stones to make the Pyramids and Machu Pichu?

After Sarah and I studied the prints, I called neighbors Steve and Joe over to look at the circles and footprints (Circle Photo 11). I thought they might have some different interpretations of the tracks in the snow.

Our neighbors were looking at the intact circle in Circle Photo 11. The other two circles were difficult to see in this photograph due to the number of dog and children tracks that went through them earlier. I photographed Joe and Steve from the roof of the house. I was up there looking for similar prints. I saw no other tracks, circular or otherwise, on the roof or anywhere else around the house. Later I went up on top of the mesa and looked down on the entire valley with binoculars. From that commanding position I still did not see any other circular prints or suspicious tracks.

In Circle Photo 11, circle one, "B", was closest to the east side of the house and kitchen area. This circle was within 12 feet of the kitchen wall. Circle two, "C," was the middle circle. All the circles seemed to be made in the same manner and each had footprints, a center point, and melted areas around a center core. They appeared to be

Circle Photo 11: Three circles in the snow

Circle Photo 11 with overlay: A. Neighbors Joe and Steve looking at the beam-down tracks. **B.** Circle 1, 10′ from the east wall of the kitchen. **C.** Circle 2. **D.** Circle 3, the undisturbed circle. **E.** Direction of drag marks and footprints coming out of D, heading to driveway and house. **F.** Flower pot located 12 feet from the kitchen's sliding glass door. **G.** Center of circle 3, D. **H.** Footprints from people coming to look at the circles. **I.** Drag marks and footprints coming out or into circle 1, B and circle 2, C.

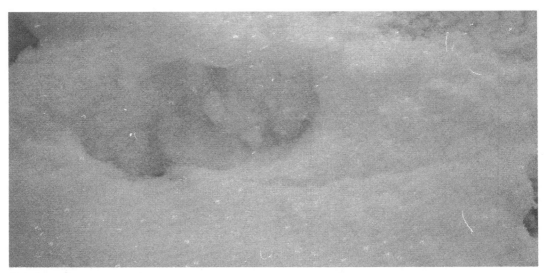

Circle Photo 12: Star person's 7 ½" footprint in the snow near the kitchen's east wall and circle 1.

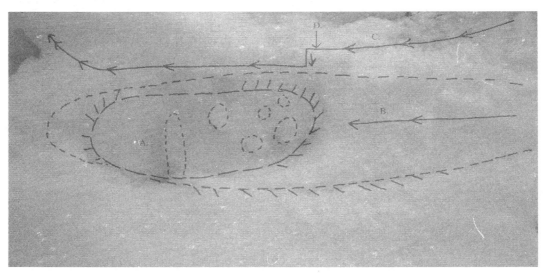

Circle Photo 12 with overlay: A. 7 ½" star person's footprint with strange marks on sole of boot or snow crumbs that fell into the impression. **B.** Direction of footprint going through the snow as it slid horizontally, skimming the snow surface then coming straight down into the snow, making the foot's distinct impression. **C.** Cross section schematic of the foot moving into the snow, making the foot's impression, then coming out of the snow. **D.** Compare this footprint to the 4 ½" footprint made outside the circle in Circle Photo 7. The walls of the 7 ½" footprint are straight up and down and the foot crushed and compressed the snow to make the print. The cold snow was also brushed as the foot slid into it before coming down to make the impression in the snow. The foot in Circle Photo 7. came straight down and the impact made the snow react strangely to this star person's foot, boot or...? The snow in Circle Photo 12. was the same temperature as in the Circle Photo 7. The 4 ½" foot exploded the snow; the 7 ½" foot compressed the snow.

near clones of the intact circle, "D".

Circle one and two, "B" and "C," were made on sloping land, yet the track maintained a perfect circular path. The beam was adjustable and altered its vertical dimension as it traversed the irregular contours of the land. Circle one and two, "B" and "C," were difficult to map because of the number of dog, children, and adult footprints that went through them. To complicate matters, it appeared something, or someone, had been dragged in or out of the two circles. Prints were obliterated that could have helped tell a more complete story of that night. I wished the first two circles had been as pristine as circle three, "D." Maybe I could have reconstructed what was being moved in and out of the circles. That could have told us volumes about how I interacted with whoever was in the two other circles.

Joe was an avid outdoorsman and former owner of a sporting goods store. He was an outfitter, cross country ski guide, and ski instructor. Joe had seen and analyzed a lot of snow in his life and said he had never seen prints like these before. Nor did he know how or who could have made them.

Closest to the kitchen and circle one, "B," I discovered two unusual footprints that were outside the circle. I photographed what I thought was the left footprint (Circle Photo 12). This larger alien footprint measured seven and one-half inches long and its matching footprint was seven feet away and appeared to fit the right foot. A stride of that distance from someone with a seven and one-half inch foot, was in my mind, very significant.

The footprint indicated that the hard edged boot or shoe slid horizontally through the snow for over a foot and then dropped straight down which ruled out the possibility that the individual jumped from where I found the first footprint in the snow seven feet away.

Had the person jumped in a normal fashion, gravity would have the boot slide at an angle to a stop, not skim horizontally and then drop vertically. The boot was then lifted more or less slightly forward and straight up out of the snow. The same walking process was repeated in the second print I found. If this seven and one-half inch footprint was compared to the four and one-half inch footprint found in Circle Photo 7, it would be apparent that there was a great difference in the walking manner and the response of the snow to the walker's boot or shoe.

The four and one-half inch foot in Circle Photo 7, came straight down into the snow which appeared to splash away from it. This didn't make sense since the snow's temperature was the same as for the seven and one-half inch footprint found in Circle Photo 12.

The snow did not splash away in Circle Photo 12; the foot goes straight down and compresses the snow in a normal fashion. I saw no tread marks on the footprint.

The gait of the person reminded me of the way herons and cranes move through the water stalking their prey; very calculating and deliberate. I imagined the boots were made of metal or some heavy material that made the wearer walk as it did. The larger footprints were moving northeast toward the driveway and could have intersected the smaller star people flying me back to bed. After the second step, I found no more seven and one-half inch footprints; they just disappeared maybe into the air or were lost under the dogs' and children's footprints.

■　■　■　■　■　■　■　■

Sunday afternoon January 15th, I found my Friday night bottle of beer on the drafting table in the studio. It was half full and partially flat. The Bronco started on the first try that same afternoon. I finished breaking a drivable trail through some small snow drifts to the main road by 4:00 p.m. The wound on my wrist healed up almost overnight. The spot was quickly replaced by premature white hair. In 30 years, the artery under the bite mark will show signs of distress and will be lumpy and no longer smooth like the visible artery on my right wrist.

I still wondered how, why, and when were the circles created on that cold weekend in January of 1984 (Circle Photo 13).

For a few days after January 15th, I believed that I would never be of interest to star people again. It was my belief at the time that whatever had been injected into me when I was nine was taken from me on Friday night. To me, the wound on my wrist was evidence of its extraction. I envisioned a mechanical suction device with teeth attached to my wrist over the artery. The suction device then sucked out most of my blood, leaving just enough to keep me alive. I considered myself an emptied Petri dish and would no longer be of value to them. Or maybe I was a delicious Bloody Mary? I felt relieved, like I had paid my final dues for being initiated into this "special" fraternity of people.

Circle Photo 13: Me looking down at the circle, closest to the house.

Circle Photo 13 with overlay: A. Circle 1, A, closest to the east wall of the kitchen. **B.** Circle 2, B, with human, dog, and alien footprints going to and from centers of circles A and B. **C.** Intact circle 3, C. **D.** Center of circle A with footprints. **E.** Main path of children and dogs from kitchen door or southeast end of the house to the barn and driveway. **F.** Me pondering circle A, with drag marks. **G.** Flower pot on east patio by kitchen wall.

The noises Breana heard Saturday night really muddied the intellectual water as to when the circles were made. Her account of three sharp thuds from something hitting the kitchen floor on Saturday night complicated matters. I was convinced the circles manifested themselves on Friday night. However, could it have been only one circle was made with me in it on Friday night or Saturday morning?

The other two circles could have been made on Saturday night. Perhaps the three thuds Breana heard were three star people being beamed down into the kitchen. The star people were then beamed up outside the house after they took something from the kitchen. Possibly, whatever was taken struggled and thus created the drag marks by the two circles? If that were the case, then the analysis of previous events made by Ben, the president of the Metropolitan UFO Society, in 1983, was a mind blower. I was beginning to realize that he might be way ahead of the left brained intellectuals who were pondering the UFO phenomena.

For several days after January 15th I do not have any more dreams or flashbacks of the ride in the alien craft. I feel vindicated in my new thoughts that I am not usable anymore. I think I'm too old to be of some biological value. Part of me feels like a member of a sleeper cell waiting to be called up to help with-who knows what. My more analytical left brain thinks I am just another discarded hunk of humanity.

※　※　※　※　※　※　※　※

Following the weekend of January 13th-15th, I couldn't get the thought out of my head as to how I was materialized out in the snow as I believed. I showed no visible changes in my physical appearance. I then thought if I could be broken down into a zillion little atomic particles I would or could become invisible if my particles were spread out over a large area. To be materialized, I first would have to be dematerialized.

If that were possible and I was reconstructed, what could keep the star people from also dematerializing themselves and their craft? They could just hang around in space as minute spread out particles. At the proper time and by the proper entity, these billions of particles could be reconstituted and materialized. The materialized person and craft would appear to magically come from out of nowhere and burst forth right before your eyes.

Aliens might also reverse the process and disappear in front of you as so many UFOs seemed to do. If it were possible to dematerialize/materialize what would keep them from cloning each molecule of a dematerialized person? Maybe there is another me in another dimension or parallel universe with a birth mark.

They could do what so many people report seeing UFOs do; split and go in different directions, just like an ameba splitting in a big Petri dish. The ability to dematerialize or materialize, would explain many mysteries attributed to ufolks inter-dimensional capabilities.

Perhaps I wasn't sick on the 14th and 15th from the bite I received on the night of the 13th, but by the materialization process. Maybe I had a case of radiation sickness.

I was filled with lots of crazy new ideas about ufolks and their apparent ability to dematerialize and materialize. The only evidence that supported the idea was footprints in the snow and the sounds that Breana heard in the kitchen Saturday night. But who would have believed my thoughts about the materialization process without hard physical evidence?

What a big disappointment. For four years, Sarah and I had hoped for evidence of some sort to substantiate the reality of aliens and related unexplained events that occurred in and around the house. Now the only tangible evidence we had would soon melt away. To my knowledge, there was no way we could make casts of the prints in snow and prove ufolks existed. Of course, I had the wound on my wrist but I never thought about seeing anyone about it. Had it persisted and become infected, I would have sought help. If I told our family doctor that I got bit and my blood sucked out of my body by an alien, I would be laughed out of his office. I kept my mouth shut and my eyes and ears open.

In the dead of night, when I couldn't sleep, I kept mulling over what had happened and the conundrum of the circles. At times, I thought left brained researchers were right. They thought star people were just using us for their own biological purposes; that they had sinister motives when interfacing with us, and that humanity was in grave danger.

For that brief moment my faith was shaken and I became apprehensive of our future. Then I flashed on some good experiences and feelings I had while in their presence. I was thankful for the work they did on my head to improve my health, and I hoped, my cognitive processes. I kept the faith, what else could I do?

My confusion as to where I stood with these people was made even more frustrating by a flashback I had 12 days after the January 13th abduction.

THE STRINGY THING | JANUARY 25, 1984

I wake to the rapid and heavy beating of my heart. The bed is shaking and the covers are rustling where they touch the left side of my chest. At first I panic and wonder how long my heart can pound out its rapid, heavy rhythm. I touch my chest and can feel it bulge with each heartbeat.

Just last week, I told Sarah how quiet my heart was and how interesting it was to see the expression on nurses' faces when they first try to find my pulse: controlled panic and alarm, tinged with curiosity.

My pulse is usually about 50 BPM and difficult to detect. Now I can't stop my heart from racing with such a ferocious beat. There isn't any evidence I have been sweating; I just wake to the incredible pounding of my heart. Jesus, it is beating as fast and hard as I've ever known and the intensity of each beat is so severe that the antique brass/iron bed shakes rhythmically in response to my heart's deep throbbing. I hear each beat as the left side of my chest bulges against the bedding.

What to do? I keep thinking: *Slow down, try not to panic, don't move, concentrate on controlling the pace, then control the intensity of the beat.* As I lie here trying to focus on my heart, all sorts of ideas flash through my mind and finally the events of January 13th to 15th surface again.

More bizarre ideas and feelings flash through my mind, seemingly out of context to what is now happening to my body and mind. My heart keeps beating like a runaway train. As I consciously try to slow my heartbeat down, flashbacks of looking out the studio windows flood my mind's eye. I am looking out the south windows; it is dark outside. The studio is cold. There are patches of new windblown snow on the bottom edges of the south facing window moldings.

The light from inside the studio illuminates the ground outside. I can see the partially snow covered patio bricks and the barren peach tree on the patio. But I can't see out to the driveway beyond my small brick patio area. Inside, I'm working on a design or getting ready to work. I am in a very calm mental state.

As I gaze out my studio windows, a light brown, translucent thing comes floating into view. The unknown entity is a thin, filmy, stringy, nebulous object traveling from west to east about five feet off the ground. What I see is unlike anything I have ever seen or heard of before. The weird creature is alive, slowly wiggling around itself and in space. It is drifting along at a slow rate of speed and I can't tell head from tail. Surprised by what I see, I quickly become fully alert, then very aggressive. Heading for the door with my T-square I plan to intercept this strange thing going by the window toward the barn side of the studio.

I come out of my flashback, my heart is still racing. Is my heart going to explode if it doesn't calm down? My mind slips back into an altered state again and struggles to get out of this flashback and the feeling of a great, sucking aggressor eating me up. A desperate fear sweeps over me. Soon I come back to reality and know why my heart is pounding so hard. I think I have confronted the thing in the ditch or some other strange aggressive stringy creature.

▨　▨　▨　▨　▨　▨　▨　▨

Was my flashback a metaphor for what happened to me when I was on board a ship with giant people? Perhaps I fought my abductors from attaching a long sinister-looking, sucking device to my wrist. Did I sublimate the horrendous experience in the craft with this strange dream? If my flashback wasn't a metaphor, did the blood sucking stringy thing happen the same night I was abducted? Did it happen shortly after I walked down to the studio to work?

If it were the same night, then Ben, the president of the Metropolitan UFO Society, could be right in his evaluation of my January 13th abduction. I had talked to Ben on Monday January 16th. His opinion of the night of January 13th was so bizarre, but what if he were right. To believe as his group and he did, was way beyond my imagination or what a rational belief system would tolerate. But faced with this flashback, I may not have a choice but to accept their other-worldly ideas about reality.

As I lay there slowing my heart down, I kept regretting that I didn't go down to the studio Saturday morning the 14th. Maybe I could have seen my tracks, where they led to, and some evidence as to what happened to me. If my tracks were there by the west door of the studio and lead toward the ditch, I would know Ben was right. But by the time I felt good enough to go down and look for tracks, the kids, Sarah, and the dogs had tramped all over the snow by the studio while feeding the rabbits and horses. There was nothing to see in the packed, three day old snow. I kept thinking of Ben's interpretation of the 13th; it was so crazy.

Ben envisioned we were living in an area where an astral rip existed. He said I had been put there by the ufolks to act as the guardian of this astral rip. I was allegedly there to keep creatures from entering our world from other dimensions. He said that entities came from three other dimensions besides our own. The lower levels of this ascending hierarchy were inhabited by low level spirits that were harmful.

According to Ben, the night the circles appeared, the highest level ufolks came out to collect those entities which had gotten through the rip. The drag marks in the circles could have been made when the star people dragged the entities off to be taken back to their dimension. No wonder Breana heard the three sharp thuds in the kitchen on Saturday night. I thought all the circles were made on Friday night, so, what was the reality? Maybe the thuds she heard were made when the ETs materialized inside the kitchen. Once inside, these ufolks grabbed the lower level spirits. They could have dragged these spirits out of the kitchen, through the snow and beamed them up. Could the ETs have grabbed the thing with big talons I had heard walking around the kitchen for years?

If those two circular tracks outside the kitchen were made on Saturday night, the third undisturbed circular print could have been made on Friday night when I was returned by the star people, after I confronted the stringy thing down at the studio. The stringy thing must have gotten the best of me and sucked most of my blood out.

For my own sanity, I hoped the ufolks intervened and took me somewhere on their ship to revive me or maybe bring me back to life. They then returned me. My footprints in the circle, the bite mark on my wrist, my unusual sickness, and the first and second flashbacks bore witness to my surreal experience that weekend.

In one terror-filled flashback, I have gone from a nuts and bolts normal, confused person, to a far out astral projection new age geek. Change your point of view and everything you see changes too! What Ben told me continued to resonate in my mind when I reevaluated the past, the circles, and events of January 13th-15th and the 25th.

No matter how I tried to imagine astral planes, or other dimensions I could not. The best a non-scientific person like me could envision was dimensions existing like soap bubbles clustered together. At their touching points, passage between two bubbles or dimensions was possible, but you would have to know the vibrational password or have an astral tube to travel through. Maybe the craft that blasted out of our yard in 1981 was going up an astral tube. That was the best way I could imagine different dimensions existing alongside ours. Ben's description made it sound like dimensions could be interwoven and glommed together.

Mixing the various dimensions was an impossible idea for me to grasp or imagine. Our neighbor, who experienced the missing time, must have walked into an invisible portal and another dimension. Perhaps that was what happened to me on the night of the 13th. Then I was beamed down early on the morning of the 14th. Could the bright light I used to see for a second when I was heat-setting by the downstairs windows, be an entry into another dimension?

When Charma saw the invisible thing following her and I saw nothing it was obvious she was sensitive to a wavelength that I was not. At the time, it was thought our visual precepts and dogs' were similar, except they saw in black and white. Later it was believed they did see in color. Then, strong scientific evidence suggested that dogs and cats saw things that existed on the ultraviolet wavelength. Perhaps, spirits existed on this vibrational level and that was why dogs and cats often perceived them when we did not. What I wouldn't have given for a pair of ultraviolet glasses while living in Plum Creek Valley.

Considering the wound on my wrist and my sickness that I attributed to a loss of blood, the idea popped into my head that maybe the myth of vampires feeding off man was not so absurd. I recalled my incident with the black cat with big yellow-green eyes in 1970 that I told Leo Sprinkle about. After my visit with Leo, and my new awareness of my past abductions, I believed that black cat eventually transformed into the person whose face I saw in the window and who abducted me that same night. What would it take to go from a bat, wolf, or cat and turn into a blood-sucking vampire, werewolf or humanoid-looking alien?

Almost all ancient cultures believed in some kind of shape shifter that morphed from one creature into another. Maybe the first flashback I had in 1980 was about the peasants coming after us with torches because we were shape shifters and morphed into-who knows what? A horrible thought, but one I believed could be a reality.

Ancient man's lives were totally interlaced with nature's rhythm. They lived close to Mother Earth. Their lives depended on observations and responses to natural phenomena. Watching TV wasn't an option; just like life at the Bartok's in the 1980s. That was one reason my family became aware of phenomena others did not.

Around the campfires or tending flocks of sheep at night, early man's vantage point was perfect to notice all the evening mysteries that stars, meteorites, and cosmic orders conjure. Unusual nighttime events were noted and recorded. They became part of the tribal and cultural lexicon that enthralled, frightened, and formed the social mythology that was the glue that kept early civilizations together. Most of the Native American tribes in the plains region believed in shape shifters. As an example, the White Buffalo Calf Woman was a goddess they had seen shape shift into a brown, red, black, yellow, and white buffalo.

Then there was Kukulkan, the Mayan god of wisdom, the winds, etc., who morphed into the Plumed Serpent. He was often depicted in three dimensional sculptures sticking his head out of a serpent's mouth. The metamorphism was locked in stone for eyes that can "see" to see. So my experience was not new. It just so happened I experienced what others had already seen, believed in, talked, and written about for eons.

If I chose to believe Ben's interpretation, I could feel reassured that the ufolks had not turned against me for talking about them with others. I could keep my faith in their motives of helping mankind and I was still in their good graces.

My simple world of just dealing with life, star people, and Indian spirits now was so much more complex. On the one hand, if the ufolks bled me as I first thought, why? Was it time to take some kind of needed cocktail out of my system? Or was I being punished for openly talking about our experiences while at the RMUFOC, or to Leo Sprinkle, or to the Metropolitan UFO Society? Could it be because I couldn't gut up and go out to meet the star person on the deck, last January, 1983?

"Our task must be to free
ourselves by widening our circle
of compassion to embrace all
living creatures and the whole
of nature and its beauty."

ALBERT EINSTEIN

*" To kill an error is
as good a service as,
sometimes even
better than, the
establishing of a
new truth or fact. "*

CHARLES DARWIN

CHAPTER SIX | 1985

SHOCKING | JANUARY 30, 1985

Sarah wakes me in a panic! I can barely see her face in the night light. I can tell she is really frightened, excited, and confused. She wants to tell me what has happened, but she won't; she is afraid our talking will wake Breana. Breana is sleeping in her sleeping bag on the floor next to our bed. Sarah whispers she will tell me what happened, in the morning.

The next morning, after Breana leaves the room, Sarah tells me what she experienced last night:

She is lying in bed on her back, which in itself, is rather odd since she never sleeps on her back. Her arms are by her side and she knows she is not asleep or dreaming. She feels three separate electrical shocks. Each one originates at the top of her head and travels down her entire body. Her body stiffens and lengthens with each shock. During the duration of the shock, it feels like her head is compressing down into her shoulders. The experience is not painful but very disturbing. She says she is not frightened, but more annoyed, that she has to endure this experience.

There are about five seconds between the shocks, but it isn't like she falls back to sleep and then reawakens with the next shock. She is awake, but unable to move. However, she doesn't really struggle or even try to move, as if she knows it will do no good. She is aware of her surroundings and thinks she is still in our bed and that I am on her left side. That is the side I always sleep on, now that we are sleeping in the southeast bedroom.

Even though she thinks her eyes are closed, she sees, or senses, there is a white wall beyond the foot of our bed and that she is covered with a thin, blue sheet. Sarah said it is odd that she would sense a wall, as there is not a wall beyond the foot of our bed, but a railing 12 feet away overlooking the living room below. She also thinks it is odd that she is covered with a blue sheet since we sleep under a white down comforter that has a lot more bulk and weight than a sheet. So why would she have had the impression that she was under a blue sheet? We do not own blue sheets.

After the first shock, she thinks, *It's over.* Then the second shock comes and she again thinks, *Well, this is it, it's over.* Then the third shock comes. She panics, worried that the shocks will just keep coming, not knowing when, or if, they will cease. After the second shock, she recalls me, or someone she thinks is me, who is on her left, leaning toward her and whispering, "It's okay. It's okay."

After the third shock, it all ends. She thinks she just goes back to sleep. Sometime later in the night is when she wakes me, wanting to tell me her story.

She doesn't recall anything like this ever happening to her before or since. But at the time, Sarah says she isn't surprised or alarmed when the shocks start, which makes her wonder if she had gone through this before and she just didn't remember it… yet.

■　　■　　■　　■　　■　　■　　■　　■

When Sarah finished telling me what had happened that night, I didn't know what to think. To my knowledge, this was the first time she had an experience she remembered and could describe. Sarah was like me in the beginning, puzzled and not sure anything really happened. Yet, she was circumspect as to how absolutely real the experience was. But after January 13, 1984 the link between dreams, flashbacks, and reality was pretty much a certainty in my mind.

If I had not had the sore on my wrist and the circles in the snow were not discovered in the yard, that Saturday morning would have been like any other. I would have had a strange dream of being on a ship with tall people and I would have accepted it as merely a dream. But now, we knew the truth; dreams and reality were often one and the same.

The electrical shocks were a reality for Sarah, but what was their purpose? Were the shocks implemented to test or prepare her for some future event, plague, or condition? Were they testing her physical endurance or modifying her genetic code to accommodate future events on the planet? Were the ufolks preparing her for more strenuous experiments the next time she was abducted? Perhaps the shocks were part of a procedure to make her forget what might have happened during that and/or an earlier abduction.

It was my understanding that electroshock therapy was a common procedure for releasing stress in mental patients by erasing their short term memory. Maybe her short term memory was being erased or altered with each shock. Each dream or flashback produced so many more questions.

Floral swimsuit cover up

THE RAG BIZ | MAY 15, 1985

I discover Spandex after a designer calls me and wants to collaborate on designing swimwear and cover ups for her clients. Once I was given a sample swatch of white, shiny-surfaced Spandex, it doesn't take long for me to recognize how beautiful the chemicals and processes I am using will work on the high-gloss new material. Soon I am creating up to three swimsuits each studio day. Cover ups take much longer as there is a lot more material and the designs are more complex.

I am happy exploring a new venue and my work presses the traditional boundaries. I develop ideas for creating silk chiffon bodysuits as lingerie. I also start working on creating Spandex full body suits for swimmers, dancers, and skiers. I do some preliminary

Above; matching floral swimsuit: below; head sketches for full body swim/ski suit

Full body Halloween costumes   Matching swimsuits and cover ups

sketches of one-piece suits for women skiers.

After three months of trying, a new seamstress and I cannot come up with a full body suit design using Spandex material that is stretchy enough to conform to the face and neck of an adult woman. The big problem area is between the chin and clavicle. The material makes the wearer look like she has a "chicken neck". Until a more stretchable Spandex comes along, I put the project on hold.

I don't give up on the idea of a unibody ski or swimwear, but when Halloween comes along, I adapt two failed experiments into unibody Spandex Halloween suits for Breana and her girlfriend. Is my inspiration coming from my experiences with star people?

Dolman swimsuit cover up with detail below left; below right, Native American inspired cover up

Kimono inspired swimsuit cover up and detail

God knows what the neighbors think when the two ufolk girls come to trick or treat. By now, our neighbors know we are half a bubble off level, or onto something they do not want to know or talk about.

I keep creating cover ups and swimwear for years. I have many good experiences and memories of this period in my life. I also vaguely remember a couple of female designers threatening me with lawsuits supposedly for stealing their swimsuit pattern designs. Pretty humorous threats since I alter, to my own tastes, the *McCall's* swimwear and cover up patterns I buy at Cloth World.

At one point, the Broadway Southwest company wants me to sell my swimwear and cover ups in their new store in a west Denver shopping mall. "Sir" Sean's big break into swimwear fashion! Just as I begin gearing up to create fantastic swimwear for Broadway

Southwest, it goes belly up in Denver and retrenches back to its Texas home base. Shortly after that, I somehow find myself under contract designing swimwear and surface design for an Italian firm in New York. After a while, they want my soul and I can't teach and keep up with their constant demands. My salary at the university is a joke, but I love teaching and it is steady money.

So I say *goodbye* to New York. The rag biz is a bitch and they ride you like a rented pony until they have sucked you dry of all your ideas and energy. Then you are just another piece of meat and are kicked out on your ass onto the street like a putz. The star people are much more humane.

■　　■　　■　　■　　■　　■　　■　　■

When I looked at my sketches of the second-skin unibody swim or skiwear, I was somehow reminded of the star person Scott described seeing in the tree. Maybe that was where I got my inspiration. Or maybe it was from my previous abductions.

EFFERVESCENT SPOTS | MAY 22, 1985

I wake to the sensation that my whole body is having an incredible shock-induced muscle spasm. All the muscles in my body are flexed tight as they possibly can be. I am having a whole body cramp. My body is literally compressing itself onto itself by using my own muscles to crush me. After the first great compressing cramp stops, there seems to be a moment or two before the second compressing flex begins again. There is no pain, just this tremendous fear I am going to implode from every direction and end up a gooey wad of bloody flesh, broken teeth, and crushed, splintery bones. In my absolutely terrified state, I manage to mutter in my mind, *Evil, Go Away*!

Immediately the spasm stops. I am out of breath and want to cry with joy. The seizure seemed to stop when I commanded it to stop. God, I can't make heads or tails out of what just happened. I saw nothing; no electrical shock, no people, nothing! My body just heaved itself into a parabolic arch as it tried to compress itself to death. As the event happened, I thought my teeth would explode from the force I put on them. I feel my body; it seems to be three dimensional. I don't experience pain to my appendages, core, or head. I run my tongue around the inside of my mouth; everything feels intact. My teeth are not chunks of porcelain floating around in a mouth full of saliva like I think they will be.

I wake Sarah up and tell her about my experience. Her eyes tell me that she knows what I am describing. I have blurted out the unmentionable word, *Evil.* My soul sinks in disbelief. I have used that awful word others use in conjunction with UFOs. The word terrifies me. Would the word *Stop!* have had the same effect?

I don't want to think these people are evil, in my heart they are well meaning and helping us in ways that are incomprehensible to us. I must have suppressed the experience until now; and probably Sarah and I experienced the shocks and cramps at the same time. It just takes me longer to let the experience come from my subconscious to the surface. Did I terminate the shocks in my flashback or when they were administered to me?

■　■　■　■　■　■　■　■

Months later, I wondered if the shocks were associated with a strange depression in my left thigh. In February or early March, I noticed a tingling sensation in a small indentation about midway in my left frontal thigh muscle. At first, the one-quarter inch diameter spot only tingled, but at times there was the sensation that the area was effervescing; like a fizzing deep down in my thigh muscle. It felt like bubbles coming up through the heavy belly muscles of my thigh; they tickled as they rose to the surface.

I got the distinct impression the spot was atrophying. Eventually, the spot became cold and partially numb. By the end of April 1985, there was a larger concave area developing over the spot that was tingly. I thought maybe whatever it was would go away on its own, but the depression kept expanding in its slow, insidious way. By mid-June I was really concerned. I felt a slight tingling sensation developing in my right thigh and in exactly the same spot as it was on my left thigh! There was a hint that the severity of the affliction would develop to the same degree that the left thigh had.

Near the end of June I decided to see our family doctor. By then the center of the area on my left thigh was almost totally numb. The outer edges seemed swollen ever so slightly and this donut ring around the numb spot was tingly and felt like it was still effervescing. What the hell was I going to tell our doctor? "ET's hooked me up to an electrical device and shocked me with such force that it killed my muscle tissue and cells in that area?" At least that is what I thought had happened. I had never had anything like this happen before in my life.

I played it dumb and simply asked our doctor if he would take a look at my left thigh muscle. At first he didn't see anything, and then I had him run his fingers over the area. Bingo! I could tell by his facial expression he found the spot, and that he was puzzled.

"We should take a biopsy from the spot," Dr. Zimmerman said.

He then added, "I have never seen or heard of anything like this before."

Dr. Zimmerman took two biopsies; one shallow and one deep, right from the middle of the depression. The biopsies were sent to Chicago. After two weeks he called and said the area was benign.

"I have no idea what caused the depression or is causing the tingling and numb sensations in your thighs," he commented.

I was relieved to know the area was benign, but the mysterious indentation continued to tingle. I kept telling myself the tingling and depression came with the territory of being chosen and possibly improved upon. The loss of feeling in my left thigh area persists to this day.

When I reflected on our two similar experiences, I realized the only difference was Sarah had three sequences of shocks, jolts, compressions, or whatever one might call the experiences, and I only had two. I was shaken by what had happened to us both, but also concerned as to how I had stopped the process of being imploded in on myself.

EPHEMERAL IMAGES | MAY 30, 1985

I **am now creating banners** on four by eight foot pieces of chiffon. I like the results. What intrigues me the most is the way the material allows the images to appear and disappear as one moves around the hanging sheet of translucent material, viewing it from different angles. The visual effect reminds me of the

Chiffon banner, "Ebony"

Chiffon banner, "Judy Judy"

Chiffon banner, "Star Girl with Sparkler"

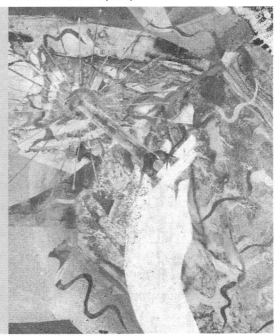

Detail of "Star Girl with Sparkler"

way events occur around the house and in our minds. The ephemeral, appearing and then disappearing, images on the chiffon are symbolic to me of life in Plum Creek Valley. I like the way the material moves with the slightest breeze that traverses through the house. The chiffon material looks like it is constantly breathing and animates the images painted on its surface. For a local salon, I create three large banners to add ambiance to their shop's interior design theme. One of the women I paint looks like she is from the future. I can't help but think I am subconsciously creating her from memory. In her hand is a sparkler.

FAMILY TIES | JUNE, 1985

On late night talk shows, I hear that not only are people seeing UFOs, but people are also being abducted. No surprise there, but then I hear something that piques my interest. The talk show host states that according to some UFO experts, abductions often occur in the same families. These experts allege that abductee lineages run from father to daughter, daughter to son, son to daughter and so on. After hearing their theory, I feel as though this may be the case with me.

■　■　■　■　■　■　■　■

Mother had probably been abducted. I remembered her talking about seeing strange lights at night. When she was a young girl, she and my grandparents lived on a farm located east of Spring Hill, Kansas. The farm was not far from the future Olathe Naval Air Base. Mother said the lights hovered around close to the ground and moved randomly back and forth across a big field east of their farm house. The lights seemed to be looking for something on the ground, she thought. She saw the strange lights on many occasions. My experiences told me that when you saw unusual lights you were going to be, or had been, abducted. Mother was a nature lover and spent a lot of time by herself in the woods and taking care of the farm animals. Perhaps she had an experience with ufolks while by herself in the woods near the farm house.

Of course, I thought I had been abducted when I was nine. Was it destiny with no way out? They were going to follow me and my family wherever we moved until the baton had been passed to new generations. That meant Breana was the new standard bearer. However, since Sarah had been having flashbacks, it meant Scott probably was also an abductee. Scott refused to talk to us about most of his experiences. He did, however, talk to his school friends about the "live skeleton in the tree," and some entities he called "clot hoppers." We knew nothing about other occurrences, until his friends mentioned the events to us after they also had experiences in and around our home.

Now I felt I knew why the ETs were hanging around Grandpa's farm when Jimmy was almost taken. Or perhaps he had already been taken and had just been released when Grandma stuck her head out the porch door and yelled, "RUN, JIMMY! RUN!!" His experience could have been similar to mine when I was 19 and at Grandpa's pond. When they return you, it is often difficult to know the difference; am I coming or going? Could the UFOs have been hunting around the Olathe Naval Air Base since its inception or before?

After seeing Leo Sprinkle, I had often thought seeing or sensing a star person after an unusual dream meant they were checking on me. I believed it was during those times I must have really had a problem with the abduction and they were concerned about my mental and physical state.

The first night we saw the lights around the house, I firmly believed I was abducted. Then they dropped me off and waited to see if I were still alive. Once they saw me crawling around on the bedroom floor with my revolver headed for the sliding glass door, they left. I thought the exact opposite at that time. I foolishly thought I had caught them before anything had happened to us. The next day I could not talk. Maybe I screamed my bloody head off during the abduction and in the process, strained my vocal cords to the point I was hoarse.

The face in the window in 1970 was probably checking on me before leaving. The loud whack on the living room glass door in 1980 could have been a trigger mechanism. It could have brought me out of a trance, after they returned me back to the loveseat I was sitting on. The rectangular brownish-green shape I saw could have been the sole of an alien's shoe. The star person might have kicked the glass as he pushed off the sliding glass door with his foot and ascended to the top of our roof and out of my sight.

The thought also occurred to me that maybe Grandpa Johnson had his massive heart attack after encountering a star person as he walked in the woods south of the farm house. He never regained consciousness before dying in a Miami County, Kansas hospital. We will never know what happened in the woods prior to his heart attack.

GRAND JETE | JULY 6, 1985

I am in a dark, endless chasm, way up above four people lying on simple cots. I drift around looking down at these people way below me. The beds do not have headboards; they look like those I have seen in photographs of WWII field hospitals. The four people are all in a line with three to four feet of space between their cots. Everything is white: the cots, the sheets, and the bedding. Everyone is covered by the sheets and I can only see their heads sticking out. I see their body contours under the sheets.

There are no walls, just an endless gaping space beyond the lights around the four people. The space is vast, no stars or other natural elements suggesting I am outside. There are no breezes, smells, or sounds…nothing. The lighting around the people is soft, white, and luminous, and comes from where, I'm not sure. The figures are partially illuminated by this lighting that reminds me of fifteenth century *chiaroscuro* lighting seen in many religious paintings. The people appear to be adults but look very small. Judging by the atmospheric perspective, I must be floating in this endless space, 150 feet or more above.

One of the patients, the second from the right, is lying in a prenatal position. This person is highly animated and is violently convulsing. This pitiful body is twitching all over and violently opening and then jerking and closing and opening on itself like a jack knife. This individual appears to be going through his/her death throws. Watching this awful scene from my lofty position, I realize that the person is dying, and looks vaguely like me. I continue to watch with great concern for this person who is in such trauma.

Floating around, I have no feeling of standing or lying on my stomach. I am just there floating above this troubling scene. I cannot see my body or the tip of my nose. There is no physical me to be seen or touched, just this dramatic scene unfolding. The person continues to convulse. No one else in this line of hospital beds is moving and they are lying on their backs. I am so high up in this vast space, details of the other people on the beds are hard to identify. I need to get closer to see who these people are.

Somehow I drift down closer as my concern mounts for the person whom I think is me. When I float to within 45 or so feet from the people on the cots, I become semi-fixed in space. I continue looking down at the line of humans.

Then from the right, out of this gaping void, a tall, thin, extremely elegant looking ET enters. This person is pale, almost translucent white. He appears to be slightly shiny and glowing as I see highlights glisten on various parts of his body as he moves. He has a somewhat oversized head, a long slender neck; could be nude, but no gender genitalia is visible. There are no breasts so I assume it is a male, or neuter. I can't tell if the individual is nude or wearing a one piece, skin-tight, full body suit. His torso is short compared to his long willowy, graceful arms and legs.

This tall, graceful creature is leaping through the air performing a magnificent *Grand Jete*. His entry leap must be fifteen feet in length and five or six feet above the people on the beds. As the euphoric-looking figure comes down over the last patient on the left, he repeats the great ballet movement again and disappears out of sight into the dark void. The figure is not affected by gravity because he performs his *Grand Jete* above the people lying on the cots. To me, the figure appears to be moving in slow motion, making his graceful movements all the more magnificent.

I am reminded of the beauty of the ballerina in Norman McLaren's art film, *Pas de Deux*. After the elegant ET vaults over the last person, the one I think is me, is no longer convulsing. I am relieved and lose consciousness.

▪ ▪ ▪ ▪ ▪ ▪ ▪ ▪

The experience was very gut-wrenching, haunting, and I could not help but think my flashback was an extension of the January experiences. Was my subconscious attempting to tell me what happened on the weekend of January 13-15, 1984 or on May 22, 1985?

For the first time in a flashback, I got a good look at one of my abductors: a tall, whitish, willowy, benevolent-looking individual. Who were the other three human figures in the beds? Were they my family or just other abductees in for inspection, bumping up, experiments, or recalibration?

As silly and superficial as it might sound, I couldn't help but wonder who taught whom how to execute the *Grand Jete* with such grace and elegance, them or us? Was the ballet move just another clue that we were really them in another incarnation?

In later years, I wondered if the beautiful dancer was trying to steal my soul as it emerged from my body right before or after death. Or did the elegant one save me from dying as it leapt over me, making my soul become one with my body again?

WHAT ARE THEY LOOKING AT? | AUGUST, 1985

My teeth have been hurting for a couple of months. I finally gut up and go see our family dentist. I have a real approach/avoidance dilemma when it comes to seeing doctors of any sort.

I am reclined in our dentist's chair looking at the ceiling tile, and then inside the gigantic hairy nostrils of his assistant looming above me. She is looking down her nose at me, making me feel uncomfortable. No sooner does she start cleaning my teeth, when she abruptly stops and leaves me with a mouthful of air. Moments later the dentist shows up all wild-eyed with his assistant right on his heels. Instantly I get very nervous. Something is up. The overhead light is then jammed down in my face to get a closer look…at what?

His assistant whispers, "I've never seen anything like it in my life!"

"Neither have I!" my dentist says.

I'll never forget that moment! I think, *Jesus what are they looking at?*

He stares at me and exclaims, "It's no wonder your teeth have been hurting, you have totally crushed some of your molars to smithereens! You must be under great emotional pressure to be bruxing your teeth at night the way you have! We'll have to put crowns on some of your lower and upper molars."

Holy crap! This is going to cost us a fortune, and just when I think we are breaking out of the red. It will be painless to fix my teeth but not our budget.

* * * * * * * *

I recalled my dream of January 30th of that year, and thought maybe I crushed my molars when I felt compressed by the cramps, shocks or…?

I had stopped the shocks/cramps from compressing my body in on itself by saying in my deepest, gruffest mental voice, *Evil, Go Away!* Again, I reluctantly became circumspect as to the motives of the entities that came into our house at night. Could it be I was wrong? Had these entities come to hurt us, not enlighten and prepare us and our children for the future? I felt a little bitter and betrayed. Up until the last year, signs seemed to indicate we were being helped physically, spiritually, intellectually, and emotionally by the visitors. Again, I wasn't sure what to think.

LET ME IN | AUGUST 27, 1985

Scott rushes into our bedroom to wake us up. I am already awake. Scott is alarmed. He says something is trying to get into his room by working the screen to his sliding glass door back and forth. I think the door is shut and locked and whoever or whatever it is, cannot get inside. Once the noise of the frantic attempt to open the screen door ceases, there is a loud, dull THUD. The noise is so loud it can be heard throughout the house. Scott and I go out on his deck and check the door. It is locked. I don't find, see, feel, or smell anything. It's just a pitch black beautiful, starry, summer night.

* * * * * * * *

I began to think the heavy THUD we occasionally heard over the years, was an invisible entity launching itself off into the air, in this instance, away from Scott's sliding glass door. But I didn't know for sure; it was merely a guess. Perhaps this was the same entity that made the large nine foot circular prints in the snow across the ravine in 1980.

This entity must have leapt along like a frog as it moved around the neighborhood. I believed it was also the same one that wiggled its way through the balcony screen door of the family room, the night Charma almost jumped to her death. I couldn't help wondering why it was so frantic to get into Scott's bedroom. Was something even more bizarre chasing it?

"And while I stood there
I saw more than I can tell,
and I understood more than I saw,
for I was seeing in a sacred manner
the shapes of things in the spirit,
and the shapes of all shapes
as they must live together as one being."

BLACK ELK, LAKOTA SHAMAN

"All our knowledge has its origins in our perceptions."

LEONARDO DA VINCE

CHAPTER SEVEN | 1986

ARTSY FARTSY SCIENCE | JANUARY, 1986

It is late at night. I am working in the studio. Out of the corner of my ear I listen to a late night talk show host discussing a book titled, *The Chariots of the Gods* by Erich Von Daniken. I can't believe the conversation I hear. This Von Daniken guy is so far ahead of his time and is courageous to challenge traditional western values and ideas about civilization, God, and UFOs.

Up to this point, I have not read any books about ETs, and have tried to distance myself from any outside ideas about UFOs, star people, and their existence. I am determined to weigh all the facts myself and arrive at my own conclusion, free of outside influences. I don't want my thoughts or views, based on personal experience, to be influenced by "experts" who were perhaps biased, uninformed, publicity seekers, kooks, or hoaxers. I try to keep an open mind and not have too many preconceived ideas.

Von Daniken talks about aliens that were seen by past civilizations. His work is based on research that is right in front of mainstream anthropologists. His creative genius sees right through the veneer that encoded the reality of the past. Mainstream anthropologists poo-poo Eric Von Daniken's ideas about ancient aliens having a positive influence on past and present civilizations. After all, they are mainstream "scholars" and their divine right to tell us what happened in the past could not be challenged by "no-bodies" like Von Daniken.

■ ■ ■ ■ ■ ■ ■ ■

Von Daniken really sparked my imagination about the origins of the species and how we evolved. Soon, my mind flashed onto my research of South American Pre-Colombian Indians and North American Native Americans and their cultures. I recalled the surprise of seeing the huge sculptured heads found in the Yucatan Peninsula of Mexico of the Olmec gods. The Olmec culture existed from roughly 1500 BC to 900 BC before the mysterious emergence of the Mayans. Olmec artists sculpted gigantic, realistic-looking 22 ton heads of their gods out of basalt rock. The heads they created out of this very hard, black rock looked like Africans not Mayan people indigenous to the Yucatan Peninsula. The Mayan gods and populace were painted as reddish-brown in color by artists of that time. The Mayan facial features were anything but African, as my drawing depicts.

How was it possible that the African features of the Olmec heads were indigenous of people who lived thousands of miles east of the Yucatan Peninsula? Had the basalt heads made the trip from Africa during the continental drift when South America moved west away from Africa so many geological years ago?

Drawing of Olmec God

Drawing of Mayan man

It was said that the anthropologist, Louis Leakey, thought that some sort of island crossed from Africa to South America. I think that island was a spaceship loaded with Olmec gods who attempted to seed the Yucatan Peninsula with their genes or race. The Mayan civilization developed and lived "next door" to the Olmec civilization. I believe the Mayans outperformed the Olmecs and they mysteriously disappeared from the Yucatan Peninsula. Perhaps the Olmecs were rescued by a spaceship from their dimension, and they returned home, or they were taken back to Africa by their gods. A more imaginative scenario could be that some galactic federation evicted the Olmecs because they had moved out of the territory allotted to them. Were they made to go back to Africa? Maybe Kukulkan and his Mayans from a different planet or dimension had dibs on the Yucatan Peninsula, and the Olmecs had to go.

Did Darwinian evolution have little to do with the original development of the human species, as most scientists were taught to think? Knowing what I knew and had experienced, I believed the real missing link in Darwin's theory of evolution was the alien factor.

My artsy fartsy idea was probably not a new one, but for me the UFO connection explained phenomena I had always wondered about. How could modern man come out of Africa, wander around the world morphing into the various races and their permutations when they lived in close proximity to one another? I couldn't understand how the East Indians could look so different from their Chinese neighbors or the Olmec from their Mayan neighbors.

I realized how obvious, and unscientific, my thoughts were about evolution. The first time I looked at a world map after hearing about continental drift, I was in high school. It was visually obvious to me that the West African coastline was once joined to South America's east shore line. They fit together, like pieces in a puzzle. I wondered then why South Americans and Africans looked so different from each other.

In 1596, Abraham Ortelius came up with the revolutionary concept of continental drift. Like me, Ortelius probably based his assumption on the visual similarities of the two opposing shore lines he evidently saw on a map. He wasn't blinded by mainstream dogma of the day. Along the way, many other geologists came to the same conclusion. An eon later, 1958, the theory and mechanics of continental drift was finally accepted by the scientific community.

What I couldn't fathom, was how Ortelius found a map with Europe, Africa, and

North and South America on it. His observation was made roughly 100 years after Columbus discovered America. Who mapped these continents for Ortelius to draw his conclusions from? Or did he have an out-of-body or alien experience and saw the coastline from outer space?

It was late, so I decided to quit working in the studio and go to the house and to bed. I would review my ideas in the morning. Strange ideas hatched late at night, while listening to talk radio, don't always make as much sense in the morning.

Sometime before morning light, it occurred to me that if all of modern mankind shared the same genome, as scientists alleged, then there must be only one God creating all these other gods who were coming out of the heavens and creating people in their own image. Civilizations and subsequent religions were based on the teachings of each particular god (ufolk) from a different dimension or planetary system. I could live with my idea of evolution which popped into my head that night.

MIDDLE OF NOWHERE | FEBRUARY, 1986

It is 1986. Mom and Dad have retired and are living in our jointly-owned summer home in Buena Vista, Colorado. Mother is diagnosed with multiple melanoma. We sell the summer house so they can buy a home closer to doctors who specialize in her affliction. We have some unexpected money from the sale of the summer house. After several months of looking, we buy an old broken-down, abandoned ranch in Park County, Colorado.

The location of the ranch is perhaps the last place in the world we would have expected to buy anything. We know the area well. For 16 years, we have driven through the county on our way to Buena Vista. The south half of Park County always seemed windy, cold, dusty, dry, forbidding, uninhabited, and bleak; a real unpleasant place to be if you don't have to be there. The old ranch, however, has some redeeming qualities that override all these negative aspects.

It is located not far from a river that empties into a large reservoir filled with trout. The ranch itself has many springs on it and a stream runs through the property. The panoramic view from the house east is magnificent as its overlooks green, sub-irrigated hay fields, the reservoir, and Pikes Peak.

I begin planting trees around the old ranch house to beautify and to create much needed wind breaks. The house and ranch date to the 1860s, and no one has planted a tree anywhere on the ranch house grounds. I have reforested two properties already and consider myself an expert at locating, procuring, planting, and nurturing my favorite mountain tree, the quaking aspen.

It is late April, I have driven 100 miles from Plum Creek to our new ranch. I locate, dig, ball, haul, plant, and stake thirty aspen trees around the old house and its sun deck. It is dark when I leave the ranch, and head back home. Thirty minutes later, I'm directly across the reservoir looking toward our new summer ranch home. I am stunned. In the early light of a full moon, I see a landscape that is almost identical to the desolate moonscape shown to me in my flashback when the aliens were perusing through my mind and planting seeds there in 1980. At the time, I thought the image on the luminous wall in front of me was a moonscape I used in a piece of art I had created in the early 1970s!

The landscape I now see in the moonlight is a colorless, black and white version of an old lava flow that is now covered with short grasses that has been overgrazed. The landscape looks almost identical to the moonscape I saw on the aliens' luminous wall! I stop the truck and look across the lake and where the ranch is located. Flashing on my experiences with the aliens, I think, *Is this a coincidence or my destiny?* This is the first time I have ever related what was shown to me in a flashback with reality as I know it to be. I get home and tell no one about what I have seen and think.

This old broken-down ranch soon becomes my pet project. It is so damned dilapidated and ugly, it needs me. I'm in love. The stark reality of the bleak, lonely, remorseful-looking corrals, barns, sheds, bunk house, log cabins, and the house, just beg for me to make them right and happy again. They want their dignity back and I'm going to give it to them.

I have done all I can to our home in Plum Creek without spending large amounts of money to add more square footage to the house. I would rather have a main house in Plum Creek and an escape ranch just in case all else goes to hell and we need a refuge.

The children are wise and old enough to watch for rattlesnakes. The sprinkler system is watering the grass and keeping the trees around the house and studio alive. I can now devote some energy to saving this old place. Going to the ranch as often as possible, I begin to plan the changes I will make in the future. It would be overwhelming to think about all that needs to be done, so I do one thing at a time. Starting with redoing the shallow, hand dug basement, I work my way up.

In the past, a wild horse had fallen through the sloping cellar door to the basement and was trapped there. With nothing to eat and a desire to get out, the poor beast thrashed around until it had totally torn up or destroyed the electrical boxes, electrical wiring, hot and cold water tanks, as well as the gas and water lines. The poor animal was allegedly saved by a local rancher looking for some stray cattle.

The horse that was trapped in the basement chewed on the floor joists until they were so weak that I had to replace them. It will be years before the smell of the horse's urine, imbedded in the dirt floor, fades away. To help rid the lingering urine odor, I remove six inches of dirt in the basement floor area. I re-face the vertical decaying dirt walls with rocks and mortar.

There is never a time that I am down in the basement screwing around with the electrical or plumbing that I do not feel compassion for the poor horse. No telling how much time it had spent trapped in this dreary, black widow spider infested space, with nothing to eat or drink.

As I work on the mechanical parts of the house, I keep planting trees each time I go down to the ranch. Soon, I have the finicky Onan generator up and running, the plumbing, gas lines, water tanks and water lines replaced or fixed; and the cellar door repaired. We now have fresh water from the well to the house and electricity when the generator is running.

A small creek runs through the new property, and upstream above the house, an old pond had washed out. We have the pond reinstated, and also dig a trench from the pond outlet to the house. In front of the house, we have a pond excavated to create a fishery and to use in case the house catches fire. From the trench that feeds the house pond, I create a gravity feed sprinkler system to water the hundred or so trees I have planted. Soon, we have trout brought to the ponds, which are now surrounded by plenty of aspen trees. A new dream begins to form in my mind. I start to love this place called South Park.

Both barns on the property have circular, metal plaques with a silver star on each gabled end. The strange plaques are about 18 inches in diameter and have a big silver star on them. I do not know what the symbolism on the plaques mean and would not know for some time to come. When I do find out, I am not surprised. I would also think I know why the owners were in such a rush to sell the property.

On one of my solo trips to the ranch, I am cooking dinner on the gas range. For some reason, I step outside the house and when returning, find I cannot get back in. I am locked out! I check all the doors and windows and cannot get back into the house. I would not be concerned, but I have food cooking on the stove that can catch fire and smoke up the whole house or even start a fire in the kitchen.

I am desperate and finally force my way into the house through an old dilapidated sliding glass kitchen back door. Getting inside just in the nick of time, I keep the food from burning. I go check the door I had just gone outside through and realize the deadbolt has been turned to the lock position! I could not have done that myself just by shutting the door as I went out. The knob that activates the deadbolt is old and difficult for me to lock. Now, I understand what I am dealing with. I go into a rage and scream, "If you ever do that again I will burn this house and every building on this ranch to the ground and you will not have a place to haunt or live! Do you hear me; your ass will be out in the cold!"

■　■　■　■　■　■　■　■

I meant business. I had nothing to lose. This place was a shambles and I could do without spending my time repairing it! Had I not had so many experiences in the Plum Creek house, I would not have known what to do. Don't take crap off any spirit who offends you. They will have you by the psyche if you do.

I was never bothered again in a negative way. In the years to come, we had many unusual and some touching moments with the spirits who appreciated all we did to save this little ranch on the high barren prairies of South Park. It turned out, that the star symbols on the two barns' gabled ends were there to ward off evil spirits.

On Sarah's and my wedding anniversary, we are all down at our new summer ranch installing a barbed wire fence around the main house, soddie house, log outbuildings, bunk house, and of course the outhouse. We have been there for two days and have seen no one. We do not have TV, and only lights and running water when I turn on the noisy, temperamental generator. Normally we use Coleman gas lanterns to light the house at night. We are hungry to see anyone whom we could talk to.

On this evening, Sarah gets her guitar, and we all sit out on the front steps of the ranch house. She starts playing and we all begin singing the Cat Steven's song, "Moonshadow". I find the lyrics to this song prophetic on this dark, moonless night. Some of the lyrics are as follows:

Yes I'm being followed by a moon shadow
Moon shadow, moon shadow
Leapin' and hoppin' on a moon shadow
Moon shadow, moon shadow

And if I ever lose my hands
Lose my power, lose my land
Oh, if I ever lose my hands
Oh, I won't have to work no more

And if I ever lose my eyes
If my colors all run dry
Yes, if I ever lose my eyes
Ooh, I won't have to cry no more

Yes, I'm being followed by a moon shadow
Moon shadow, moon shadow
Leapin' and hoppin' on a moon shadow
Moon shadow, moon shadow

"Did it take long to find me?"
I asked the faithful light
"Oh, did it take long to find me
And are you gonna stay the night?"

As we all sing along to "Moonshadow," we are looking east toward the reservoir and the back side of Pikes Peak. We begin to notice a beautiful, soft white light coming from behind a small rolling hill, three-quarters of a mile in front of us. The light looks like it comes from a car's head lights that are facing the low, round-topped hill. We are seeing the small hill silhouetted against the diffused white light, creating the illusion of an aura. We continue singing and watching the soft white light out of the corner of our eyes and mind. The light stays the same and does not move or change in direction or intensity.

I think we are all secretly hopeful someone is coming to see us; how exciting. We keep singing and then all of the sudden, the soft light bursts into an explosion of bright, focused white lights erupting upward into the night sky. It is as if a thousand white roman candles go off at once! There is no sound.

As the brilliant light thrusts itself skyward, it emits three gigantic balls of light. They are the most beautiful colored spheres I can imagine. The glowing spheres are composed of multiple colors that form a luminous, opalescent color harmony. For me, the spectacular spherical light show is joyous, magical; a religious experience.

We are totally spellbound as these pearlescent orbs of light slowly drift back down to earth and vanish behind the hill where the soft light came from. All is now black again, the light show is over, our eyes adjust, the stars and Milky Way are back out. I am stunned, silenced, and bewildered by what we have seen. I am then immediately electrified and have this strange feeling I am being left behind by the people dropping these beautiful spheres of light.

I tell everyone to get into the car. They do not want to, but when Sarah, Scott, and Breana see me heading toward the car they are right on my heels, afraid to stay at our dark house by themselves. I recklessly drive the rock-strewn, two-track ranch road in the direction of where the lights came from. As I race with free abandon down the road, I frantically blink our car lights on and off to attract our departing visitors' attention. *Come Back! Come Back! Come Back!* my mind screams out. Of course our visitors do not come back, by now they are thousands of miles away.

I drive east to the county road, Soda Creek, then south to Salt Creek road and right again. The two-track road we are traveling on gets narrower and narrower. The tracks become less and less visible until they are just dark smudges in our headlights. Finally, the grasses in and around the road are so high that we can hardly see the two-track ahead of us. At that moment, we see the decaying corpse of a cow in the road. In the bright headlights, the body looks ghastly. Sarah, Scott, and Breana scream in unison, followed by shouting to take them back to the house. I have had enough too.

Did I find them or did they find me, or us? I guess the beautiful lights aren't going to stay the night. Moon shadow, moon shadow.

■   ■   ■   ■   ■   ■   ■   ■

Author's note: As Sarah and I were working on the final selection of photographs for this book, I realized that 6 year old Breana's 1983 drawing, of an alien sitting on a porch, looked almost identical to the ranch house we purchased years later. We never saw this ranch house until 1986, three years after her drawing was made.

Breana created her drawing in her first grade class, just days after Scott saw the star person

6 year old Breana's drawing she made in 1983 with the "nice alien" on the doorstep. Compare her drawing to the photograph of the ranch house we purchased 3 years later in 1986.

in the tree and the one looking in the window at him. Included in her drawing was a star person sitting on the front porch, perhaps waiting for me to come out and say, "Come on in and we'll talk."

Our Plum Creek home was a modernist house design with a flat roof. The front of our home had white stucco siding, floor to ceiling glass doors and windows, balconies, and brick/rock patios. Her drawing showed a gabled roof and porch roof with wood shingles: raised wood porch, two horizontal windows downstairs, two small windows upstairs, and steps or foundation. Our house was nothing like that. Her drawing was created in color and part of the house was colored red. The ranch house, when we purchased it, was red.

DUCK WEED | JUNE 8, 1986

The next day, I walk down to the area where we saw the lights originate from behind the hill. At the base of this knoll is a very active spring that spits out duck weed just as our little spring in Plum Creek Valley does. I walk around the lushly vegetated area the spring gurgles from, and see nothing that suggests people or a craft was ever there last night. The sedges and rushes have not been trampled down. There are no swirl marks or tripod prints in the grasses. Away from the spring and its little creek, the soil is dry and covered with blue grama and short prairie grasses.

I do my ritual spiral walking pattern away from the spring looking for signs of any nature that will let me know who was there last night. I spend a long time working the area and find nothing. The spring is at the base of the hill and emanates from a perched aquifer. I walk to the top of the hill that is perhaps 50 to 75 feet above the spring.

There is an old 1950s-style, abandoned mobile home parked there. I walk around the old worn out trailer, and as I do I get the strong feeling not to go inside. The hair on my neck stands up and I get goose bumps. Maybe I'm goosey and spooked by our experience last night. I hurry to get away from the old mystery trailer that overlooks the spring, the reservoir, and the South Platte River basin.

* * * * * * * *

Years later, we bought the land that the spring and the trailer were on. We adjudicated the spring and named the active water source, the Sarah Spring.

Around this time, an old timer told us that there were graves of five Ute Indians buried not far from the mobile home. We ventured to the site, and found five teardrop-shaped areas on the top of the knoll that were created by unusual colored lichens. We couldn't find these strange lichens in such abundance any other place except over the five teardrop spots.

During this time, we also found out that the Utes and the Plains Indians used this land for their battles over the right to hunt mountain bison, elk, deer, and the like during the summer months. Not more than two miles away to the east, Zebulon Pike, the explorer, met all the Indians in the area at a rendezvous in 1798. The Indian connection to the land was everywhere on this vast high plains prairie. We found the remnants of a giant prayer wheel on our land. It was only about 200 yards from the alleged grave sites.

PREMONITION | JUNE 9, 1986

Driving back home to Plum Creek Valley, the thought occurs to me that the incredible lights of two nights before were a signal that confirms my premonition on April 27th. I (we) must be where they want me (us) to be. I don't feel fearful, controlled, violated, anxious, or used.

I am mildly excited and feel confident we have a special positive relationship with these people. But why do they want us to live or spend weekends out here in the middle of nowhere? Are they isolating us for their own use as I think they had done to me at the pond in 1959 and in the Plum Creek Valley from 1980 to now?

Is there going to be an apocalyptic event or plague and they want us where we will be safe in this remote uninhabited environment? Or are we here for some kind of purpose that will be revealed in the future or never? I have no idea as to what our purpose might be, or if there is one. What can someone like me do for people who are so far, intellectually and technologically, ahead of our civilization? And what can a normal person possibly do out in this high plains desert where there are so few natural and cultural resources to create with? What is important here that I do not see or acknowledge?

At home, a whole new bizarre world is about to open up and continue to give us a glimpse of the many different ETs who come in and out of our world. Our imagination will be challenged and tantalized by their presence, coming and going. But at this moment at home in Plum Creek Valley, I am cautiously euphoric, a bit anxious, but reassured to know I am (we are) evidently part of some cosmic plan. We are not alone in the universe and there is life after life. I feel if we and others let these star people into our lives, all cultures will benefit as early civilizations had. Instead of discord, the world would experience harmony and a lasting peace.

I intuitively know I am where I'm supposed to be in South Park. Although Sarah and the kids may not agree, I feel our family is privileged to be contactees. No matter what trials and tribulations nonbelievers will put us through by their ignorance, religious bias, jealousy, and denial, I feel that we will ultimately benefit from our liaison with our elusive and mysterious ancestors.

"And those who were seen dancing were thought
to be insane by those who could not hear the music."

FRIEDRICK NIETZSCHE

BOOK TWO

FLASHBACKS 2

The flashbacks and paranormal activities continued. A second memoir is in the planning stages and will include events from 1986 to 2015. *FLASHBACKS 2* will feature paranormal encounters of the children, their friends, the dogs, relatives, some of our neighbors, Sarah and myself.

Some very strange entities emerge from out of the ground, fly away and then are seen disappearing back into the ground. Huggy and Charma chase after people running through the tree tops of the coniferous forest south of the house. Scott, a friend, and the dogs are chased by an invisible thing down the mesa through native shrubs, and small Gamble Oak trees. Another of Scott's friends describes his experience with an ET and strange looking mastodons.

Traditional ideas about the creatures called Big Foot and the Thunderbird are challenged. More beam-down sites are discovered with my foot prints in them. Scott is wooed by the wolf clan spirit that converted Huggy and Charma to his sun dancing pledges. A shaman visits and startling discoveries are made. Although surrounding trees are untouched, the sacred cottonwood tree in the ravine has its top blown out by some unknown force.

An infrared photograph is shown for the first time revealing cigar-shaped UFOs in a cloud over the Martin Marietta Corporation, a producer of high tech satellite components for NASA.

I unknowingly begin my mission in South Park. Years after we move from there, I understand what I was to do and did.

In a flashback, I have a terrifying eye ball to eyeball encounter with a tall praying mantis-type star person who subdues and surprises me.

Doodle drawings I did in the 1970's, depicting people working on personal computers with feedback wires implanted in their head, is vindicated as a reality for me in a vivid "dream". Another flashback takes me to Hell. I am given a tour that is so horrific that my subconscious will not allow me to see and experience it until 2013.

After my brief tour of Hell I think I know why man has an ancient preoccupation with the union of man and beast. The doodle of a human with a horse head in place of his own I did in the 70's now has new meaning. I find doodles depicting the event in Hell that date to my first year in graduate school and probable abduction.

The continuing paranormal experiences revealed in *FLASHBACKS 2* suggest to me good and evil ETs exist and are still struggling for control of mankind.

"For my part I know nothing with any certainity,
but the sight of the stars makes me dream."

VINCENT VAN GOGH

SEAN BARTOK

"A single dream is more powerful than a thousand realities."

J. R. R. TOLKIEN

ACKNOWLEDGEMENTS

I want to express my love and gratitude to **Sarah, my wife who was my** toughest critic, and ardent cheerleader. Without her help the book would not have been produced. Support from Leo Sprinkle was indispensable. His council, empathy, vision and friendship gave me courage to keep the faith when events were overwhelming. Without Huggy's and Charma's diligence in defending the family I would not have been aware of the many paranormal events going on, in and around the house, and the enlightenment that came from those revelations. I am grateful to the children for their faith and trust in me. I am grateful to MUFON and Ethan Rich for their wisdom and encouragement; and for allowing parts of Ethan's report to be reprinted in the book.

I appreciate the support, council, and friendship of all the believers whom I have met, their encouragement and advice. Thanks to our good ancestors who opened my mind to the reality of their existence and other dimensions.

Additional acknowledgement for the use of "Moonshadow" lyrics:

Words and Music by Cat Stevens
Copyright (c) 1971 Cat Music Limited
Copyright Renewed
All Rights Administered by BMG Rights Management (US) LLC
All Rights Reserved Used by Permission
Reprinted by Permission of Hal Leonard Corporation

SEAN BARTOK

SEAN BARTOK

"Everybody is a genius. But if you judge a fish by its ability to climb a tree, it will spend its whole life thinking it is stupid."

ALBERT EINSTEIN

ABOUT THE AUTHOR

Sean and his wife, Sarah, have been married for 48 years, and have two children and four grandchildren. He and his wife live in a rural town in Colorado. Sean enjoys working in his studio, consulting, collecting, researching, and participating in outdoor activities with his friends and family.

Adopting a pen name to protect his family's and his privacy was a difficult decision. Sean is proud of his legal surname and his accomplishments in art, design and education that are documented in: *Marquis' Who's Who in the West; Marquis' Who's Who in America* (33 years); *Marquis' Who's Who in the World*, the above published by Marquis' Who's Who in New Providence, New Jersey; *International Who's Who in Education*; published by International Who's Who in Education, Cambridge, England, *The International Who's Who of Intellectuals* published by The International Biographical Centre, Cambridge England; *Distinquished 2,000 Americans* published by The American Biographical Institute; *International Registry of Profiles*, Cambridge, England; *International Book of Honor* published by The American Biographical Institute. His service to the community earned him inclusion in *Who's Who in Colorado* published by Ty Publishing, Ltd..

Sean has worked as a professional art director for a major U.S. corporation; university professor of art, design and design history; entrepreneur; developer and owner of a fly fishing ranch; inventor of a U.S. utility patent; company president; freelance artist; design consultant; and first-time author.

■　■　■　■　■　■　■　■

For the collector or the skeptic, quality prints of the beam-down circle series are available for purchase on **www.seanbartok.com**. None of the 32 year old negatives or the prints from them have been touched up or modified in any way, and contain dust, scratches and blemishes. The website includes additional photographs of the circle not seen in the book.

Sean's paintings, banners, and fashions found in this book may also be seen in color on his website, **www.seanbartok.com**. Many of Sean's artworks may be purchased as originals, prints, or museum quality *giclees*.

"There is nothing in a caterpillar
that tells you it's going to be a butterfly."

R. BUCKMINSTER FULLER